Early Jewish Writings and New Testament Interpretation

ESSENTIALS OF BIBLICAL STUDIES

Early Jewish Writings and New Testament Interpretation
C.D. Elledge

An Invitation to Biblical Poetry
Elaine James

Ancient Israel's Neighbors
Brian R. Doak

Sin In The New Testament
Jeffrey Siker

Reading Hebrew Bible Narratives
J. Andrew Dearman

The History of Bronze and Iron Age Israel
Victor H. Matthews

New Testament Christianity in The Roman World
Harry O. Maier

Women in the New Testament World
Susan E. Hylen

Early Jewish Writings and New Testament Interpretation

C.D. ELLEDGE

OXFORD
UNIVERSITY PRESS

Oxford University Press is a department of the University of Oxford. It furthers the University's objective of excellence in research, scholarship, and education by publishing worldwide. Oxford is a registered trade mark of Oxford University Press in the UK and certain other countries.

Published in the United States of America by Oxford University Press
198 Madison Avenue, New York, NY 10016, United States of America.

© Oxford University Press 2023

All rights reserved. No part of this publication may be reproduced, stored in a retrieval system, or transmitted, in any form or by any means, without the prior permission in writing of Oxford University Press, or as expressly permitted by law, by license, or under terms agreed with the appropriate reproduction rights organization. Inquiries concerning reproduction outside the scope of the above should be sent to the Rights Department, Oxford University Press, at the address above.

You must not circulate this work in any other form and you must impose this same condition on any acquirer.

Library of Congress Cataloging-in-Publication Data
Names: Elledge, C. D. (Casey Deryl), author.
Title: Early Jewish writings and New Testament interpretation / C.D. Elledge.
Description: New York, NY : Oxford University Press, 2023. |
Series: Essentials of biblical studies |
Includes bibliographical references and index.
Identifiers: LCCN 2022061035 (print) | LCCN 2022061036 (ebook) |
ISBN 9780190274580 (hardback) | ISBN 9780190274597 (paperback) |
ISBN 9780190274610 (epub)
Subjects: LCSH: Jewish religious literature—History and criticism. |
Bible. Old Testament—Criticism, interpretation, etc., Jewish. |
Bible. New Testament—Relation to the Old Testament. |
Judaism—History—To 70 A.D. |
Church history—Primitive and early church, ca. 30-600.
Classification: LCC BM485.E55 2023 (print) | LCC BM485 (ebook) |
DDC 296.1—dc23/eng/20230207
LC record available at https://lccn.loc.gov/2022061035
LC ebook record available at https://lccn.loc.gov/2022061036

DOI: 10.1093/oso/9780190274580.001.0001

Paperback printed by Marquis Book Printing, Canada
Hardback printed by Bridgeport National Bindery, Inc., United States of America

For Annabelle and Elijah
(Sirach 30:4–5)

Contents

Series Introduction ... ix

1. Forms of Scripture in Early Judaism ... 1
   Early Judaism ... 1
   Canon and Noncanonical Literature ... 6
   Apocrypha, or Deuterocanonical Books ... 10
   Pseudepigrapha ... 13
   Dead Sea Scrolls ... 19
   Philo and Josephus ... 19
   This Book ... 20

2. The Glory of Wisdom ... 23
   The Dimensions of Wisdom ... 23
   Sages and Scribes ... 25
   Wisdom Writings ... 25
   The Wisdom of Jesus ben Sira ... 27
   The Wisdom of Solomon ... 34
   Wisdom in the New Testament ... 41

3. In the Last Days ... 54
   Apocalyptic Literature ... 54
   Apocalyptic Thought ... 57
   1 Enoch ... 59
   Post–70 CE Apocalypses ... 70
   4 Ezra ... 73
   2 Baruch ... 78
   Apocalypse of Abraham ... 80
   Apocalypticism in the New Testament ... 83

4. Rewriting Scripture ... 97
   Explicit Interpretation ... 97
   Implicit Interpretation ... 99
   Rewritten Scriptures ... 100

Jubilees	102
Biblical Antiquities (*Liber Antiquitatum Biblicarum*)	113
Scriptural Interpretation in the New Testament	120
5. In the Wilderness	128
The Community of the Dead Sea Scrolls	128
Scriptural Manuscripts and Their Interpretation	134
Rule Documents	138
Legal Writings	142
Psalms, Hymns, Prayers	145
Wisdom and Apocalypticism	147
The Dead Sea Scrolls and the New Testament	150
6. Jews, Greeks, and Romans	157
Philo of Alexandria	157
Philo and the New Testament	166
Josephus	170
Josephus and the New Testament	181
Notes	187
Glossary	191
Works Cited	195
Index of Sources	201
General Index	205

Series Introduction

The past three decades have seen an explosion of approaches to study of the Bible, as older exegetical methods have been joined by a variety of literary, anthropological, and social models. Interfaith collaboration has helped change the field, and the advent of more cultural diversity among biblical scholars in the West and around the world has broadened our reading and interpretation of the Bible. These changes have also fueled interest in Scripture's past: both the ancient Near Eastern and Mediterranean worlds out of which Scripture came and the millennia of premodern interpretation through which it traveled to our day. The explosion of information and perspectives is so vast that no one textbook can any longer address the many needs of seminaries and colleges where the Bible is studied.

In addition to these developments in the field itself are changes in the students. Traditionally the domain of seminaries, graduate schools, and college and university religion classes, now biblical study also takes place in a host of alternative venues. As lay leadership in local churches develops, nontraditional, weekend, and online preparatory classes have mushroomed. As the number of seminaries in Africa, Asia, and Latin America grows, particular need for inexpensive, easily available materials is clear. As religious controversies over the Bible's origins and norms continue to dominate the airwaves, congregation members and even curious nonreligious folk seek reliable paths into particular topics. And teachers themselves continue to seek guidance in areas of the ever-expanding field of scriptural study with which they may be less than familiar.

A third wave of changes also makes this series timely: shifts in the publishing industry itself. Technologies and knowledge are shifting so rapidly that large books are out of date almost before they are in print. The internet and the growing popularity of ebooks call for flexibility and accessibility in marketing and sales. If the days when one expert can sum up the field in a textbook are gone, also gone are the days when large, expensive multi-authored tomes are attractive to students, teachers, and other readers.

During my own years of seminary teaching, I have tried to find just the right book or books for just the right price, at just the right reading level for my students, with just enough information to orient them without drowning them in excess reading. For all the reasons stated above, this search was all too often less than successful. So I was excited to be asked to help Oxford University Press assemble a select crew of leading scholars to create a series that would respond to such classroom challenges. Essentials of Biblical Studies comprises freestanding, relatively brief, accessibly written books that provide orientation to the Bible's contents, its ancient contexts, its interpretive methods and history, and its themes and figures. Rather than a one-size-had-better-fit-all approach, these books may be mixed and matched to suit the objectives of a variety of classroom venues as well as the needs of individuals wishing to find their way into unfamiliar topics.

I am confident that our book authors will join me in returning enthusiastic thanks to the editorial staff at Oxford University Press for their support and guidance, especially Theo Calderara, who shepherded the project in its early days, and Dr. Steve Wiggins, who has been a most wise and steady partner in this work since joining OUP in 2013.

Patricia K. Tull
Louisville Presbyterian Theological Seminary

1
Forms of Scripture in Early Judaism

A classic feature of many religions has been the role of authoritative writings, often called "scriptures." Religions are adamant about the authority, wisdom, mystery, and beauty of their scriptures. Yet complex questions emerge when we ask what counts as "scripture" and how such writings emerged within the historical experiences of a religion. This is especially the case for Judaism and Christianity. Near the close of the first century CE, Judaism would preserve a collection of scriptural books known today as the Hebrew Bible. Another name for this collection is the *Tanak*, an acronym that includes three major divisions: the Torah, the Prophets, and Writings. It is also called *Mikra* (that which is read aloud, especially in the synagogue).

As for the Christian Bible, a more extended development transpired throughout the first four centuries of its emergence—and beyond. Christians would accept the writings of the Hebrew Bible as their Old Testament, preserving them in a different order and typically reading them in the Greek translation known as the **Septuagint**. Their Greek scriptures also contained additional writings not found in the Hebrew Bible. These included writings designated by later Christians as **Apocrypha** or **Deuterocanonical** Books. The collection, of course, further expanded to include the early church writings that formed the New Testament, which itself was attested in varied arrangement and content among the earliest surviving collections.

Early Judaism

An important feature of the formation of scriptures is that Jews and Christians would ultimately exclude a vast range of popular religious literature from their scriptural collections. Many of these books were originally composed during one of the most fascinating environments in the study of religions, a historical era sometimes called "Early Judaism" or "Ancient Judaism" (see Box 1.1). "Second Temple Judaism" further designates the Judaism that flourished from the Persian restoration of the Jerusalem temple (515 BCE) until its destruction by the Romans (70 CE).

The geographical parameters of Early Judaism range beyond the ancestral homeland of Palestine to the **diaspora** communities that flourished in Babylonia, Egypt, Asia Minor, Greece, and Rome. Its historical parameters are understood differently by modern historians. Yet they commonly include the Hellenistic (332–63 BCE) and Roman (63 BCE) eras in the centuries prior to the reformulation of Jewish tradition achieved by early rabbis and codified in the Mishnah (ca. 200 CE). Prior to the full emergence of this "Rabbinic Judaism," however, many colorful strands of religious belief and practice flowed through the Jewish community.

Box 1.1 Major Events in the History of Early Judaism

BCE (Before Common Era)	
Alexander's Conquests	334–323
Septuagintal Translation	third century
Hellenistic Reform Movement	175
Maccabean Revolt	167–164
Hasmonean Dynasty	ca. 140–63
Roman Rule in Palestine	63
Herod the Great	37–4
Roman Rule in Egypt	30
CE (Common Era)	
Great Jewish Revolt	66–70
Diaspora Revolt	115–117
Bar-Kochba Revolt	132–135
The Mishnah	ca. 200

The experiences of Early Judaism in the Hellenistic era reveal how Israel's earlier traditions were creatively adapted to the seismic changes that Alexander's conquests brought to the Near East (334–323 BCE). The subsequent spread of Greek culture, or **Hellenization**, fractured the Jewish community internally, as conflicting factions pursued competing alternatives for how to live out the ancestral faith under Greek dominion. One of the most intense political expressions of these conflicts erupted in the Hellenistic Reform (175 BCE), in which pro-Hellenistic Jews enacted cultural, religious, and legal reforms that endeavored to transform the city of Jerusalem into a Greek *polis*. They were supported in their radical initiatives by the Greek emperor Antiochus IV Epiphanes, infamous throughout subsequent Jewish tradition. In the **Maccabean Revolt** (167–164 BCE), the Maccabean family fought to assert practices of Jewish religion threatened by the Reform, including circumcision, sabbath, and temple sacrifice. After their revolutionary triumph over Antiochus and his pro-Hellenistic partisans, the heirs of the Maccabees, the Hasmoneans, established a prosperous political dynasty in Jerusalem (ca. 140 BCE). Hasmonean leadership, however, would only provoke intense sectarian opposition from other sectors of the Jewish community. It is within this environment that the first historical references to the three famous "sects" of ancient Judaism are to be found: the Pharisees, Sadducees, and Essenes (see Box 1.2).

Bringing an eventual end to the **Hasmonean Dynasty**, Rome experimented with varied strategies for governing ancient Palestine (63 BCE). The most successful involved political friendship with King Herod the Great, whose lengthy reign (37–4 BCE) secured Roman interests in the region, while promoting Jewish prosperity internationally. Herod's leadership gloriously renovated the Jerusalem temple (20s BCE), making it a renowned centerpiece of Jewish civilization. Yet this delicate pro-Roman/pro-Jewish alignment was defended with a bloody sword and proved difficult to maintain after Herod's death.

As revolutionary factions gained momentum, three catastrophic revolts would contribute to the gradual demise of Early Judaism. The **Great Jewish Revolt** against Rome (66–70 CE) would see the destruction of the Jerusalem temple and the massive upheaval of earlier Palestinian society. Yet 70 CE was far from the end of Jewish nationalism and revolutionary fervor. After prolonged conflict in major

> **Box 1.2 The Three Jewish Sects**
>
> According to Josephus, three religious "classes" or "schools" "practice[d] philosophy" (*War* 2:119–66; *Antiquities* 18:11–25). These included the Pharisees, Sadducees, and Essenes. Differences in theological beliefs and social organization distinguish the schools. The aristocratic Sadducees emphasize free will, deny rewards in the afterlife, and are contentious toward one another. Severe in matters of judgment, they abide only by the written Torah in their religious practice. Pharisees enjoy popular appeal and are renowned for their legal interpretation, which emphasizes certain "traditions from the fathers" not written within the Torah (*Antiquities* 13:296–97). Lenient in matters of judgment, they live simply, believe in an afterlife, and emphasize cooperation between free will and determinism. Essenes form an altogether distinct communal order in which they practice asceticism, adhering to deterministic beliefs and a positive view of the afterlife. Josephus's accounts testify to how differing theologies and social behaviors characterized competing sectarian movements in Early Judaism.

urban environments, a **Diaspora Revolt** (115–117 CE) raged in North Africa, Cyprus, and Mesopotamia as Jewish revolutionaries destroyed pagan temples and massacred Greek populations. The unrelenting Roman response devastated many of the diaspora communities that flourished in these regions. The **Bar-Kochba Revolt** (132–135 CE) in Palestine waged another failed attempt at political liberation from Rome. These revolts intensively disrupted the social and religious structures that had characterized earlier Judaism.

Since the origins of Rabbinic Judaism and Christianity are to be found within this setting, Early Judaism may be regarded as among the most generative environments in the history of religions. Rabbinic Judaism was deeply informed by the religion of the **Tannaim**, sages who had been active before the temple's destruction and offered leadership to the Jewish community in the desperate aftermath. Their interpretation of Israel's law contributed to the advancement of rabbinic **Halakhah**. This totality of Jewish legal tradition included orally transmitted sources later collected in the Mishnah and continuously deliberated throughout the Talmud. Early Jewish writings reveal a vast expanse of legal traditions that developed prior to the temple's destruction, exhibiting both continuity and discord with the emerging rabbinic Halakhah. Such is also the case with the **Aggadah**, the nonlegal, moral, theological, narrative, and mystical traditions of Rabbinic Judaism.

Jesus and his earliest followers also lived within this environment. Within its first-century context, it is perhaps premature to use the term "Christianity" to describe the actual social setting of Jesus and his earliest followers, especially if we use that term to designate a distinct world religion. While Jesus and his earliest followers appear to have challenged existing beliefs and practices in Early Judaism, so did other movements within this era. Beyond the Tannaim and the nascent church, there flourished a variety of other competing religious currents that contended for their own interpretations of how to live out the ancestral faith amid the incessant tides of imperial rule.

The literature of Early Judaism has thus stood at the forefront of attempts to understand the gradual emergence of the church and Rabbinic Judaism from the multifaceted religious context that both shared. These shared origins have remained among the factors that have most persistently linked Judaism and Christianity as mutual heirs of a common religious heritage. While scholars once confidently asserted an intentional "parting of the ways" between Judaism and Christianity in the late first-century CE, the continuing study of Early Judaism offers a more problematic tale (Becker and Reed 2003). As Daniel Boyarin (1999, 5–6) observes, "Like many twins, Judaism and Christianity never quite formed entirely separate identities. Like closely related siblings, they rivaled each other, learned from each other, fought with each other, perhaps even sometimes loved each other." Since Early Judaism supplied their originally shared, formative environment, the literature composed in this era preserves crucial evidence for understanding the later development and tensive relationships between the two religions throughout their subsequent histories.

This age was also crucial to the latest stages of the development of the Hebrew Bible itself. Late compositions like Daniel 7–12 and many of the Psalms were composed in this era. Many books were continuously edited throughout this age, as they began to develop together into larger scriptural collections. Thus, Early Judaism was not merely a later heir but was an active contributor to the literature of the Hebrew Bible.

Jewish scribes, visionaries, sages, historians, poets, and philosophers also composed a vast amount of fascinating new literature throughout the Hellenistic and Roman eras that did not ultimately appear in the later Hebrew canon. These diverse writings provide modern scholars some of the best available insights into one of history's most fertile religious contexts. The purpose of the present volume is to introduce a select number of important genres and collections of these writings and to discuss their implications for interpreting aspects of New Testament literature and Christian origins.

Canon and Noncanonical Literature

From a contemporary perspective, many of these writings may be categorized in some sense as "noncanonical." This categorization, of course, assumes the formation of a biblical **canon** or exclusive collection of scriptural books. The term "canon" derives from a Greek word denoting a straight rod or beam utilized to measure or maintain the structure of other materials. A *kanōn* might align the intricate threads of a woven tapestry or guide the precise measurements of a skilled mason or carpenter. As applied to intellectual culture, the ideal models for literature, philosophy, or architecture might be designated as *kanones*. Christians would apply this term to the collection of their scriptural texts. Amid stormy controversies, these writings provided an authoritative guide, metric, or model for distinguishing between truth and falsehood, worship and abomination.

An important feature of canon in Judaism and Christianity is that their collections ultimately became exclusive. Some writings were included, while others, however popular, were omitted. The scriptural canons of Jews and Christians also became closed, so that no new writings were added. For the Hebrew Bible, it appears that such an exclusive scriptural collection first emerged among early rabbinic leaders near the end of the first century CE, although some scholars still argue for an earlier or later context. For the Christian Bible, the closure of the canonical process transpired through a much later development, first traceable to the fourth century CE. Moreover, the canonical process transpired differently among global populations within Christianity, leading to differences among the canons of Catholic, Protestant, Eastern Orthodox, and Oriental Orthodox churches. Since the closure of the canonical process began relatively late in the histories of Judaism and Christianity, what "scripture" may have meant in earlier settings remains a more open and enticing question.

Canons as Inclusive

One way to appreciate the situation is to recognize two features of canon. As Lee McDonald (2012) advises, one feature of canon *positively* asserts that a writing represents an authoritative scriptural document. This emergent sense of canon came relatively earlier. The Torah or Pentateuch, the first five books of the Hebrew Bible, received strong, even essential acceptance throughout much of Judaism in the Hellenistic and Roman eras, even among communities that were otherwise at odds. The Prophets are continuously utilized as religious authorities, even if questions persist about what texts were referenced by this categorical term. Passages of Psalms are also frequently referenced in varied ways in the literature of Early Judaism and the nascent church.

One may recognize an early, formative sense of canon among the Dead Sea Scrolls, an early Jewish literary collection from Palestine. The scrolls contain manuscripts from the Hellenistic era up until the Great Jewish Revolt. Approximately 25 percent of the scrolls comprise copies of all the books found in the later Hebrew Bible, with the possible exception of Esther. They attest numerous copies of each of the books of the Torah, with Deuteronomy registering the most, at twenty-nine. Each of the Prophetic books is found in multiple copies, with Isaiah registering the largest number, at twenty-one. While their numbers are often fewer, most of the texts featured as Writings in the later Hebrew Bible appear. This includes thirty-six manuscripts that preserve portions of Psalms in varied compositions.

New Testament writings likewise cite every book of the Torah as scripture. Deuteronomy is most frequently quoted, with over forty citations. Most of the Prophetic books are cited, with Isaiah registering over sixty citations. Among the Writings of the Hebrew Bible, passages of Psalms are quoted over seventy times; Job, Proverbs, and Daniel are also cited. Even conceding that quotation alone does not reveal a writing's canonical status, one finds the broad contours of the eventual books of the Hebrew Bible throughout the pages of the New Testament.

Testimonies from Ben Sira (early second century BCE), Josephus, and *4 Ezra* (late first century CE) share the view that Law and Prophets constituted essential categories of scripture. Ben Sira's Prologue further references "other books that followed them"; Josephus references "four" additional books containing "hymns to God and instructions for human life" (*Apion* 1:38–40; cf. Luke 24:44). These sources, however, do not identify specific books or their sequential arrangement. Josephus enumerates the total collection of scriptural books at twenty-two (five law + thirteen prophets + four hymns/instructions); *4 Ezra* identifies twenty-four public books to be read by all people (14:45). These enumerations appear to converge in large measure with the eventual twenty-four books of the Hebrew Bible.

Even so, as Timothy Lim (2013) and other scholars advise, the 22/24 book enumeration may describe the scriptural collection of the particular Pharisaic-rabbinic movement that would hold increasing sway in the decades following the temple's destruction. The scriptural collections of other movements may well have remained more, or less, expansive.

Canons as Exclusive

Even as canons positively include authoritative scriptural books, they ultimately possesses a delimiting and *negative* characteristic. Canons became exclusive collections with boundaries. Thus, many popular, even authoritative writings were ultimately excluded. Indeed, such selectivity would have been meaningful and necessary only amid a much larger array of popular religious literature that held value within the Jewish and Christian communities. McDonald (2012) counsels that this exclusive feature of canon emerged late and that it is anachronistic to assume that it prevailed in the centuries prior to the closure of the canonical process. There is sufficient evidence to believe that in Early Judaism a more expansive sense of authoritative texts prevailed, one that included writings that would not appear within the later Hebrew Bible.

The Dead Sea Scrolls and New Testament again provide illuminating instances. Writings later known as *Jubilees* and portions of *1 Enoch* appear to have held some type of religious authority among the authors of the scrolls. Manuscripts of *Jubilees*, in fact, register nearly as many copies as Genesis (fifteen to sixteen), a number surpassed only by Deuteronomy, Isaiah, Exodus, and portions of Psalms. The New Testament also cites or alludes to texts that ultimately did not feature in the Hebrew Bible. Among the clearest examples, Jude explicitly cites a portion of *1 Enoch* as an authoritative prophecy that foretells the demise of the wicked and the final triumph of God's justice (v14).

Most striking in this regard is a passage from *4 Ezra*, where "the twenty-four books" of the Hebrew Bible comprise a public declaration for the masses. Yet for "the wise among your people" remain "seventy [books] that were written last. . . . For in them is the spring of understanding, the fountain of wisdom, and the river of knowledge" (14:45–47).[1] *4 Ezra* may suggest that the fullest wisdom was to be found beyond the writings of the Hebrew Bible alone, within seventy divinely revealed, esoteric books, in which the most profound waters of understanding flowed.

In yet a different case, the Prologue to Ben Sira presents the book as an essential complement to "the law," "prophets," and "other books." It offers functional training in the written and spoken word, skills essential for keeping the law and advancing its fame among "outsiders." In this instance, existing scriptural books may yet be wedded to secondary, supportive works, like Ben Sira, that refine their interpretation and application to the problems of daily life. The Prologue recommends awareness that canons may contain internal gradations of authority that complement and support one another.

Studying the so-called noncanonical literature of Early Judaism today thus requires a kind of dual vision. Even as modern readers study these documents centuries after the closure of the canonical process, we must also acknowledge that they were originally composed and utilized within a range of diverse communities that held their own particular assumptions about what constituted scripture. Since the authors of the New Testament also lived in an era prior to the closure of the canonical process, their own theologies and arts of expression may have been meaningfully informed by traditions preserved within noncanonical literature.

Apocrypha, or Deuterocanonical Books

One later category superimposed upon a collection of early Jewish writings is that of the Old Testament Apocrypha. These works were written within the Hellenistic and Roman eras, in both Palestine and the Diaspora. Several were originally composed in Hebrew or Aramaic (Tobit, Judith, 1 Maccabees, Sirach, Baruch). Yet after their composition, they came to be known primarily in Greek translation, as they circulated together with the Septuagint.

As Jews (and, later, Protestants) established their scriptures upon Hebrew manuscripts rather than the Septuagint, they excluded these Greek writings, forming a more selective scriptural canon. Roman Catholic and Orthodox churches, however, included these books, incorporating a wider range of the Jewish traditions of antiquity among their scriptures. Catholics and Orthodox share the inclusion of Tobit, Judith, Baruch, Letter of Jeremiah, Sirach, Wisdom of Solomon, 1–2 Maccabees, plus additions to Daniel and Esther. Greek Orthodox further include 3 Maccabees, Psalm 151, and 1 Esdras, with Prayer of Manasseh and 4 Maccabees often presented in an appendix. In its own apocryphal appendix, the Latin Vulgate Bible includes the Prayer of Manasseh, 3 Esdras (= Greek 1 Esdras), as well as the apocalypse of Ezra (known in other contexts as 2 Esdras, *4 Ezra*).

The term "Apocrypha," meaning "hidden away," "obscured," or "concealed," is ambiguous at best. More pejoratively, it may convey that these writings are of uncertain origin and meaning. More positively, it may imply that they are reserved for those of sufficient maturity to interpret them properly (cf. *4 Ezra* 14:46–47). Another description applied by Catholics in the 1500s and further utilized in Orthodox circles is that they are Deuterocanonical Books: scriptural works deemed canonical secondarily or later in history than other books (see Box 1.3).

Orthodox Christians have also referred to them as *Anagignōskomena*, literature that is "to be read" by those seeking

> **Box 1.3 The Term "Deuterocanon"**
>
> Sixtus of Siena (1520–1569) described "Deuterocanonical" writings as those that came into later historical recognition by the church, after the time of the apostles. Deuterocanonical literature encompassed the Apocrypha, as well as the New Testament books of Hebrews, James, Second Peter, Second and Third John, Jude, and Revelation. Sixtus even included passages not attested in many ancient manuscripts (the ending of Mark, Luke 22:43–44, John 8:1–11).

> **Box 1.4 Luther on the Apocrypha**
>
> In prefaces to the Apocrypha, Martin Luther (1483–1546) offers an individualized critical valuation of each book. Judith "would be a noble and fine book, and should properly be in the Bible," were it not for its purely fictional literary character. Even so, it remains "a fine, good, holy, useful book," one that "preaches" through dramatic elements (*Luther's Works* 35:337–53). Similar praise attends Wisdom of Solomon, Tobit, Ben Sira, 1 Maccabees. Other works, such as Baruch, however, fare worse, containing "nothing that one could not find better in Aesop."

instruction (Athanasius, *Festal Letter* 39) (Gallagher and Meade 2017). In early Protestant Bibles, these writings were separated from the Old Testament and published in a special section (see Box 1.4). Catholics and Orthodox, however, integrate most Deuterocanonical works among the Old Testament writings themselves.

Narratives

Several works provide narrative renditions of the historical experiences of the Jewish people. First Esdras reviews historical episodes that span the reign of Josiah, the Babylonian conquest, and the restoration of Judah under the Persians. The book of Baruch recounts the penitential prayers and wise admonitions of this faithful scribe of the prophet Jeremiah. First Maccabees narrates a patriotic rendition of the Maccabean Revolt and the gradual emergence of the Hasmonean Dynasty. Its pro-Hasmonean tendencies hail the Maccabean family as saviors and liberators of Judaism. Second Maccabees offers a different portrait of these events that highlights festival observance in the Jerusalem temple, the piety of Judah the Maccabee, and the Jewish martyrs' faith in resurrection. Fourth Maccabees takes a more philosophical vantage of the Jewish martyrs interpreting their heroism as the triumph of godly "reason" over the "passions." Unrelated to these events, 3 Maccabees concerns an imagined threat to Judaism posed by the Ptolemaic Empire in Egypt.

Tobit and Judith, two masterpieces of storytelling, promote serious religious values through the suspenseful adventures of their protagonists. Tobit recounts the story of a righteous man taken into exile in Nineveh after the fall of Israel to Assyria. Through the faithfulness of Tobit's family, the author portrays an ideal picture of Jewish piety regarding sacrifice, prayer, burial, almsgiving, marriage, and fidelity to the temple. Judith transpires within a fanciful historical setting that was nevertheless familiar to Jewish experiences in antiquity. Threatened with extermination by the Assyrians, Judith, a courageous widow, saves her people and the temple through an artful interplay of beauty, wisdom, and faithfulness to Jewish law. Poetic hymns and prayers accent both works, offering models of devotional piety within the drama of trial and deliverance.

Additions

Several Additions supply further episodes to the Greek versions of Esther and Daniel (Susannah, Prayer of Azariah and Song of the Three Young Men, Bel and the Dragon). Such additions reveal an interpretive culture in which Jews read these popular books with a sense of inquiry and imagination, contributing expanded content where they believed it was warranted.

Wisdom and Apocalyptic Literature

Finally, wisdom and apocalyptic compositions appear in the collection. The Wisdom of Jesus ben Sira and the Wisdom of Solomon provide sapiential compositions that may be compared with the so-called wisdom literature of the Hebrew Bible (e.g., Job, Proverbs, Ecclesiastes). The Latin Vulgate further includes the apocalypse of 2 Esdras (known elsewhere among the Pseudepigrapha as *4 Ezra*), which recounts Ezra's apocalyptic visions after the fall of Jerusalem to Babylon.

Pseudepigrapha

The Old Testament **Pseudepigrapha** comprise writings that Christians later judged to be "falsely ascribed" to the authorship of ancient worthies like Enoch, Abraham, Moses, David, or Solomon. Many of these writings utilize the literary art of **pseudonymity**. The authors of pseudonymous works did not write in their own names, but attributed their compositions to exemplary figures of the sacred past. Through this powerful literary device, they fortified the authority of their writings, as though the stream of divine revelation in earlier contexts flowed into their own, later times. How the ancients heard the scriptural voices of "Moses," "Abraham," or "David" may thus have encompassed an expansive range of traditions beyond the writings of the Hebrew Bible alone.

Pseudonymous authors invited meaningful comparisons between the world of the past and the pressing issues of their own times. Even pseudepigrapha that do not utilize pseudonymous authorship frequently craft their compositions within earlier settings that become paradigmatic for interpreting their contemporary circumstances and promoting their religious claims.

The writings collected as pseudepigrapha have varied for centuries, a process initiated by J. A. Fabricius's (1713, 1723) modern collection of over three hundred writings. The early twentieth-century collection by E. Kautzsch (1900) included twelve works, and that of R. H. Charles (1913), seventeen. The prevalent contemporary collection by

J. H. Charlesworth (1983–85) amassed over sixty writings. A team of scholars continues to supplement and expand earlier collections (Bauckham, Davila, and Panayotov 2013–). Dates of authorship range widely among the works collected by Charlesworth, with the earliest (*Ahiqar*) dating prior to 500 BCE and the latest (the *Apocalypse of Daniel*) to the ninth century CE.

Many writings are not fully preserved in their original language of composition but survive in Greek, Latin, Syriac, Ethiopic, Coptic, Arabic, Armenian, and Slavonic translations. For this reason, scholars continue to make important discoveries in the language, rhetoric, and theology of these writings by studying the fullest range of manuscript witnesses.

In the pseudepigrapha, one witnesses a larger historical process of transmission in which many popular writings within ancient Judaism came to be translated, edited, and reinterpreted in the early church, thus playing a formative role in the development of Christian thought (Stone 2011). Given the complexity of this process, it is not always immediately clear whether one is reading Jewish, Christian, or even pagan literature. Presuppositions about the lines defining Jewish and Christian traditions in antiquity also strongly influence how one addresses this ongoing interpretive problem.

Some scholars emphasize that the Pseudepigrapha ultimately represent a Christian collection, since it was not Judaism but the church that was primarily responsible for their transmission in later antiquity. Indeed, the church is likely to have preserved those earlier writings most conducive to its own religious interests (Bauckham, Davila, and Panayotov 2013–). Robert Kraft (1994, 55–56) thus advises, "it is premature to distill from these writings information about pre-rabbinic Judaism before they are thoroughly examined for their significance as witnesses to Christian interest" (see also Himmelfarb 2018). On the other hand, transmission by the church alone does not obviate the possibility of the originally Jewish context of individual pseudepigrapha, any more than it does for writings such as 1 Maccabees, Ben Sira, Tobit, or Judith. Scholars today thus examine each of these writings on an individual basis according to historical criteria to determine its particular characteristics (Davila 2005; Collins 2022).

Such a methodology only further deepens appreciation for the vast internal complexity of this collection. Versions of individual writings were composed prior to Christianity and represent originally Jewish compositions, like portions of *1 Enoch, Jubilees,* and the *Psalms of Solomon.* Other writings, like the *Odes of Solomon,* were probably composed by early "Jewish-Christians" late in the first century. Still others, like the *Testaments of the Twelve Patriarchs* and *Sibylline Oracles,* may contain originally Jewish compositions that were also reworked by Christian scribes. Portions of the *Sibylline Oracles,* as well as *Ahiqar,* appear to have been neither Jewish nor Christian. The religious origins of writings like *Joseph and Aseneth* remain contested.

The categorization "pseudepigrapha" is modern, Western, perhaps even condescending (Reed 2009). Some scholars prefer to describe this literature as simply "beyond the canon." Yet this designation also has limitations, since many of these writings were composed prior the closure of the canonical process. The question thus remains as to how the ancients viewed these writings. The strong attestation of *Jubilees* and portions of *1 Enoch* among the Dead Sea Scrolls demonstrates that some of these writings possessed significant authority in sectors of Early Judaism prior to the origins of Christianity. We have also seen that a passage found in *1 Enoch* is quoted as prophecy in the book of Jude. They did not, however, ultimately feature in the Jewish canon of scripture. Nor did the majority of these books appear in later Christian canons.

Yet significant exceptions appear within particular church collections. Fourth Maccabees, sometimes numbered among the Pseudepigrapha, appears within Codex Sinaiticus (fourth century CE) and other collections.[2] The *Psalms of Solomon* concludes the table of contents in Codex Alexandrinus (fifth century CE), separated by a space. The apocalypse of *4 Ezra* appears in Syriac Codex Ambrosianus (B), the apocryphal appendix of the Latin Vulgate, and Gennady's Old Church Slavonic Bible. The apocalypse of *2 Baruch* registers within Codex Ambrosianus (B) as well. *Jubilees* (*Kufale*), (*First*) *Enoch,* and *4 Ezra* (*Izra Sutuel*) number among the Old Testament writings of the Ethiopian Orthodox (Tewahedo) Church.

Since the Pseudepigrapha represent an eclectic collection, it is challenging to classify their contents. In the Charlesworth edition, the following literary categories are utilized: (1) Apocalyptic Literature (and related works); (2) Testaments; (3) Expansions of the "Old Testament" and Legends; (4) Wisdom and Philosophical Literature; (5) Prayers, Psalms, and Odes; (6) Fragments of Lost Works. Even so, these headings merely represent "broadly conceived literary types.... Any system for ordering these documents has weaknesses" (Charlesworth 1983–85, 1:xvi). Other editions have classified their contents according to the scriptural ancestor whose story provides the literary setting for each work (e.g., "Adam," "Moses," "Solomon").

Apocalypses and Related Works

Literary apocalypses, like *1 Enoch*, *4 Ezra*, *2 Baruch*, and *Apocalypse of Abraham*, feature prominently among the Pseudepigrapha. These originally Jewish apocalypses emerge from the Hellenistic era (portions of *1 Enoch*), as well as the aftermath of the Great Revolt against Rome (*4 Ezra*, *2 Baruch*, *Apocalypse of Abraham*). They offer immense comparative value for understanding the apocalyptic rhetoric and theology of the biblical apocalypses, Daniel and Revelation. *Second Enoch* represents an important work for understanding how apocalypticism further contributed to Jewish and Christian mysticism. Within a broader range of revelatory texts, the *Sibylline Oracles* record the supposed oracles of a sibyl, one of the legendary prophetesses of antiquity. The oracles often preserve pagan and Jewish renditions of sibylline lore that were later edited by Christians. Later Christian apocalypses, like the Greek *Apocalypse of Daniel*, illustrate that the apocalyptic tradition did not perish from the church but persisted well beyond its first century.

Testaments

Testaments portray the final admonitions of illustrious ancestors to future generations, often their own descendants or successors, just prior to their deaths. These precious "last words" form a rhetorical vehicle for addressing later audiences. The *Testaments of the Twelve Patriarchs* offer the final admonitions of each of the Israelite ancestors. Their speeches draw upon moral lessons exemplified within the ancestors' scriptural biographies (Gen 29–50). The *Testament of Job* reflects on Job's experience of suffering just prior to his death, providing a fascinating reinterpretation of the scriptural book. Testaments also frequently forecast the calamities and eschatological redemption that will come upon future generations.

Expansions and Legends

Several narrative writings retell, expand, and reimagine earlier scriptural and legendary narratives. In the retelling of earlier traditions, authors subtly—and sometimes drastically—interweave their own interpretive agendas. Two prominent examples are the book of *Jubilees* and the book of *Biblical Antiquities*. Such narratives are invaluable resources for understanding the interpretive traditions that surrounded scriptural writings in Early Judaism (see Chapter 4).

The *Letter of Aristeas* advances an idealized, apologetic narrative that recounts the Septuagint translation in Ptolemaic Egypt. The name "Septuagint" derives from the legend of the seventy-two sages who translated their scriptures into Greek in seventy-two days (*septuaginta* = seventy, LXX), under the sponsorship of King Ptolemy II Philadelphus (d. 246 BCE). The sages not only produce an impeccable, harmonious translation; they further counsel the king in a philosophical symposium on the virtues of wise governance. The narrative legitimates the Greek scriptures of Egyptian Judaism, as well as the flourishing of Jewish rights within the Ptolemaic Empire.

Joseph and Aseneth recounts how the Egyptian "daughter of Potiphera, priest of On," came to marry Joseph (Gen 41:45, 50). The author's entertaining romance wishes, above all, to explain the patriarch's dubious intermarriage with a non-Israelite. As Aseneth turns away from Egyptian deities, she converts to the worship of Israel's God, as though she has passed from death to life, from darkness into light. After their marriage, Aseneth plays a wise, judicious role within Joseph's administration in Egypt.

Wisdom and Philosophy

The Pseudepigrapha also contain explorations of wisdom. In the case of Pseudo-Phocylides's *Sentences*, a Jewish author pseudonymously ascribes his own poetic instructions not to Israel's ancestors but to the celebrated Greek sage Phocylides of Miletus. In so doing, the unknown author, who probably wrote in the first century CE, makes the venerable Greek sage a spokesperson for Jewish ethics—even imitating his poetic maxims in well-crafted Greek hexameters. Pseudo-Phocylides paraphrases the Decalogue (or Ten Commandments), offering his own synthesis of Jewish and Greek morality on poverty and wealth, sexual behavior, and care for the dead.

Prayers, Psalms, Odes

Prayers and psalms were a crucial feature of early Jewish piety and are well represented among the Pseudepigrapha. In the *Psalms of Solomon*, a Jewish author imitates the styles of the book of Psalms, producing eighteen poems that reflect upon the aftermath of Rome's advent in Palestine and the collapse of the Hasmonean Dynasty. The perplexity of the psalmist ultimately gives way to hope in God's own kingship, which will one day be restored through a Davidic messiah (chs. 17–18). The *Odes of Solomon* probably arose from Jewish-Christian circles late in the first century. Utilizing daring imagery, the *Odes* explore the intimate, mystical relationship between believers and the Lord.

Fragments

Finally, the Pseudepigrapha include fragments of writings that have survived antiquity only as quotations within other works. Many of these illustrate the attempt to render Jewish tradition in the literary genres of Greek antiquity, including history, epic, and tragedy. Other fragments defend the historical antiquity of the Jews and their cultural contributions to the Hellenistic world. Such literary and apologetic strategies deeply informed the works of Philo and Josephus, as well as later Christian apologists.

Dead Sea Scrolls

Until the middle of the twentieth century, interpretations of Early Judaism depended heavily upon Deuterocanonical Books, Pseudepigrapha, Philo, Josephus, the New Testament, and rabbinic traditions. Yet in 1947 the discovery of the Dead Sea Scrolls unveiled another vast collection through which to understand this crucial era. The scrolls preserve manuscripts in Hebrew, Aramaic, and Greek that range from the third century BCE to ca. 68 CE. We have already observed how the scrolls shed important light on questions of scripture and canon. Their discovery also unveiled previously unknown writings that must now be factored into discussions of early Jewish religion. The movement that preserved the scrolls opposed the Jerusalem priesthood, as well as the Pharisees. Against these two competing movements, they advanced their own interpretation of Jewish law, which they believed to have been uniquely revealed to their own leaders in an age of spiritual deception. The surprising discovery of such adamant claims forever challenged assumptions that Pharisaic or priestly leaders held sway over Early Judaism and advanced continuing awareness of the religious diversity of this era.

Philo and Josephus

Finally, two individual authors, Philo and Josephus, each composed prolific literary works that open additional vistas into Early Judaism. Philo of Alexandria (ca. 20 BCE–ca. 50 CE) composed some of the most sophisticated exegetical works in Western history, achieving his own distinct synthesis of scriptural tradition and philosophy. The works of the historian Flavius Josephus (37–ca. 100 CE) provide essential evidence for understanding the historical, religious, and political environments of Early Judaism. While there are important differences between them, both wrote in Greek and self-consciously interacted with Hellenistic culture, literature, and philosophy. Both of these authors lived on within Christianity as compelling models for exegesis, philosophy, and history, yet proved less useful for Rabbinic Judaism.

This Book

The remaining chapters of this book treat select aspects of these collections that have proven essential for understanding the literary, historical, and theological dimensions of ancient Judaism and the early church. The literary achievements of Early Judaism prove that this era was far from an age of silence between the Old Testament and the New. Nor did the authors of these writings imagine that they somehow lived within an intertestamental vortex, stranded somewhere between the revelations to Israel and the church. The surviving literature of this era actually exceeds the volume of the Christian Bible and warrants serious consideration in terms of what it can teach readers today about the larger religious world from which much of the Hebrew Bible and New Testament emerged.

Any attempt to treat the vast literature of this era must remain selective. The first three chapters focus on three literary traditions reflected among the Deuterocanonical Books and Pseudepigrapha. These include wisdom writings (Chapter 2), apocalyptic literature (Chapter 3), and attempts to rewrite earlier scriptural narratives and laws (Chapter 4). These widespread literary types reflect the ongoing legacy of Israel's traditions within Early Judaism and remain central to the interpretation of New Testament literature. Two further chapters treat the Dead Sea Scrolls (Chapter 5) and Philo and Josephus (Chapter 6). Each of these offers a distinct vantage upon the historical experiences, literature, and religious concerns of ancient Judaism. In pursuing this agenda, the following perspectives will be paramount.

1. We are only secondarily reading noncanonical literature. Many of these writings were composed long before the closure of the canonical process. This means that in their formative contexts, their authors may well have believed that their religious claims were decisive. Some claimed the mantle of revelatory authority. Even those who did not explicitly do so often presented their compositions as essential enhancements to scriptural traditions that addressed urgent functional needs within their communities. Their earliest audiences, too, may have found that some of these writings possessed unsurpassed wisdom for addressing their own religious questions and needs.

2. *The writings of Early Judaism are exceptionally diverse, originating from different religious movements and regional environments.* To read any of these writings as representative of the totality of ancient Judaism would result in a distorted view of what was originally a more varied panorama. The picture of Early Judaism that scholars construct today must be gradual, patient, and inclusive, relative to the remarkable adaptability of Jewish traditions to differing contexts. In the present volume, individual chapters will reveal the inherent tensions that exist even among different wisdom writings, apocalypses, and Dead Sea Scrolls. It is further cautioned that we are typically hearing the voices of technically trained literary elites in these works, a specialized stratum within the total Jewish population of antiquity. Beyond literature, a wealth of inscriptional and archaeological evidence offers material insight into "normal, everyday life" (Goodman 2002, 48) beyond the dire religious problems explored within literary circles.

3. *The study of these writings is essential to understanding the larger history of the Hebrew Bible and the New Testament.* These writings offer some of the earliest evidence for understanding how Israel's traditions were intensively studied, reinterpreted, and courageously lived out in the Hellenistic and Roman eras. Moreover, they bear eloquent witness to the early Jewish literary and theological heritage that would live on in varied ways within the New Testament and in the literature of Rabbinic Judaism. While the New Testament authors drew heavily from writings found in the Hebrew Bible, they did not do so in a vacuum, but viewed Israel's traditions through the interpretive assumptions of their early Jewish environment. In attending seriously to the literature of this era, we may thus encounter a range of popular traditions that shaped the literatures and theologies of the New Testament. It is further the methodology of this book to take seriously the distinctive implications that individual books/collections may offer for interpreting the New Testament. Yet does this literature have meaning only in terms of what came before it or what would come after it?

4. The study of this literature is illuminating in its own right. Even if there is immense historical value to these collections, a distorted view of their contents can emerge if they are viewed only as inhabiting a liminal realm upon the inexorable timeline of normative religious traditions. Negative perceptions have viewed them as a decline from the ascendant heights of the religion of the Hebrew Bible or as an imperfect anticipation of the religious problems that would later be resolved within the church and Rabbinic Judaism. They have been viewed as legendary rather than historical, esoteric rather than inviting, dubious rather than authentic, postbiblical rather than biblical. One corrective to this tendency is to think critically about the religious world within each text in its own historical setting. That is the approach taken in the present volume, recognizing that this remains necessary before generalizing about the larger epoch-making developments that this era would inspire. Such a journey into the worlds of early Jewish writings will involve its own distinct encounters with one of history's most creative religious environments.

2
The Glory of Wisdom

A frequently encountered religious ideal among early Jewish writings is the concept of wisdom. The writings preserved in the Hebrew Bible attest concern for wisdom within the religion of ancient Israel, as well as in the history of Judaism after the Babylonian Exile. Scholars frequently classify the scriptural books of Job, Proverbs, and Qoheleth (Ecclesiastes) as "wisdom literature," due to their specialized interest in the concept of wisdom. Beyond these three books, concern with wisdom animated many sectors of postexilic Judaism, generating a diverse range of new "wisdom" or "sapiential" compositions. Two of the most significant examples are the Wisdom of Jesus ben Sira (also called Sirach, Siracides, Ecclesiasticus) and the Wisdom of Solomon, both of which feature today among Deuterocanonical Books (Apocrypha). The present chapter explores the variant presentations of wisdom in these two writings, further explaining their value for understanding aspects of New Testament literature.

The Dimensions of Wisdom

An essential characteristic of wisdom is its all-encompassing character. Those who pursued wisdom did not seek specialization in a particular sphere of knowledge. Nor were they simply concerned with logical reasoning. Wisdom comprised a holistic intellectual, moral, practical awareness regarding the character of God, the nature of the created world, and the proper place of humans within it. Wisdom may approach sublime subject matter concerned with the deity's wise governance of the cosmos, the full extent of which is impossible for humans to comprehend (Job 38:1–42:6; Sir 24:28–29). Yet wisdom may equally deal with everyday affairs of sound judgment within this magnificent order that will lead humans away from self-destruction and toward happiness. From the transcendent to the practical, wisdom proves challenging to define, precisely because it is ultimately concerned with the interrelatedness of everything.

The diverse wisdom writings of Early Judaism illustrate a number of tensions and developments when compared with the wisdom books of the Hebrew Bible. In the Hebrew Bible, approaches to wisdom range from the more conventional to the more subversive. The book of Proverbs, for example, serves the more conventional purpose of affirming traditional communal expectations and familial order. Yet Qoheleth and Job hold conventional values up for critical examination—perhaps even rejection. One controverted issue among biblical wisdom books concerns divine justice, or what is sometimes called **theodicy** (see Box 2.1). How does God's justice work amid the mysteries of creation and the realities of human experiences? Job and Qoheleth provide little confidence in how to resolve this question and even ridicule facile solutions. Yet Proverbs reflects greater assurance that God faithfully rewards the righteous and punishes the wicked. Deliberations on wisdom also concern **epistemology**, the question of what humans can know and how they know it. Job and Qoheleth offer skepticism concerning human understanding amid the wonders of creation, while Proverbs remains more optimistic that humans can indeed acquire sufficient wisdom to live well.

When compared with these works, early Jewish wisdom writings tend toward more optimistic approaches to theodicy, epistemology, and conventional beliefs. In spite of their crucial differences, they are generally more interested in maintaining the integrity of traditional beliefs than in subverting them. They are confident that God is not ultimately hiding wisdom from humans, even if they differ in how it is to

---

Box 2.1 Theodicy

Religion and philosophy often concern the problem of "divine" (*theo-*) "justice" (*-dikē*) amid the imperfections of the cosmos and the realities of suffering. While the term originated in the European Enlightenment, it may be used to describe a major concern within early Jewish literature.

be acquired or where it may be found. They are further convinced of the reliability of divine justice and offer their own fascinating theodicies.

Sages and Scribes

The sages who authored wisdom compositions are frequently unknown. Only in the case of Jesus ben Sira, a Jerusalem scribe of the early second century BCE, do we know the historical identity of a particular author. If Ben Sira is a representative instance, the authors of wisdom compositions were technical literary and rhetorical specialists, known as **scribes**. As experts in the cultural and legal traditions of their respective nationalities, scribes occupied a particular place within Near Eastern societies, where knowledge meant power. Jewish scribes of the Hellenistic and Roman eras, in particular, advised the priestly aristocracy and populace on the basis of their expertise in the interpretation of Jewish law and cultural tradition. Their "wisdom" preserved a broad range of cultural knowledges and instructed future generations in how to win honor and avoid shame by meeting communal expectations.

The scribes aspired to preserve their own understandings of tradition amid the social and political pressures of their times. Since they depended upon the support of their patrons, divisions in the aristocracy just prior to the Maccabean Revolt factionalized scribes into conflicting parties. Such conflicts facilitated rival interpretations of Jewish law, scriptural traditions, and the concept of wisdom itself. Scribes also pursued wisdom in a context in which Hellenistic culture was predominant and threatened to diminish the value of Jewish tradition. Thus, they faced the dual challenges of contending against internal rivals, while also legitimating their interpretations of Judaism within the more global intellectual context of the Hellenistic age. This social environment nourished the creative flourishing of diverse approaches to wisdom.

Wisdom Writings

The literary skills of scribes are apparent within wisdom compositions. Much of the literature is poetic, yet it remains difficult to define a single genre or structure to "wisdom literature." Two basic styles of presentation are common. The **wisdom instruction** offers itself as the teaching of a sage to an envisioned audience. A classic example may be found at the beginning of Proverbs, which addresses parental instructions to children: "Hear, my child, your father's instruction, and do not reject your mother's teaching" (Prov 1:8).[1] The style of the wisdom instruction may be found throughout much of the book of Ben Sira, where the lived experiences of the renowned Judaean scribe supply a reservoir of wisdom for younger generations who will one day serve the same role. The Wisdom of Solomon presents itself as the wise king's instruction to the rulers of the earth. The characterization of the sage's own biography, as well as the envisioned audiences they address, create colorful literary contexts for conceptualizing wisdom.

Another style of presentation is the **wisdom hymn**, typically a poem exploring a particular theme. The hymns within wisdom literature may dwell upon creation, human experiences, or wisdom itself. The book of Proverbs, for example, contains an extended hymn that personifies wisdom as a wise and elegant woman who persuades youths to hear her instruction (Prov 8:1–9:6). Ben Sira and Wisdom of Solomon also preserve their own poetic hymns on "Lady Wisdom" (e.g., Sir 24; Wis 10). Such hymns fully display the literary imagination and poetic skill of wisdom authors.

Further supporting these two larger styles of address stands an array of smaller instructional units. The individual sayings of the wise are often termed "maxims," "aphorisms," or "proverbs." They offer brief observations promoting a particular idea. Such sayings may range from self-evident truisms to enigmatic riddles. Qoheleth offers the truism "Two are better than one" (4:9). Of course, companionship is better than total isolation, even if it is beneficial to be reminded of this. Many sayings of the wise, however, possessed a cryptic or "dark" character that provoked deeper thought (Prov 1:6; Psalm 49:4). Ben Sira thus acknowledges "the subtleties of parables . . . the hidden meanings of proverbs" (Sir 39:2–3) that demand intense analysis.

Artful similes and comparisons highlight many proverbs: "A new friend is like new wine; when it has aged, you can drink it with pleasure" (Sir 9:10). Prayers are found within wisdom writings (Wis

9:1–18; Sir 36:1–17). **Beatitudes** provide poetic statements of blessedness upon particular persons, often followed by a brief explanation: "Happy is the husband of a good wife; the number of his days will be doubled" (Sir 26:1). Ben Sira and the Wisdom of Solomon express their own wisdoms as they creatively adapt these traditional literary styles of instruction.

The Wisdom of Jesus ben Sira

The Wisdom of Jesus (Yeshua) ben Sira recounts the teachings of a Jewish sage who was active in Palestine in the early second century BCE. The book was composed in Hebrew, yet also circulated in Greek through his grandson's laborious translation, which he began after arriving in Egypt in 132 BCE. Ben Sira himself, however, appears to have written sometime between 200 and 180 BCE, prior to the Hellenistic Reform and Maccabean Revolt. While the grandson's Greek translation later featured among Deuterocanonical Books, modern discoveries have unearthed Hebrew manuscripts, so that a substantial portion of the book may be studied in Hebrew today.

Ben Sira remained of interest in later Rabbinic Judaism, a relatively rare phenomenon among Deuterocanonical writings. Although some rabbis rejected public Sabbath readings of Ben Sira, it remained valuable within rabbinic deliberations, even if it did not feature within the later Jewish canon.[2]

Literary Context

Complexes of similar materials suggest the book developed gradually out of earlier compositions (Collins 1997). The clearest example is the "Praise of the Ancestors" (chs. 44–50), which provides a stylistically consistent review of how wisdom was historically embodied in the worthies of Israel's past. The poem on Lady Wisdom in 24:1–22 appears to represent a distinct composition that was further expanded (cf. 14:20–15:10, 34:14–20). Other portions of the book offer clusters of similar literary material (e.g., 7:34–9:16, chs. 39–43). Autobiographical remarks accent portions of the book (24:30–34, 33:16–18), revealing the sage's own self-understanding and experiences.

Some compositions, however, may not actually have originated with Ben Sira. The revolutionary tenor of 36:1–22 seems alien to Ben Sira's more moderate sociopolitical thought (Collins 1997). Remains of 51:13–30 are attested elsewhere among the Dead Sea Scrolls in a collection of psalms (*11QPsalm^a*) and may not have originated with the sage. Since the book became a popular instructional handbook, it was copied many times, thus contributing to variant readings and the gradual incorporation of additional materials.

Its style and subject matter are often comparable to Proverbs, which probably served as a literary and conceptual model. The book has also been compared with collections of Greek maxims. Ben Sira shares several topics of concern with the maxims of the famous Greek sage Theognis of Megara, especially on the subject of friendship (DeSilva 2004). The concerns of Ben Sira also occasionally intersect with late Egyptian wisdom books, like the *Instruction of Phibis* (Phebhor) (Sanders 1983). Ben Sira may have been informed by such Hellenistic literary models, even as he praised the excellence of Jewish wisdom.

Social Setting

Ben Sira wrote as a technically trained scribe who held a specific status within Judaean society. He insists that the work of the scribe differs from that of the farmer, blacksmith, and potter (38:24–34). Such skilled professionals "maintain the fabric of the world" (38:34), yet the scribe's vocation requires leisure and even travel (34:11–12, 39:4). Instead of the plow, furnace, and wheel, the scribe's tools are the specialized rhetorical skills of literary analysis and public expression (4:24). These arts prepared scribes to stand in the assembly of the people and offer precise counsel that would preserve the Jewish community from imminent threats (15:1–5, 21:17, 38:33).

Speaking from this social location, Ben Sira offers valuable perspectives on religious and social issues in the generation prior to the Maccabean Revolt. Above all, he faithfully supports the present structures of priesthood, temple, and sacrifice that preserve tradition and offer coherence to Judaean society (7:29-31, 34:21-27, 35:1-12, 45:6-26, 50:1-21). His instructions on wealth and poverty (4:1-10, 5:1-8, 11:14-28, 13:1-26, 29:1-28, 31:1-11, 35:13-26), family and kinship (7:18-28, 25:7-26:18, 36:26-31, 42:9-14), happiness and adversity (2:1-11, 14:3-19, 30:14-25, 33:1, 39:17-35) further advance his own distinct interpretation of conventional aristocratic values.

His admonitions on wealth and poverty strive to mediate justly amid the socioeconomic fissures of his society, often inspired by the moral awareness of Israel's prophets (34:21-27) (DeSilva 2004). Among later church authors, in fact, his sayings are repeatedly cited in affirmation of almsgiving, humility, and mercy toward the poor.[3] At the same time, Ben Sira may seem comfortably detached from deeper conflicts between rich and poor (Collins 1997). While he exhibits a keen awareness that the rich may exploit the poor (13:1-24), his instruction typically seeks to ameliorate existing social conditions rather than overturn them. He is fully aware that foolish and unjust rulers may devastate their people, yet ultimately confides, "The government of the earth is in the hand of the Lord, and over it he will raise up the right leader for the time" (10:4).

In his treatment of wives and daughters, he exhibits unusual misogyny, even when compared with the standards of his time (25:13-26:12, 42:9-14). On the management of household slaves, he is highly ambivalent. On one hand, he advocates continuous labor and strict discipline (33:25-30). One the other, he warns against injustice (33:30) and even counsels, "If you have but one slave, treat him like a brother, for you will need him as you need your life" (33:31). His social outlook further reveals the anxiety that in the best of times, all could change, suddenly and unpredictably, for the worse (11:1-28) (Sanders 1983). The sage's "conventional" attitudes thus remain animated by his own anxious, cautious viewpoint:

> In the time of plenty think of the time of hunger;
> in days of wealth think of poverty and need.
> From morning to evening conditions change;
> all things move swiftly before the Lord.
> One who is wise is cautious in everything. (18:25-27)

Perhaps such anxieties were well founded, as Ben Sira lived amid religious and political tensions that would soon erupt in the Maccabean Revolt.

Creation

As with the wisdom literature in the Hebrew Bible, creation is an essential concern for Ben Sira. Creation is gloriously designed in an everlasting order, filled with all things essential to human flourishing (16:26–30). It contains no malevolent forces that lead humanity tragically to its demise. Ben Sira is thus no ascetic, but freely encourages the dignified enjoyment of all the pleasurable blessings of creation (14:11–19, 31:12–32:13). Likewise, the deity has generously poured wisdom upon all creation. Wisdom abides with "all the living according to his gift" and is readily accessible to those who love God (1:10). Humans have been created with the capacity to attain wisdom: "He filled them with knowledge and understanding, and showed them good and evil" (17:7). Careful observation of the world and reflection upon human experiences thus offer reliable guides to understanding. Ben Sira takes a more optimistic view of epistemology than some of his predecessors (Job 28, 38:1–42:6). Although God's own complete knowledge remains incomprehensible, there is sufficient wisdom for human happiness generously displayed throughout the creation (Sir 42:15–43:33). Cosmic order and human understanding are well aligned.

Lady Wisdom

Several hymns personify the beauty and power of wisdom in the form of Lady Wisdom. She was created "before the ages, in the beginning," and will never cease (24:9). This universal, ethereal presence now dwells among humans and openly offers the fruits of instruction to all who seek her. For Ben Sira, she makes her home in Israel, where the Creator commanded her, "Pitch your tabernacle in Jacob, and in Israel receive your inheritance" (24:8):

> Before the ages, in the beginning, he created me,
> and for all the ages I shall not cease to be.
> In the holy tent I ministered before him,
> and so I was established in Zion.
> Thus in the beloved city he gave me a resting place,
> and in Jerusalem was my domain.
> I took root in an honored people,
> in the portion of the Lord, his heritage. (24:9–12)

With this overture to the national tradition of Israel, the sage offers a distinct development beyond the wisdom writings of the Hebrew Bible.

Job, Proverbs, and Qoheleth approach wisdom universally, without explicit reference to the national story of Israel. Even in the hymns to Lady Wisdom in Proverbs, which seem to have had profound influence upon Ben Sira, she may be found in the city (Prov 1:20–21, 8:3), in the reign of just kings (8:15–16), and in the divine presence (8:22–31)—yet explicit mention of Israel's own national traditions remains elusive. Ben Sira, however, leaves no doubt that divine wisdom has found a unique home within Israel's own particular traditions.

This is especially apparent in Ben Sira's development of the intimate relationship between wisdom and Israel's law. The very wisdom in which the cosmos was created fills Israel's law, which "pours forth instruction like the Nile," the Tigris, and Euphrates (24:25–27). While Proverbs emphasizes faithful adherence to parental instruction (Prov 1:8), Ben Sira insists that the practical disciplines of legal observance are fundamental to the pursuit of wisdom (Sir 1:26):

> Whoever fears the Lord will do this,
> and whoever holds to the law will obtain wisdom.
> She will come to meet him like a mother,
> and like a young bride she will welcome him.
> She will feed him with the bread of learning,
> and give him the water of wisdom to drink. (15:1–3)

Ben Sira otherwise avoids technical treatments of how to observe particular laws from the Torah, viewing its commandments in very generalized terms. Meditation upon the law, as well as publicly conversing about it, comprise the daily habits of the wise (6:37, 9:14–16). Honoring parents (cf. Exod 20:12) is repeatedly demanded (Sir 3:1–16, 7:27–28). Adultery (cf. Exod 20:14) is excoriated (Sir 23:16–27). The poem "Praise of the Ancestors" integrates the role of the law throughout its reminiscence upon Israel's history (chs. 44–50). The importance of priesthood, temple, and sacrifice are continually emphasized (7:29–31, 34:21–35:13, 38:11, 45:6–26, 50:1–21).

The observance of the law is further complemented with a prophetic sense of justice toward the poor, orphans, widows, and even slaves: "Like one who kills a son before his father's eyes is the person who offers a sacrifice from the property of the poor" (34:24 [Isa 66:3]; cf. Sir 4:1–10, 7:20–21). Ben Sira, in fact, is so serious about the law that even the great sage must concede, "Better are the God-fearing who lack understanding than the highly intelligent who transgress the law" (19:24; cf. 33:2–3).

The fusion of the wisdom tradition together with Israel's law represents one of Ben Sira's greatest contributions as a sage. Indeed, his grandson's preface would interpret the book as an inspiration for all who seek knowledge and deeper observance of Israel's law. Even so, interpreters debate Ben Sira's ultimate purpose. Was he prioritizing Israel's law above and against the diverse wisdoms of the Hellenistic age? Or did he rather view the law itself within a larger cosmic framework that was ultimately concerned with universal wisdom? At the very least, Ben Sira creates a position of honor for Jewish law, history, and tradition in an environment in which Hellenistic culture held primacy. Ben Sira persuades his readers that the one who faithfully practices the law lives in accord with the very wisdom that fills the entire creation.

Since wisdom is ultimately from God, one must pray for it: "If the great Lord is willing, he will be filled with the spirit of understanding; he will pour forth words of wisdom" (39:6). Such spirit-inspired instruction may be compared to prophecy (24:32–33). In these cases, wisdom genuinely emerges from a kind of divine inspiration. Even so, Ben Sira is quick to discourage dreams and speculative practices (34:1–8; cf. 3:21–25). In an environment in which apocalyptic revelations and philosophical speculation were popular, Ben Sira discourages these practices as pathways to wisdom. In contrast, the law provides an unwavering guide (34:8).

Good and Evil

Thus far, it may seem that the sage emphasizes the more optimistic side of human possibilities. Yet Ben Sira is aware of suffering and deeply attuned to deliberations on divine justice that troubled earlier sages (e.g., Job, Qoheleth). A distinguishing conceptual feature of his wisdom is its "doctrine of opposites" (11:14, 33:14–15, 39:17–35, 42:15–25). Good and evil, life and death—all things are twofold, in antithetical pairs: "Look at all the works of the Most High; they come in pairs, one the opposite of the other" (33:14–15). This doctrine of opposites expresses Ben Sira's orientation to theodicy. Suffering and prosperity are both simply contrasting parts of the fullness of creation, each of which ultimately serves its own divinely ordained purpose. Ben Sira warns that even the wise will be tested by adversity, and his instruction offers consolation to the righteous in their afflictions:

> Accept what befalls you,
> and in times of humiliation be patient.
> For gold is tested in the fire,
> and those found acceptable in the furnace of humiliation.
> Trust in him, and he will help you;
> make your ways straight, and hope in him. (2:4–6)

Such temporary afflictions encourage humble, ethical behavior, while also revealing the insincerity of sinners (2:1–18; cf. 4:17–19, 6:18–32, 32:24–33:3).

Humans have also been empowered with the freedom of will to make their own informed choices and experience the consequences (15:11–20, 16:24–17:24). Moreover, the deity allows abundant, patient, merciful provisions for repentance from sins (17:25–29, 21:1–3). Thus, there is no evil with God. The things most essential to life—"water and fire and iron and salt and wheat flour and milk and honey"—will abound to the blessing of the righteous, even as they bring evil consequences to sinners (39:26–27). In this sense, human freedom further magnifies the duality that exists within creation. In contrast with other competing wisdoms of his time, Ben Sira develops this theodicy without reliance upon an afterlife—a belief he discourages (41:1–14). The world as presently constituted remains sufficient to ensure the faithful execution of divine justice.

The Wisdom of Solomon

Ben Sira's approach to divine justice might well classify as a "theodicy of good fortune," an approach to human experience that views the world as ultimately sufficient as it is. One encounters a different approach in the Wisdom of Solomon, where God's justice will resolve innocent suffering in an afterlife and a final judgment upon sinners. Like the Greek translation of Ben Sira, the Wisdom of Solomon takes us to the context of Egyptian Judaism, where the work was written in Greek sometime during the first century BCE/first century CE. This setting and date are suggested by its linguistic style, its concern with the Gentile cults of "Egypt" (Wis 11–19), as well as conceptual affinities to writings of Egyptian Judaism that were also involved in a thoroughgoing dialogue between Israel's traditions and Greek philosophy. The book became very popular in early Christianity and would later circulate among the Deuterocanonical Books. Unlike Ben Sira, no evidence exists for its reception within Rabbinic Judaism.

Literary Context

The title of the book reflects a pseudonymous poem in chapters 6–9, in which the author (sometimes called "Pseudo-Solomon") takes on the persona of the wise king to instruct rulers in how to acquire wisdom and govern righteously (6:1–3, cf. 1:1). Two other main units begin and end the work, although there is little consensus on their precise boundaries. The first unit provides a poem that explores wisdom through the experience of the suffering righteous, who is saved by God from the wicked (chs. 1–5). The final unit offers an exploration of wisdom through a historical review of select episodes from Genesis through Exodus 17, especially focusing on how divine justice was vindicated in the events surrounding the exodus. These three overlapping and stylistically diverse units are nevertheless considered to be the work of a single author.

The Suffering Righteous

Pseudo-Solomon first instructs readers concerning the wisdom that should guide one's interpretation of innocent suffering (chs. 1-5). Since wisdom is a pure and immortal spirit, she will never dwell in the midst of blasphemy, deceit, and slander—false discourses that lead to death (1:6-11). For "God did not create death" (1:13-16; cf. 11:24-26). Only through the envy of the devil and the deeds of the wicked did death enter into the world at all (2:24). With this claim, the author clearly reveals dualistic assumptions regarding the origin of evil in the world (see Box 2.2). Thus, the innocent suffering and death of the righteous do not originate with God. To vindicate this line of reasoning, the author's clever theodicy poem imitates the false discourse of the wicked (2:1-20), then utterly refutes their mistaken worldview (2:21-4:20).

"The wicked" believe that life is short, with no promise of an afterlife (2:1-5). On this basis, they advocate the indulgent pursuit of pleasure. Their hedonistic lifestyle leads to moral indifference, as they oppress the innocent (2:6-20). Their apparent freedom to

---

Box 2.2 Dualism

Ancient thinkers sometimes made sense of reality by dividing it into two contrasting opposites, a tendency known as "dualism." Anthropological dualism divides the human into contrasting opposites, such as "body" and "soul." Spatial dualism organizes the cosmos into conflicting spheres, such as "heaven" and "earth." Temporal dualism emphasizes the contrast between this present age and the world that is to come.

crush the righteous with impunity vindicates their immoral philosophy: "Let our might be our law of right" (2:11). Wisdom's depiction of the wicked is likely drawn as a somewhat exaggerated caricature of Epicurean philosophy and earlier Jewish wisdom. Like Epicureans, the wicked subscribe to a psychophysical understanding of the soul that envisions its dissipation into the air at death (2:2-3).[4] Like Qoheleth (9:7-10) and Ben Sira (14:11-16), they discourage the likelihood of an afterlife and encourage the enjoyment of material pleasures within present existence.

The author is quick to refute such assumptions. Wisdom is keen to "the secret purposes of God" (2:22), which include the hope of immortal life for the righteous. Their affliction is but a temporary trial that refines them, like fire, into everlasting life (3:5-9):

> [T]he souls of the righteous are in the hand of God,
> and no torment will ever touch them.
> In the eyes of the foolish they seemed to have died,
> and their departure was thought to be a disaster. . . .
> But they are at peace.
> For though in the sight of others they were punished,
> their hope is full of immortality. (3:1-4)

They only "seemed to have died" (3:2) from the false perspective of the wicked, yet in reality, their souls enjoy immediate, everlasting peace in the presence of God. The wicked, however, who have "made a covenant" with death (1:16; cf. Isa 28:15-18), will suffer in the present life for their folly. Rather than prosperous descendants, they leave behind only the destructive consequences of their sins (3:10-4:20). The wicked even renounce their own distorted philosophy later in the poem, astonished at God's hidden plan to redeem the righteous (5:1-16).

The theodicy poem concludes with a rousing presentation of the deity as a divine warrior, taking up arms to execute final judgment throughout the cosmos (5:17-23):

> The Lord will take his zeal as his whole armor,
> and will arm all creation to repel his enemies;

Box 2.3 Eschatology

Eschatology is concerned with the "last things" of creation and history, a subject treated with deep imagination and variety in early Jewish writings. Apocalypses, in particular, are concerned with these questions. Yet Wisdom of Solomon demonstrates that eschatological beliefs also became relevant to some sapiential writings.

> he will put on righteousness as a breastplate,
> and wear impartial justice as a helmet;
> he will take holiness as an invincible shield,
> and sharpen stern wrath for a sword,
> and creation will join with him to fight against his frenzied
>   foes. (5:17–20)

With this strong emphasis upon dualism, the afterlife, and eschatology, Wisdom stands apart from Job, Proverbs, Qoheleth, and Ben Sira by adapting apocalyptic traditions into its instruction (Winston 2003). The result attests the development of a more "eschatologizing wisdom" in Early Judaism (see Box 2.3).

The Spirit of Wisdom

In the extended autobiographical poem of chapters 6–9, Pseudo-Solomon explores his experience of pursuing wisdom, as well as its implications for just governance. Indeed, the first lines of the book are presented as an instruction to rulers (1:1), whom God will judge more severely than others for the position of authority they have been given (6:1–11). The autobiographical poem thus summons all rulers to seek wisdom as their highest duty. It is through wisdom alone that rulers may govern justly and administer God's own perfect "kingdom" or "reign" over the world (6:17–20; cf. Prov 8:14–16). Though of royal lineage (7:1–6), it was only through humble prayer that Solomon himself received "the spirit of wisdom" (7:7; cf. 1:6). While God's plans are veiled in "mystery" (2:21–22, 7:21), wisdom ultimately presents no epistemological barrier to humans. The prerequisites to wisdom are primarily ethical. Those who are humble and practice righteousness open their hearts to the presence of wisdom.

Alongside its spiritual, ethical dimensions, wisdom initiates the king into vast categories of knowledge: cosmology and the elements, time and the seasons, the calendar and astrology, the nature of animals, the powers of spirits, human reasoning, botany and its medicinal properties (7:17-20). The passage provides a fascinating window into how the author understood the diverse concerns of instruction in wisdom. In other writings, Solomon was indeed known as a master of these disciplines (1 Kings 4:29-34; Josephus, *Antiquities* 8:42-45). Pseudo-Solomon praises wisdom as the mother of all these beautiful facets of reality (7:12).

As in Ben Sira and Proverbs, wisdom is personified as a heavenly being, who has come down to instruct fallible humans (9:10). Yet Wisdom takes a bold step beyond its predecessors by characterizing Lady Wisdom as a "spirit" that may presently indwell the righteous: "Wisdom will not enter a deceitful soul, or dwell in a body enslaved to sin" (1:4). The language of wisdom's descent into the human soul describes wisdom on a mystical, philosophical plane. Other passages of the work further explore the characteristics of the soul, its enlightenment, and even its immortality through the pursuit of wisdom (8:13, 17; 9:17; 10:16; 12:1). It is Lady Wisdom, in fact, who has passed "into holy souls in every generation," making them "friends of God and prophets" (7:27).

More than dwelling in righteous souls alone, however, the author boldly declares that Lady Wisdom is a universally pervasive force that sustains and renews all things:

> For Wisdom is more mobile than any motion;
> because of her pureness she pervades and penetrates all things.
> For she is a breath of the power of God,
> and a pure emanation of the glory of the Almighty;
> therefore nothing defiled gains entrance into her.
> For she is a reflection of eternal light,
> a spotless mirror of the working of God,
> and an image of his goodness. (7:24-26)

Though she is one, she pervades and "renews all things" throughout creation (7:27; cf. 12:1). She equipped Solomon to build the earthly temple in Jerusalem based upon a heavenly model designed by God at the creation. She is able to reveal such mysteries, since she herself was present at the throne of God's glory even before creation (9:8-10). While she remains subordinate to God, Wisdom is also presented as an extension of divine nature into the world. It is in wisdom that humans may have the most accessible experience of divine power and goodness—virtues that may guide rulers and preserve civilizations from destruction.

Wisdom and Tradition

Finally, the book concludes by exploring the character of divine wisdom through the narratives of Genesis through Exodus 17 (Wis 10-19). This section of the book shares with Ben Sira the basic assumption that wisdom has been embodied in Israel's own historical experiences. A rapid historical review (10:1-11:26) reveals how "Wisdom" saved the human race from destruction in the cases of Adam, Cain, Noah, Babel, Abraham, Lot, Jacob, Joseph, and especially the Exodus. Yet curiously, the names of figures from the scriptural narratives are not mentioned, nor is "Israel" directly named. Perhaps this is an indication that the author emphasizes what is universal about the scriptural narratives, interpreting them upon an abstract, spiritualized plane in which divine wisdom has acted throughout history to redeem the world.

God's justice upon non-Israelites consumes the author (chs. 11-19), as he produces one of the most sustained explorations of the topic among early Jewish writings. Wisdom utilizes the Exodus narrative creatively, forming a strong correspondence between the Egyptians in the scriptural text and the predominant Graeco-Egyptian culture of the author's own time. Likewise, the redemption of the Israelites in the scriptural narrative offers ultimate assurance that the righteous will also be redeemed from present endangerment.

The author hopes to demonstrate, often through clever scriptural interpretation, that "the very things by which their enemies were punished" ultimately became measures of redemption for the Israelites

(11:5). Thus, the waters of Egypt were polluted by blood, yet water sustained the Israelites in the wilderness (11:4–14). The heavens sent forth storms against the Egyptians but manna for Israel (16:15–23). Darkness and the horrors of night seized the Egyptians, even as radiant light from the pillar of fire illumined Israel's path (17:1–18:4). The idolatry of the Egyptians in worshiping senseless animals resulted in the very plagues in which "irrational creatures" destroyed their land (16:1–3). Thus, "one is punished by the very things by which one sins" (11:16). Divine justice is also administered differently among Egyptians and Israelites: the former are proportionately punished for their evils, while the latter are instructed and disciplined for their ultimate benefit (12:19–22, 16:4–6; cf. 2 Macc 7:30–36).

On the basis of Egyptian idolatry, Wisdom argues that the Gentiles have been unwilling to recognize the greatness of God manifest in creation (Wis 13:1–9). This leads them to worship created things as idols, rather than the creator. Such idolatry, in turn, becomes "the beginning and cause and end of every evil" (14:27). Wisdom's blistering attack on idols even reveals a familiarity with **euhemeristic** theories about the origins of Gentile cults (see Box 2.4). Idols arose through the veneration of departed family members and the idolization of human kings (14:12–21). Their worship ensnares humans in immorality through elaborate rituals that include infanticide, sexual transgression, and violence—so that "riotous blood and murder possess all" (14:25). In the plagues against the Egyptians, God transforms nature itself (19:6–21; cf. 5:15–23), demonstrating the creator's ultimate justice to punish the wicked and save the righteous.[5] Wisdom's virulent attack

---

Box 2.4 Euhemerism

Named for the Greek mythographer Euhemerus, this theory proposed that the worship of the gods originally arose from historical events and human persons. In the surviving fragments of his *Sacred History*, Euhemerus presents Ouranos, Kronos, and Zeus as a line of human kings who came to be worshiped as gods. The Wisdom of Solomon appeals to euhemerism in its vehement criticism of idols (14:14–25).

on Gentile cults may be read as an attempt to preserve Jewish identity within the author's own polytheistic Egyptian context.

Comparing Ben Sira and Pseudo-Solomon

Comparisons between Ben Sira and Wisdom of Solomon fruitfully illustrate the shared interests and diverse approaches that characterized early Jewish wisdom. The two books represent a temporal distance of some two centuries. They chart a geographical span from Jerusalem to Egypt. They are mutually concerned with Lady Wisdom, creation, theodicy, and practical ethics. Both locate divine wisdom in creation, the Torah, and the historical experiences of Israel. At the same time, sharp differences are apparent.

Ben Sira speaks in his own voice, as a technically trained scribal authority. Wisdom speaks pseudonymously through the voice of the archetypal wise king. Ben Sira recounts both the spiritual and technical features of acquiring wisdom. Wisdom is far more concerned with the spiritual, mystical apprehension of wisdom, as it descends into the very souls of the righteous. Ben Sira's theodicy emphasizes the glorious sufficiency of life in the present world, as suffering and prosperity each serve a divinely ordained purpose within the totality of creation. Wisdom, however, depends more heavily upon dualism, the afterlife, and eschatology. Through the "envy of the devil," wickedness and death entered a perfect creation—yet the power of wisdom presents a countervailing force that bestows righteousness and immortality. Ben Sira actively discourages apocalyptic thought, yet Wisdom creatively adapts it, anticipating the future advent of the divine warrior to restore justice throughout the cosmos.

Wisdom in the New Testament

The shared interests and impasses between Ben Sira and Wisdom of Solomon reveal a broader diversity that may be observed among other contemporary writings. Among Deuterocanonical Books, Tobit (4:5–19) and Judith (8:8, 14, 28–30; 11:20–23) develop their own presentations of sapiential ideals, which are embodied in the wise counsels and actions of their lead characters. Like Ben Sira, Baruch (3:9–4:4) insists that divine wisdom is to be found in Israel's law, yet equally chastises Israel for rejecting her through its legal transgressions.

Among writings later designated as Pseudepigrapha, wisdom features prominently in *Ahiqar*, the *Letter of Aristeas*, and the *Sentences* of Pseudo-Phocylides. As we shall see, previously unknown wisdom writings also surfaced among the Dead Sea Scrolls, and Pseudo-Solomon's Egyptian contemporary, Philo of Alexandria, was further invested in the pursuit of divine wisdom (Chapters 5–6). The prevalence of wisdom throughout these otherwise diverse writings from different sectors of Early Judaism reveals just how crucial this religious ideal was during the era of Christian origins.

Readers of the New Testament will find that the early church also concerned itself with questions of wisdom. Not only did New Testament authors repeatedly study and quote the wisdom writings of the Hebrew Bible, but they also wrote in an environment in which wisdom remained an urgent problem within both Jewish and Graeco-Roman traditions. In the opening units of 1 Corinthians (1:18–3:23), Paul deliberates concerning how the perennial ideal of "wisdom" was to be reconciled with the "gospel" that he preaches, even quoting from the book of Job as he concludes his argument (3:19). The book of James distinguishes between dualistic wisdoms at work in the world: one is earthly and demonic, while the "wisdom that is from above" inspires peace, humility, and righteous works (3:13–18). Such explicit discussions reveal how defining proper "wisdom" was central to maintaining communal harmony within the early church.

Historical Jesus

Jesus's own relationship to wisdom also comprises a significant theme within the gospel literature. Among the Synoptic Gospels (Matthew, Mark, Luke), Jesus's teaching often intersects with traditional themes found in wisdom instructions. This is especially the case in a collection of sayings shared by the Gospels of Matthew and Luke but missing from other gospels. Scholars have explained their presence in both

> **Box 2.5 Q Hypothesis**
>
> Matthew and Luke share a number of nearly identical sayings of Jesus, often termed the "double tradition." The Q Hypothesis proposes the existence of a sayings "source" (*Quelle* in German) to explain the independent use of these materials in Matthew and Luke. Q may have represented an early collection of Jesus's sayings (approximately 230 verses) dating prior to the Great Jewish Revolt. Much of Q coincides with the interests of Jewish wisdom writings.

Matthew and Luke as arising from an earlier literary source that both independently utilized, often called the "sayings source" (*Logion-Quelle*) or "Q" (see Box 2.5). The prevalence of wisdom among the Q-sayings strongly indicates that its editors interpreted Jesus through a sapiential lens. The possibility that many of these sayings may have originated in Jesus's own activity would further imply that wisdom was an important concern of the historical Jesus himself.

The Q-sayings depict Jesus explicitly speaking of (Lady) "Wisdom." In one instance, Jesus implies that he and John the Baptist have been "her children":

> For John the Baptist has come eating no bread and drinking no wine, and you say, "He has a demon"; the Son of Man has come eating and drinking, and you say, "Look, a glutton and a drunkard, a friend of tax collectors and sinners!" Nevertheless, Wisdom is vindicated by all her children. (Luke 7:33–35)[6]

Jesus criticizes the hypocrisy of his contemporaries who reject both John's ascetic behavior and his own, more indulgent attitude toward banqueting. Yet paradoxically, his opponents have failed to realize how the manifold activity of Wisdom has inspired the seemingly opposite behaviors of John and Jesus. In this instance, Lady Wisdom speaks in many ways. Jesus further implies that he and John, in spite of their differences, are among "her children," a metaphor utilized in Ben Sira to describe those who devote themselves to Wisdom: "Wisdom teaches her children" (Sir 4:11).

In yet another instance, Wisdom speaks with prophetic warning concerning the impending wrath that is coming to the present generation:

> For this reason the Wisdom of God said, "I will send them prophets and apostles, some of whom they will kill and persecute," so that this generation may be charged with the blood of all the prophets shed since the foundation of the world. (11:49–50)

In directly revealing Wisdom's admonition, Jesus presents himself as her messenger, prophet, or interpreter. The utterance further assumes that Lady Wisdom speaks as a prophet and has, indeed, been the origin of prophetic activity throughout Israel's experience. The relationship between wisdom and prophecy may also be identified in Ben Sira, who claims, "I shall pour forth instruction like prophecy" (Sir 24:33; cf. 39:1, 6). It is even more explicitly developed in Wisdom of Solomon, where "in every generation" Lady Wisdom "passes into holy souls and makes them friends of God, and prophets" (Wis 7:27; cf. 11:1).

Several additional Q-sayings reference the wise and wisdom. In a surprising subversion of most conventional approaches to wisdom, Jesus "rejoices in the Holy Spirit" that God has "revealed to infants" realities that have been otherwise hidden "from the wise and discerning" (Luke 10:21). The belief that wisdom ultimately comes through prayer as a divine gift can certainly be found in Ben Sira (39:5–8). The Wisdom of Solomon relies even more heavily upon this conviction. Wisdom comes primarily by inspiration from God (Wis 7:7, 9:1–11). Thus, Wisdom even makes "the tongues of infants speak clearly" (10:21). Jesus appears to emphasize an even more radical implication of such spirit-inspired wisdom, one that subverts the status and specialized training of professional scribes (Luke 11:52). In spite of the failure of the scribes, Jesus views the present as a unique moment for the revelation of wisdom. The queen of the South traveled across the earth "to listen to the wisdom of Solomon, and indeed, something greater than Solomon is here" (11:31).

The attempt to locate the sayings of Jesus within the world of early Jewish wisdom is thus demanded by traditions found in the gospels themselves. Yet as this brief survey has emphasized, early Jewish reflection on wisdom was diverse. An ongoing question in New Testament research remains how to qualify *the kind of wisdom* that Jesus taught.

One prominent approach, represented by John Dominic Crossan (1992), regards Jesus's teaching as a Jewish adaptation of Hellenistic, Cynic wisdom. Jesus's instructions on itinerant preaching (Luke 10:2–12), for example, bear strong resemblance to comparable Cynic practices (Diogenes Laertius, *Lives* 6:22–23). Cynics attempted to reduce intellectual problems to their barest necessities, flouting custom and subversively criticizing luxury, hypocrisy, and social convention. Like Jesus, they also utilized brief, sometimes paradoxical aphorisms. For Crossan, Jesus's Jewish-Cynic wisdom was located within Galilean peasant society, posing significant contrasts to the wisdoms that developed among professional Judaean scribes, like Ben Sira. The idea that Jesus utilized Cynic wisdom may seem surprising, yet Ben Sira and Pseudo-Solomon offer precedent for how earlier sages mediated between Greek and Jewish wisdoms.

Another feature of Crossan's (1992) interpretation is that Jesus's wisdom was not concerned with future judgment or the end of the present age. He may even have ridiculed eschatological beliefs. Instead, Jesus emphasized the present "reign" or "kingdom of God" over creation and human life, and he called human beings to live in accord with it. Crossan supports this argument with examples from sapiential literature, including Wisdom of Solomon, where God's present "reign" or "kingdom" is a reality already found throughout creation (Wis 6:3–4, 17–20; 10:10). The more future-eschatological features among the gospel traditions originated with his later followers rather than with the wisdom of Jesus himself.

Other scholars, however, have argued for a stronger eschatological component to Jesus's wisdom. Ben Witherington III (2000), for example, interprets Jesus as a "prophetic sage," one whose instruction was predominantly Jewish (not Greek) and blended both late prophetic and wisdom elements. While Jesus speaks on his own authority like the sages, the content of his teaching also frequently concerns prophecy (Luke 6:23, 7:26, 11:32, 11:47–48, 13:34, 16:16). Indeed, Wisdom herself speaks prophetically of coming judgment (11:49–50). According to Witherington, Jesus was a sage whose wisdom included an urgent eschatological teaching about God's coming kingdom.

The Wisdom of Solomon offers strong precedent for such an "eschatological wisdom" during the time that Jesus lived. The Wisdom of Solomon attests a developing trend within Jewish thought that adapted future eschatological hopes to traditional wisdom themes. Wisdom compositions among the Dead Sea Scrolls also reflect a coalescence of wisdom and eschatological hopes (see Chapter 5). Daniel Harrington (1996, 91) thus counsels that "wisdom teachings from first-century Palestine most likely had a strong mixture of sapiential and apocalyptic material." If this is the case, then the eschatological element in Jesus's wisdom need not have originated exclusively among his later followers. It may simply have been a concurrent feature of his own prophetic and eschatological blend of wisdom.

The Prologue to John

The importance of wisdom among the gospels extends to the presentation of Jesus found in the Gospel of John. While John differs substantially from the Synoptics, its Jewish-Christian authorship continued to envision Jesus in sapiential terms, as the wisdom of God "made flesh" within the world. Wisdom thus became crucial to John's **Christology**, or theological interpretation of Jesus. This "wisdom Christology" is especially evident in the opening unit of John, often called the Prologue (1:1–18). The Prologue may have been written relatively late in the complex editorial process that formed John's gospel in the late first century CE. Some have also considered the possibility that it was originally an independent poem added to John.

In any event, the Prologue stands as a compelling interpretation of the book that introduces its major themes and symbols. It is not until verse 17 that the name Jesus Christ is mentioned. The earlier stages of the Prologue utilize the term *logos* or "Word" to refer to the preexistent Christ. The term *logos* had an extensive philosophical history in Stoicism, where it designated the universal presence of divine reason, structuring the cosmos and making it intelligible to humans (see Box 2.6). The Prologue moves from the preexistent work of the *logos* in

> **Box 2.6 *Logos* in Stoicism**
>
> The concept of the *logos* has a celebrated history in Greek philosophy. Stoics used the term to describe the universal reason that structured the cosmos and made it intelligible to human inquiry. The Stoic Cleanthes describes Zeus as "rightly guiding the universal *logos*, which ranges throughout all things" (*Hymn to Zeus*, 12–13). He has also "fitted together all things into one, good with evil, so that there is one everlasting *logos* throughout all things" (19–20). Jewish thinkers reinterpreted the *logos* concept, as illustrated in Philo and *4 Maccabees*.

creation to its physical embodiment upon earth, where it reveals the divine glory. In its embodied from, the *logos* is rejected by "his own," yet the author's community receives the *logos*'s revelation of divine glory, grace, and life.

One important dimension of the Prologue's complexity is its creative utilization of wisdom traditions. The very claims made about the *logos* in John were also made about Lady Wisdom. Both are preexistent with God before the creation. In Ben Sira, Lady Wisdom declares her everlasting harmony with God: "Before the ages, in the beginning, he created me; and for all the ages I shall not cease to be" (Sir 24:9; 1:4). The Wisdom of Solomon likewise reveals the intimate accord between God and Lady Wisdom before the world began: "She . . . knows your works and was present when you made the world" (Wis 9:9). John also insists that the Word "was in the presence of God" "in the beginning" (John 1:1–2).

Like Lady Wisdom, the Word participates in the creation of the world. Proverbs presents Lady Wisdom at God's side in the creation (Prov 8:22–31). For Ben Sira, God "poured her out upon all his works" (Sir 1:9). The Wisdom of Solomon regards her as "the fashioner of all things" (Wis 7:22); reaching from one end of creation to the other, "she orders all things well" (8:1). The Prologue, too, emphasizes the activity of the *logos* in creation, as "all things came into existence through him" (John 1:3).

Wisdom proceeds forth from God, bearing a unique, intimate relation to the creator. In Proverbs, she is the first of God's works, continually dwelling in the divine presence and rejoicing at the glory of the creation (8:22–31). In Ben Sira, she comes forth "from the mouth of the Most High" (24:3). Like a priest, she ministers before God within the tabernacle (24:10). The Wisdom of Solomon develops the God-Wisdom relationship perhaps more intimately than any other early Jewish writing: "For she is a breath of the power of God, and a pure emanation of the glory of the Almighty" (7:25). Wisdom is "radiance (beaming forth) from everlasting light, a spotless mirror of the working of God, an image of his holiness" (7:26).[7] The imagery of the Wisdom of Solomon permits the interpretation that she is not merely a created companion but rather a genuine extension, reflection, or effluence of the very deity. These features of the Wisdom of Solomon would make it an important Christological document within the later history of Christianity. No less than Augustine would draw explicit connections between John's Prologue and the Wisdom of Solomon: "Is not Christ after all that Wisdom of God 'that penetrates all things by its purity' (Wis 7:24)," "the Wisdom of the Father, of which it is said, 'It is the radiance of the eternal light' (Wis 7:26)?"[8]

In John, the intimacy of the *logos* with God is like "the only (child)" (1:14), who dwells within "the bosom of the father" (1:18). Not unlike Lady Wisdom, who is a reflection of divine light, a mirror image of God's nature (Wis 7:25–26), Jesus claims that the one who has seen him has also seen God (John 12:45; 14:7, 9). Although Jesus remains dependent upon God, the Prologue ultimately follows the implications of such intimacy to the conclusion "The *logos* was God" (1:1, 18). For John, the reflection of divine nature was so clear, so pure, so complete, that the quality of "God" could not be withheld. In making Jesus "equal to God" (5:18), "one" with God (10:30, 33), John gradually presses the boundaries of earlier wisdom to their most radical extent. Even so, the Wisdom of Solomon may offer a precedent for appreciating how Lady Wisdom could also be envisioned as a genuine image of the divine glory itself.

Lady Wisdom may further provide a meaningful paradigm for interpreting some of John's predominant symbols and metaphors. In Ben Sira, God "causes her tent to rest" in Israel, commanding her, "In Jacob *make (your) tabernacle*, and in Israel receive (your) inheritance" (24:8; cf. v10).[9] In John, the preexistent Word "became flesh and *made a tabernacle* among us" (1:14). In this specific case, the Prologue utilizes the metaphor of raising a tabernacle or tent (*eskēnōsen*). The same metaphor is used in Ben Sira to describe how Lady Wisdom raised her tabernacle (*kataskēnōson*) in Israel. Elsewhere in John, the metaphor of the temple/tabernacle remains one of the most striking images of Jesus as the divine glory embodied on earth (cf. 2:21). Like Lady Wisdom, Jesus is also repeatedly to be found within the temple throughout John (2:13, 4:45, 5:1, 7:10-44, 10:22, 11:55-57, 12:20, 13:1, 18:20; cf. 4:21-24).

John's use of "light" as a symbol for the divine Word (1:4-9; cf. 8:12, 9:5, 11:9, 12:35-36, 46) is also used of Lady Wisdom (Wis 7:10, 25-26). She surpasses even the light of the sun, which ultimately fades into the darkness, yet "evil does not prevail against wisdom" (7:29-30).[10] Likewise, in Jesus "the light shines in the darkness, and the darkness did not overcome it" (John 1:5). The conviction that the one who believes in Jesus will not die but have everlasting life (John 1:4; cf. 3:16, 11:25, 14:6, 17:2-3) may also be profitably compared with the Wisdom of Solomon, where Lady Wisdom is a life-giving spirit that grants immortality (Wis 8:17; see also 1:12-15, 3:4, 6:18-19, 8:13, 15:3).

John's indebtedness to Jewish wisdom may thus help to explain some of the most crucial aspects of its interpretation of Jesus. It may further suggest that the Jewish-Christian circles in which John was written were deeply concerned with wisdom theology, so that it became entirely natural to interpret Jesus within a sapiential framework. At the same time, we must acknowledge the gospel's creative and innovative uses of earlier tradition. Perhaps what is most distinctive about the Prologue's adaptation of earlier wisdom is its profound, thoroughgoing dualism. Certainly, the Wisdom of Solomon had already conceptualized wisdom dualistically, yet John proceeds even further. The light enters into a world of darkness, where it will be threatened and rejected. The Prologue even plays upon the irony in which the preexistent and creative *logos* enters into the world, "yet the world did not know him" (1:10). Earlier wisdom could envision a mixed reception for Lady Wisdom among the wise and foolish. Some writings even declare wisdom's mission in the world a failure due to human fallibility (Bar 3:9-31; *1 Enoch* 42). John's gospel carries the story of rejected wisdom into its own dualistic frontier, shaping a distinct identity for its community as those who have uniquely received the divine glory within the conceptual darkness of the present world.

Paul on Idolatry

In his earliest surviving letter, 1 Thessalonians, Paul briefly offers a valuable window into the nature of his preaching among the Gentiles. He reminds the Thessalonians of how his gospel urged them to turn "to God from idols, to serve a living and true God, and to wait for his son from heaven, whom he raised from the dead—Jesus, who rescues us from the wrath that is coming" (1 Thess 1:9–10).[11] The passage is interesting because no sermons from the hand of Paul himself have otherwise survived. It implies that preaching against idolatry was a significant emphasis in Paul's missionary work. In the present case, the human sin of idolatry has provoked the wrath of God, which will soon overtake the whole earth, yet there remains a path of redemption for those who turn to God from idols, as Jesus will soon rescue believers from the coming wrath.

In 1 Corinthians, Paul treats the ambiguous problem of whether believers may eat meats sacrificed to idols, a question that divides the Corinthians into conflicting factions. As Paul mediates the confusing scenario, he initially affirms the freedom of believers to eat according to the discernment of their own conscience. Yet as his argument proceeds, Paul finds this a particular case in which the obligations of love and unity qualify even the most authentic claims of freedom. He thus discourages "eating in the temple of an idol" (1 Cor 8:10), further exhorting, "Do not become idolaters" (10:7), "Flee from the worship of idols" (10:14). He implies that idolatry may further be associated with sexual immorality (10:8) and fully dissociates the celebration of the church's eucharist from idolatrous feasts: "You cannot drink the cup of the Lord and the cup of demons" (10:21).

It is, however, in the opening argument of Romans that Paul offers his fullest theological treatment of the sin of idolatry and its catastrophic consequences (Rom 1:18–32). Paul's assumptions about idols share striking commonalities with the Wisdom of Solomon. Four basic claims animate Paul's spirited argument: (1) God's wrath is coming upon the world for the sin of idolatry (1:18); (2) God's wrath is justified, since humans have no excuse for worshiping idols (1:19–21); (3) the origins of idolatry arose from worshiping created things (1:22–23, 25); (4) idolatry led further to the sins of sexual immorality (1:24–27) and all other transgressions (1:28–32).

Precedents for Paul's specific arguments may be identified in the concluding unit of the Wisdom of Solomon. Like Paul, Pseudo-Solomon views idolatry as a grave sin, in which God's coming wrath will be fully justified (Wis 12:23–27, 14:8–11). The author further insists that humans are without excuse for the crime of idolatry, since the greatness of the one true God has been manifested throughout creation (see Box 2.7).

While the Wisdom of Solomon is perhaps more willing than Paul to empathize that the beauty of creation might lead one astray, even so,

Box 2.7 No Excuses

Wisdom 13:5–9	Romans 1:19–20
"For from the greatness and beauty of created things comes a corresponding perception of their Creator. Yet these people are little to be blamed, for perhaps they go astray while seeking God and desiring to find him. For while they live among his works, they keep searching, and they trust in what they see, because the things that are seen are beautiful. Yet again, not even they are to be excused; for if they had the power to know so much that they could investigate the world, how did they fail to find sooner the Lord of these things?"	"For what can be known about God is plain to them, because God has shown it to them. Ever since the creation of the world his eternal power and divine nature, invisible though they are, have been understood and seen through the things he has made. So they are without excuse."

> ### Box 2.8 Idolatry and Sexual Immorality
>
> | Wisdom 14:12 | Romans 1:24–26 |
> |---|---|
> | "For the idea of making idols was the beginning of sexual immorality, and the invention of them was the corruption of life" (cf. 14:24, 27). | "Therefore God gave them up in the lusts of their hearts to impurity, to the degrading of their bodies among themselves, because they exchanged the truth of God for a lie and worshiped and served the creature rather than the creator, who is blessed forever! Amen. For this reason God gave them up to degrading passions." |

idolatrous humanity has no excuse before God. Both authors further agree that idols arose from the worship of created things rather than the God who created them (Wis 13:1–4, 10; Rom 1:22–25).

Finally, to a remarkable degree, both authors emphasize how the sin of idolatry led initially to sexual immorality and, subsequently, to all other sins (see Box 2.8).

Paul, then, dwells more explicitly upon homoeroticism (Rom 1:26–27), a matter to which Pseudo-Solomon probably also alludes (Wis 14:26). Both authors, further, culminate their arguments with vice lists that reveal the catastrophic consequences of idolatry (see Box 2.9).

While the precise contents of their respective vice lists differ, Pseudo-Solomon and Paul emphasize how idolatry has brought humanity into an entirely dystopic state.

For James D. G. Dunn (1988, 122), the comparisons between Wisdom and Paul reveal the apostle's conversance with "a strong strand of like-minded Hellenistic Jewish wisdom theology." Paul and Wisdom may reflect common polemics against idolatry within Jewish diaspora communities. Such polemics offered a reasoned explanation for majority religious practices in Hellenistic urban environments. They also served minority Jewish communities as a powerful argument for

> **Box 2.9 The Beginning of Every Evil**
>
> | Wisdom 14:25–27 | Romans 1:29–31 |
> |---|---|
> | "And all is a raging riot of blood and murder, theft and deceit, corruption, faithlessness, tumult, perjury, confusion over what is good, forgetfulness of favors, defiling of souls, sexual perversion, disorder in marriages, adultery, and debauchery. For the worship of idols not to be named is the beginning and cause and end of every evil." | "They were filled with every kind of wickedness, evil, covetousness, malice. Full of envy, murder, strife, deceit, craftiness, they are gossips, slanderers, God-haters, insolent, haughty, boastful, inventors of evil, rebellious toward parents, foolish, faithless, heartless, ruthless." |

self-definition and exclusive faithfulness to the God of Israel. That Paul drew upon such popular arguments in one of his most significant letters reveals how his earlier formation in diaspora Judaism lived on within his theology and preaching.

3
In the Last Days

Wisdom remains a treasured ideal within a very different set of writings known as apocalypses. For the apocalypses, however, divine wisdom is not immediately accessible within the realm of current human experiences. Nor do they share Ben Sira's confidence that the present order of the world sufficiently supports the acquisition of wisdom and the administration of divine justice. The apocalypses present wisdom as a divine mystery, hidden from present human understanding and uniquely revealed to chosen recipients. An "apocalypse" (Greek: *apokalypsis*) is literally a "revelation" or "unveiling" of divine mysteries. The term appears in the New Testament book of Revelation as a title for the work: "the *apokalypsis* of Jesus Christ" (Rev 1:1).

Today, other writings that bear formal similarities to Revelation are categorized as literary apocalypses. Within the Hebrew Bible, the clearest specimen may be found in Daniel 7–12, which recounts the rise and fall of the great world empires and the eventual triumph of God's everlasting dominion. Beyond Daniel, *1 Enoch*, *4 Ezra*, *2 Baruch*, and the *Apocalypse of Abraham* illustrate the more extensive flourishing of apocalyptic literature within Early Judaism.

Apocalyptic Literature

The apocalypses differ substantially from one another, yet they commonly present themselves as revelatory literature. Writings in the apocalyptic genre describe how a divine revelation is disclosed to a chosen human recipient (Collins 1998), often an idealized figure of the past whose experiences speak to the author's later circumstances.

Literary and Historical Contexts

Brief narratives about the visionary recipient offer meaningful context for the revelation. In Daniel, revelations are mediated to a Jewish sage who serves the royal court during the Babylonian Exile of the sixth century BCE. As a survivor of the Babylonian conquest, Daniel presents a faithful example of enduring foreign dominion and holding fast to the revelation. The historical author of Daniel 7-12, however, probably wrote centuries later, in the heat of the Maccabean Revolt (167-164 BCE). By pseudonymously (see **pseudonymity**) attributing the visions to the great exilic sage, the book creates a number of powerful rhetorical effects.

Pseudonymous attribution to Daniel endows the revelation with authority and persuasiveness. As the historical author portrays the earlier course of history leading up to his own time, he employs "prophecy from the event" (*vaticinium ex eventu*). This literary device represents known historical events as ancient prophecies revealed to earlier sages like Daniel long before they would ever transpire. The course of history thus proceeds according to a predetermined divine plan. By recording a trustworthy interpretation of the past, the book positions itself as a reliable guide to present and future events as well.

Parallels between Daniel's exilic setting and the author's own, later time further imply that the Hellenistic age constituted a kind of extended Babylonian Exile (cf. 9:1-2, 20-27), a time when Israel's sovereignty had been lost and the nation remained in desperate need of redemption. Likewise, other apocalyptic authors construct remarkably creative interrelationships between earlier literary contexts and the later historical circumstances of their own times.

Revelation and Symbol

Mystery and terror characterize the revelations of Daniel 7-12. As the sage rests upon his bed at night, terrifying visions fill his head (7:1). Despite his wisdom, Daniel cannot understand the mysterious visions (7:15-16), which portray four mythological beasts rising from the sea. Only an angelic interpretation can reveal that the beasts symbolically depict "four kingdoms" (7:17). The symbols emphasize that the revelation is impenetrable by ordinary human understanding. It can be comprehended only through divine assistance. Today scholars recognize these "four kingdoms" as the great empires that dominated the Near East: the Babylonians, Medes, Persians, and Greeks. Through these symbols, the revelation offers an entirely new way to envision the great empires and God's ultimate triumph over them.

Apocalyptic authors, however, utilize symbols on multiple levels that transcend a simple correspondence with historical events (Blount 2009). Their symbols often utilize mythological imagery. The beast images of Daniel 7, for example, draw heavily upon Near Eastern mythology, depicting a world at the mercy of chaos and terror, as titanic powers rise out of the watery abyss, seize world dominion, and crush the holy beneath their feet (7:21). Their symbols also recast earlier prophetic imagery that is now fully realized within the terrors of the author's present experiences. In one example, the author of Daniel interprets the religious crimes and political arrogance of Antiochus IV Epiphanes (8:9-10, 11:36) as a fulfillment of Isaiah's earlier prophecies against the King of Babylon (Isa 14:12-15). In such cases, apocalyptic authors display their literary skills through their intensive reinterpretation of earlier prophecies.

Not all apocalypses interpret their symbols as generously as Daniel's angel. The book of Revelation and the Dream Visions of *1 Enoch* (chs. 83-90) rely much more heavily upon internal hints encoded within the symbols themselves. As apocalypses fell into the hands of later interpreters, their symbols offered a powerful interpretive grid for understanding much later historical contexts. The book of Revelation, for example, combines features of Daniel's four beasts into one, reinterpreting them as a symbol of Rome (Rev 13:1-2). The multidimensional nature of apocalyptic symbols provoked extensive reinterpretation throughout later centuries that persists within popular religion to this very day.

Time and Creation

Daniel's visions concern the shape of past, present, and future history and are often termed **temporal apocalypses**. This temporal orientation creates a formidable literary vehicle for conceptualizing the religious meaning of history. In this sense, apocalypses deal as fervently with interpreting past and present as they do with forecasting the future. Other writings present **cosmic-spatial apocalypses**, in which the mysteries of the created universe are unveiled. Enoch, for example, observes the places of the dead, the courses of the heavenly bodies, and the divine assembly where God is enthroned (*1 Enoch* 17–36). The visions offer assurance that divine order prevails throughout the cosmos, even as wickedness currently troubles the earthly realm.

Apocalyptic Thought

The composition of literary apocalypses provides an initial vantage into the more widespread influence of apocalyptic thought. The theological assumptions of apocalyptic literature, often termed **apocalypticism**, may be found in a much broader range of compositions (Murphy 2012). Yet given the variety among these writings, defining apocalyptic thought proves challenging. The unveiling of heavenly mysteries remains a persistent conceptual feature of apocalypticism. Apocalyptic theologies envision a world in which there are vast barriers between humans and God. Yet those chosen by God receive an exclusive revelation about the course of creation and history. Such revelations frequently assume **predeterminism**, since long ago God structured reality according to a divine plan that now hastens toward completion, even in spite of the apparent prevalence of evil.

Dualism

Dualistic contrasts between good and evil abound. Reality is interpreted as a conflict between two opposite principles or powers. Such **dualism** takes varied forms. Conflicting supernatural powers, such as angels and demons, may explain the current struggle between good and evil in the world. Temporal dualism emphasizes the contrast between the present age, in which evil predominates, and the future glorious age of salvation. Cosmic-spatial dualism expresses the gulf between the earthly realm, which is pervaded by evil, and the heavenly world, where God's sovereignty is fully realized. Apocalyptic thinkers frequently place themselves at the fulcrum of such dualistic structures, as God's final redemptive age now collides with the powers of this present evil epoch or as the glory of the heavenly realm descends to purify a world that has erupted into violence and chaos.

Divine and Human Agency

Apocalypticism relies heavily upon divine agency to resolve such dualistic crises, whether by God's own intervention or by the advent of angelic and messianic envoys. In most cases, the agency of present human governments will avail little to resolve the plight of creation and history. The emphasis upon divine agency often distinguishes apocalyptic thought from earlier prophetic eschatology, in which God more frequently works "in mysterious ways" through the instrumentality of earthly empires (Isa 44:24–45:7; Jer 25:1–14, 27:1–29:14).

Even so, apocalyptic theology is no flight from human agency but encourages moral vigilance. Apocalypses were often composed by disenfranchised sages, literary elites who were alienated from the centers of power. Given their social location, it is reasonable that they emphasize divine rather than earthly political solutions to the evils of their world. Nevertheless, their vast literary productivity waged an active intellectual campaign that challenged the imperial ideologies of their times. Apocalyptic ethics also envision a variety of diverse roles that the righteous may play in the final drama (Portier-Young 2011). The leaders within Daniel's community appear to have been put to the sword while instructing the multitudes in their apocalyptic interpretation of current events (Dan 11:33). Yet whether through martyrdom, revolution, or other response, apocalyptic thought emphasizes active moral courage within the darkest moment of human history.

God's Triumph

Death, of course, is not the end for Daniel's wise teachers. They will be restored to life in an eschatological resurrection (12:1–3). The resurgence of life beyond death and suffering is a consistent feature among the major early Jewish apocalypses. Eschatological justice for the suffering righteous often includes punishments upon the wicked as well (12:2). While these forms of redemption focus on human destinies, the end of the age may also see the renewal of the entire cosmos as a new creation. The national hopes of Israel may also be projected into an eschatological restoration of the temple or messianic rule. Paradoxically, apocalyptic thought looks beyond its dire, pessimistic forecast of current possibilities toward a future horizon of immense hope for human life and the entire cosmic order. Beyond the injustice and defilement of the present, God's own reign will soon triumph, restoring peace, life, and purity to a tormented creation.

1 Enoch

Even prior to Daniel and the Maccabean Revolt, apocalyptic literature flourished within circles that esteemed Enoch as God's chosen recipient of revelation. Genesis cryptically recounts how God "took" Enoch, the seventh human ancestor, just prior to the great flood (5:24). A more extensive stream of traditions within Early Judaism explores the purpose and nature of this mysterious episode (Sir 44:16, 49:14; Wis 4:10-15; *Jubilees* 4:16-26). Enoch had been taken up into the heavenly world to become the recipient of a divine revelation. Lore surrounding Enoch may originally have been inspired by Enmeduranki, the seventh Sumerian king prior to the flood, who entered the realm of the gods, received celestial tablets, and learned the arts of divination (VanderKam 1984).

Likewise, Enoch emerges in the seventh human generation (Gen 5:1-24; cf. Jude v14). He is repeatedly associated with transcendent scribal activity. He testifies to what has been written in celestial documents (*1 Enoch* 96:4, 98:1, 99:6-7, 103:1-3, 104:1). As "scribe of righteousness," he records divine edicts and angelic petitions (12:4, 13:4-7, 15:1, 39:2). Such high esteem for Enoch accompanies a conspicuous neglect for the Mosaic Torah in *1 Enoch*. This awareness leads some scholars to posit the existence of an "Enochic Judaism," a sectarian religious movement that devoted itself to Enoch's revelations and held less esteem for the Mosaic Torah, its covenant, and laws (Boccaccini and Collins 2007). As Enoch himself declares, "[N]o man shall see as I have seen" (19:3; cf. Deut 34:10–12).[1]

Indeed, Enoch's many glorified roles sometimes exceed the status of a mere human recipient of revelation. Enoch is initially "hidden" from the sins that overtake the world prior to the flood, as he dwells among the holy ones in the heavenly world (10:2, 12:1–2). He thus operates in a state of angelic holiness within the divine council. He possesses intercessory powers to plead the case of fallen angels and sinful humans before the divine throne (13:1–14:7). The multifaceted roles of heavenly scribe, intercessor, and revealer grant the figure of Enoch a unique status within apocalyptic literature.

The book called *1 Enoch* is a collection of five major units that emerged at different historical moments (see Box 3.1). The reader of *1 Enoch* today encounters some three centuries of apocalyptic lore inspired by the figure of Enoch. This, however, is the arrangement of *1 Enoch* preserved within later Ethiopic manuscripts; it would be anachronistic to assume that the work existed in precisely this form in antiquity. The earliest Aramaic copies from the Dead Sea Scrolls attest the remains of only four of the five units, lacking evidence for the Parables (chs. 37–71). In one copy, the Book of Watchers, the Dream Visions,

Box 3.1 Five Sections of *1 Enoch*

Major Units of *1 Enoch*	Possible Dates
Book of Watchers (chs. 1–36)	Third century BCE (chs. 1–5 offer a later, second-century BCE introduction)
Parables/Similitudes of Enoch (chs. 37–71)	Turn of the eras (?)
Astronomical Book (chs. 72–82)	Late fourth–third century BCE
Dream Visions (chs. 83–90)	175–164 BCE
Epistle of Enoch and Apocalypse of Weeks (chs. 91–105)	ca. 175–150 BCE (chs. 106–8 comprise later additions)

and the Epistle appear to have circulated together (*4QEnoch^c*). Two copies include the Book of Watchers and Dream Visions (*4QEnoch^{d, e}*). The Astronomical Book appears independently (*4QAstronomical Enoch^{a-d}*). These early copies indicate that Aramaic was the original language, from which these works were later translated into Greek, and from Greek into Ethiopic.

1 Enoch remained popular within the early church and is cited as a scriptural authority in Jude (vv14–15) and the *Epistle of Barnabas* (4:3–4, 16:5–6). Eventually, however, the authenticity of works ascribed to antediluvian ancestors like Enoch came into question. In spite of such prominent defenders as Tertullian (*Apparel of Women* 3:1), *1 Enoch* survived as a canonical writing only within the Ethiopian Orthodox church.

The Book of Watchers (1–36)

Enoch's revelation transpires in a moment of crucial significance for human history: just before the great flood and just after heavenly beings, the "Watchers," have violated the cosmic order through a catastrophic transgression. The first major unit in *1 Enoch*, the Book of Watchers (chs. 1–36), narrates this story and describes Enoch's revelation of how God will redeem the world from this cosmic tragedy. The story begins with phraseology very similar to Genesis 6:1–4, yet quickly breaks away into more extensive lore regarding the primal transgression of the "Watchers."

The term "Watcher" (Aramaic: *'yr*) connotes one who is perpetually awake and vigilant. The Watchers appear to represent a specific class of angelic beings (cf. Dan 4:13, 17, 23) who intercede on behalf of humans (*1 Enoch* 15:2) and preserve distinct spheres of hidden knowledge (16:3). Their sin is explained in two complementary ways. One of the Watchers, Semihaza, leads an angelic company into forbidden sexual union with human wives (6:1–7:6, 9:7–9, 19:1–2). From this vantage, their sin is an act of lustful impurity that betrays their angelic duties and violates the created boundaries between heaven and earth. Their offspring become terrorizing giants who cannibalize humans, drink blood, and defile the entire creation. Yet the Watchers are also charged with the sin of disseminating forbidden divine knowledge. Azazel and other angels teach humans secret knowledges, such as metallurgy, astrology, and magic, that lead them to violence, fornication, and religious deception (8:1–4, 9:6, 10:7–8). Taken together, the two complementary explanations urgently reveal how the Watchers' lust, aggression, and false wisdom have jeopardized the entire created order.

The myth of the Watchers has sometimes been explained as a representation of Hellenistic empire and its disruption of Near Eastern societies (Nickelsburg 2001). It has also been interpreted as a depiction of false priestly leadership within Judaism (Suter 1979). Yet the myth transcends reduction to a single set of historical circumstances, presenting a view of reality in which humans are at the mercy of powerful cosmic beings who have defiled creation. When compared with the Genesis narrative of Adam and Eve, the Watcher myth offers an interpretation of reality that is far more deterministic and less reliant upon human freedom to explain the presence of evil. Such views about reality may have distinguished the authors of the Enoch literature from other Jews within their context (cf. Sir 15:11–20).

As angels hear the cries of human suffering, they bring news of the Watchers' transgression before God. The deity dispatches Michael and Raphael to imprison the Watchers within the earth, whence they will be cast into the fiery abyss at the final judgment. The fate of the Watchers then prefigures that of all sinners at the great judgment. The righteous, however, will escape this fate and enjoy a fertile, prosperous life within a renewed creation (10:4–11:2):

> Then all the earth will be tilled in righteousness, and all of it will be planted with trees and filled with blessing; and all the trees of joy will be planted on it. They will plant vines on it, and every vine that will be planted on it will yield a thousand jugs of wine. (10:18–19)[2]

The Book of Watchers envisions an earthly eschatology in which the creation itself is healed, purified, and cleansed of the Watchers' transgression. "The end" will, therefore, restore "the beginning," as the earth is restored to its mythical, primeval purity. Within this primeval, universal eschatology, humanity itself will also be restored, as "all humans," "all nations," will become righteous and offer worship to God (10:21–22).

The Book of Watchers concludes with two resplendent visions in which Enoch is taken on a tour of the cosmos. The tours assume an ancient geography in which Enoch travels to the extremities of a central landmass bounded by waters. Although Enoch's particular geography remains unique, its concern with the wonders at the ends of the earth may be compared with ancient Babylonian and Greek sources.[3] In the first tour (chs. 17–19), Enoch, too, beholds the mysteries that lie at the ends of the earth.

This vision receives further reinterpretation in a second tour (chs. 20–36), which invests greater concern with human destinies. Enoch beholds the mountain of the dead in the far west, where the spirits of all humans are subdivided into cave-like pits according to their works (ch. 22). They will remain here, in this intermediate state, until "the great judgment," when some will be resurrected (22:13). As for the final judgment, Enoch witnesses the landscapes of eschatological reward and punishment, as the throne of God is established upon the earth (chs. 24–25). The tree of life will feed the righteous, as a renewed sanctuary is restored in the holy city. Enoch's tour concludes with further visions of the east, north, and south (chs. 28–36). Throughout his journey, he blesses the deity for the glory and justice revealed within the mysteries of the created universe (22:14, 25:7, 27:5, 36:4). The combined content of the awe-inspiring revelation unveils a righteous knowledge of the cosmos beyond the destructive wisdoms of the Watchers.

Parables/Similitudes of Enoch (37–71)

The second successive unit in *1 Enoch* addresses the reader as the "vision" that Enoch saw "the second time" (37:1), presumably after the visions that conclude the Book of Watchers. This new revelation consists of three "parables" (37:5), a term that refers not to brief symbolic narratives but rather to apocalyptic visions (chs. 38–44, 45–57, 58–69). The three Parables disclose a "vision" of unparalleled "wisdom" (37:1–5, 42:1–3, 48:1–7, 49:1–3), uniquely entrusted to God's chosen scribe, Enoch. They proceed nonsequentially, reviewing many of the same themes. Like the cosmic tours of chapters 17–36, they explore the divine assembly in the heavens (chs. 40–41, 46, 61). Enoch also beholds astonishing natural phenomena (chs. 43–44, 52, 54, 59, 60) and envisions the final judgment (chs. 50–51, 53–55, 61–64).

The dating of the Parables poses an unresolved problem, since these chapters did not feature among the earliest Aramaic copies. For this reason, some interpreters have considered the Parables a later Christian composition, yet they contain no distinctively Christian elements and remain invested in the theological concerns of the earlier Enoch literature. Allusions to a Parthian invasion (56:5–8) may reflect historical circumstances surrounding the decline of the Hasmonean Dynasty (40–37 BCE). Recent familiarity with these events would place the composition close to the turn of the eras, yet the issue is far from certain.

The Parables repeatedly affirm that divine justice will prevail over the world through the final judgment, a claim consistent with other units of *1 Enoch*. Yet the Parables take a step beyond the earlier Enoch literature in the extensive eschatological roles they assign to a messiah. Several terms describe this figure (see Box 3.2).

Such expressions reveal a context in which Daniel 7, Israel's royal theology (Isa 11:1–9; Psalms 2, 89), and the Servant Songs of Isaiah (Isa 49:6–7, 53:11) have contributed to the conceptualization of an eschatological messiah. They offer very significant precedents for messianic designations and roles found within the New Testament. For the Parables, this preexistent, heavenly figure stands within the divine assembly "before the stars of the heaven were made" (*1 Enoch* 48:2–3; cf. 39:6, 40:5). Currently hidden from the rulers of the world, he will be revealed at the end time (62:7, 69:26–29).

Box 3.2 Messianic Language in the Parables

"Righteous One" 38:2–3, 53:6
"Elect One" 39:6, 40:5, 45:3–4, 48:6, 51:4, 53:6, 55:4, 61:5, 62:1
"Messiah" 48:10, 52:4
"that Son of Man" 46:3–4, 48:2–7, 62:9, 69:26–29

The Parables model "that Son of Man" upon aspects of Daniel 7 yet also reflect significant developments. Daniel's comparative language (e.g., "one *like a* son of man") has become explicitly demonstrative (*"that* Son of Man"). While Daniel can interpret the "son of man" image as representing a more collective heavenly company (7:22, 27), the Parables literally envision a singular entity. More fully than Daniel, the Parables emphasize his angelic identity: "His countenance was full of grace like that of one among the holy angels" (*1 Enoch* 46:1).[4] Daniel envisions dominion as being "given" to this heavenly figure by God (Dan 7:14). Yet the Parables describe a more aggressive range of redemptive activities.

Enthroned in glory (*1 Enoch* 45:3, 51:2-3, 55:4, 69:29), he will execute the final judgment, overturning the thrones of kings, destroying sinners, and judging the Watchers (38:3-5, 45:3, 46:4-8, 48:8-10, 53:5, 54:2, 55:4). Alongside these political roles stand ethical, spiritual qualities. He judges the nations with the spirit of wisdom (49:3-4; cf. Isa 11:1-9) and instructs the righteous in the secrets of divine knowledge (51:2). Newness of life will characterize the day of the Elect One, as heaven and earth are renewed (45:3) and the dead are resurrected (51:1-3, 61:5, 62:14-16).

Astronomical Book (72-82)

The oldest unit within *1 Enoch* comprises a 364-day calendar revealed to Enoch by the angel Uriel (72:1). As a revelation to Enoch, these chapters remain consistent with other units, even if its contents are less a transcendent mystery than a description of how the sun and moon majestically proceed through the cosmos. The Ethiopic version, shorter than the earliest Aramaic copies, begins with a description of the "first law" of the sun, as well as additional laws governing the moon (chs. 72-74). According to these laws, the sun passes through twelve celestial gates located at the eastern and western perimeter of the earth, forming a solar year of 364 days. The moon, too, passes through these gates, yet at different times and in phases. Chapters 80-81 represent later additions, warning prophetically that "in the days of sinners" the proper calendar will be violated. These additions reflect the reality, also found in *Jubilees* and select Dead Sea Scrolls, that competing religious calendars became a point of unavoidable sectarian controversy within Early Judaism.

Dream Visions (83–90)

In the Dream Visions, Enoch discloses to his son, Methuselah, two dissimilar visions. The first concerns a cosmic catastrophe in which the habitable world is cast into the abyss (ch. 83). Presented with this terrifying reality, Enoch intercedes with God that a righteous remnant may be preserved beyond the coming flood (ch. 84). The second vision (chs. 85–90) recounts a temporal apocalypse that begins with primeval humanity, extending to the Hellenistic era and final judgment. Due to its thoroughgoing animal symbolism, the vision is also called the "Animal Apocalypse." This apocalypse provides no explicit interpretation of its animal symbols. Nevertheless, internal hints would have allowed their main features to have been understood by ancient readers.

The vision skillfully utilizes animal symbols together with color, chronology, and geography. Cows (bulls) and sheep (rams) typically represent Israel and its antediluvian ancestors. The choice reflects their ceremonially pure status, while other nations are represented by unclean creatures. Adam and Noah appear as snow-white bulls, emphasizing the purity and power of primeval humanity (85:3, 89:1). After the flood, however, Noah's sons beget the unclean creatures that will later torment Israel (89:10). Israel eventually degrades to weaker animals, as Jacob begets twelve sheep. The symbol of the sheep may evoke the Fourth Servant Song of Isaiah, which recounts Israel's sin and suffering (Isa 53:6–7), major themes throughout the apocalypse.

Predatory nations soon victimize the sheep. The author is notably consistent in assigning animal symbols to adversarial nations (e.g., "wolves" = Egypt, "dogs" = Philistines). After God saves them from the "wolves" of Egypt, they travel to the desert. This is one of the only places in the Enoch literature where the story of Moses at Sinai is acknowledged, and it is minimally presented (cf. 93:6). No specific laws are described. Yet it is clear that the sheep will construct a "house" in which to worship the deity. The house may represent the temple complex or perhaps Jerusalem. Under the rams of Israel's kings, the house enlarges to an entire city, with a high tower, where the Lord of the sheep resides. Yet the sheep go astray, abandoning "the house." When prophetic warnings fail to restore the sheep, they are blinded and the deity departs the temple before it is destroyed (89:41–67).

The sheep are then entrusted to seventy shepherds for punishment, yet their vengeance is too harsh. The identity of these shepherds remains an enigmatic feature of the vision. They appear to represent angelic guardians, since God appoints an angel from among their ranks who will record their transgressions (89:61). There is also a chronological dimension to the symbol, since "seventy" shepherds will rule over Israel. The number may envision a chronology of seventy weeks of years (e.g., 490 years; cf. Dan 9), a temporal epoch spanning the Babylonian conquest to the Hellenistic era.

When two sheep (e.g., Joshua and Zerubbabel) return to rebuild the fallen "house" and its tower, the sheep immediately place a table of polluted food before it. The vision thus instantly rejects the Jerusalem temple cult that was restored under the Persians. Predatory birds, representing the Hellenistic empires, then feast upon the sheep. As the sustained, intergenerational suffering of the sheep is expressed with agonizing pathos, Enoch's role as intercessor once again emerges. The angelic witness and Enoch petition God no fewer than four times to intervene (89:57–58, 69–71, 76–77; 90:3; cf. 84:1–6). Yet in every instance the deity remains silent to the suffering plight of the sheep until judgment has completed its predetermined course.

Finally, one great ram gathers the sheep, restores their sight, and resists the birds. It is at this moment that the deity now rises to save the sheep. The symbol of the ram, used earlier of Israel's kings, may represent Judah the Maccabee or the larger Maccabean resistance. If so, the Dream Visions were composed sometime after the initial conflicts of the Maccabean Revolt, yet prior to Judah's death (160 BCE) (Tiller 1993). This would locate the Dream Visions as a near contemporary to Daniel 7–12. As compared with Daniel, the Dream Visions may assign a more positive, redemptive role to the Maccabean resistance. The great ram's "sword" of active opposition coincides with God's final reckoning upon the abusive shepherds (90:13–15). In Daniel, however, the ultimate triumph appears to be achieved by God alone "without human hands" (Dan 8:25) and certainly without the Maccabees. The contrast illustrates how two contemporary apocalypses might have very different attitudes toward the Maccabean resistance and the agency that "human hands" may wield in bringing about redemption (Murphy 2012; Portier-Young 2011).

The apocalypse concludes with a utopian vision that transcends the political realm entirely. The deity's throne is established upon earth (*1 Enoch* 90:20; cf. chs. 24–25). The Watchers are judged and thrown into the fiery abyss, as are the seventy shepherds. God now creates a new house, from which peace reigns throughout the earth. One final snow-white bull emerges to govern this peaceful world. This is possibly the Dream Visions' presentation of the messiah. If so, the messiah does not institute the new order but rather governs it after God has brought it into existence. Unlike Israel's earlier kings (rams), he represents a different kind of leader fashioned upon the model of primordial ancestors, like Adam, Noah, and Abraham (white bulls). Subsequently, all predatory animals are transformed into white cows. In this surprising twist, Gentile nations, too, will be gathered together into God's eschatological house (cf. 10:20–22).

Epistle of Enoch (91–105)

Chapters 91–105 of *1 Enoch* comprise the Epistle of Enoch, which he reveals to his son, Methuselah. The designation "epistle" emerges from later Greek manuscripts, which describe a revelatory composition that Enoch addresses to future descendants (92:1; cf. 93:1, 100:6). In the assessment of Loren Stuckenbruck (2007), these chapters comprise an "eschatological testimony," in which Enoch swears on oath that he has beheld the heavenly tablets that attest the certainty of coming judgment (98:1, 99:6–7, 103:1–3, 104:1). On the basis of this heavenly reality, Enoch admonishes future generations, warning of the latter days, when evil sinners, "the rich," predominate. With assurances of divine justice and everlasting life, he encourages the righteous to remain faithful (104:2). In this sense, the rhetoric of Enoch's "epistle" resembles the literary **testaments** of other ancestors and sages. While its date remains uncertain, portions of the book appear to have been composed prior to (or near) the time of Daniel 7–12 and the Dream Visions.

The Epistle dualistically separates the wicked and righteous into two ways—one leading to death, the other to life (94:1–4). The artful rhetoric of the Epistle even mimics the false view of reality asserted by the wicked "rich" (cf. Wis 1:16–2:24). They presume their wealth affords them license to do as they wish (97:8–9). They believe the righteous have died in torment without reward, while they themselves meet death in the contented happiness of a full life (102:6–11, 103:5–6, 104:7). Enoch's testimony from the heavenly tablets utterly refutes their false worldview, directly confronting the wicked with apocalyptic "woes" of coming judgment (94:6–103:8). God will exalt the spirits of the suffering righteous from Sheol into the heavens, where they will experience newness of life among the heavenly hosts. In the great judgment, the wicked will even be handed over to the righteous for execution (98:12). The afflicted righteous ones themselves will thus participate as agents of divine judgment.

Apocalypse of Weeks

These chapters also contain the originally independent "Apocalypse of Weeks," which organizes history into a succession of ten epochal "weeks" from the days of Enoch until the great judgment. The proper sequence of the weeks (93:1–10, 91:12–17) has been misarranged in later editions. Righteous and wicked ages alternate throughout this temporal apocalypse, portraying a turbulent history of good and evil. While the first primeval week is righteous, the second turns wicked, as God brings "the first end," the flood, upon the world (cf. Gen 6–9). This **flood typology**, frequent throughout the Enoch literature, interprets the flood as a precedent for the final cataclysm that will engulf the world at the end of the age. Indeed, the primeval flood offers assurance that divine judgment has already begun and will faithfully complete its course. Weeks 3 and 4 then pass from the emergence of Abraham and Israel to the construction of the wilderness tabernacle.

The temple takes on increasing significance in subsequent weeks. Week 5 concludes with the building of "the house of glory and dominion." Yet spiritual blindness soon engulfs the world, as the temple is destroyed and the nation dispersed. As in the Dream Visions, there is no victorious restoration of the temple under the Persians. The seventh week remains an evil generation, yet hope arises through an "eternal plant of righteousness," a possible self-designation for the author's own religious movement (93:10). The eighth week "of righteousness" inaugurates the time of divine judgment, and the temple is finally restored, "a house ... for the Great King in glory" (91:13). As the tenth week ends, the watchers will be judged, and the vision embarks upon a transcendent horizon of innumerable weeks.

The Apocalypse of Weeks appears to have been written prior to *Jubilees* (ca. 150 BCE), where it is referenced (4:18). It has probably also influenced the later Dream Visions. A date prior to the Maccabean Revolt would locate the apocalypse as the product of a religious movement dissatisfied with the current temple and seeking its eschatological restoration.

Post-70 CE Apocalypses

Although apocalypticism cannot be confined exclusively within specific historical scenarios, two environments produced a conspicuous number of literary apocalypses. These include the Hellenistic Reform and Maccabean Revolt (e.g., Epistle of Enoch, Apocalypse of Weeks, Dream Visions, Daniel 7–12), as well as the aftermath of the Great Jewish Revolt against Rome. At least three early Jewish apocalypses emerged from this latter context: *4 Ezra*, *2 Baruch*, and the *Apocalypse of Abraham*.

The challenges of Judaism in the late first century carried on several earlier problems from the Hellenistic era, now magnified in the devastating aftermath of Rome's triumph (see Box 3.3). Living under foreign empires now meant surviving the destruction of the Jerusalem temple. Long-standing questions about proper worship and legitimate leadership now encountered the demise of the temple and its priesthood. Many religious movements vanished amid the turmoil, even

Box 3.3 Judaea Capta

The devastating collapse of Judaean society in the Great Revolt is visually attested in Roman iconography. *Judaea Capta* (Judaea Conquered) coins depict the triumph of Rome, often presenting an imprisoned war captive and a mourning woman, situated beneath a date palm (cf. *4 Ezra* 9). In the Arch of Titus, victorious Roman troops carry the sacred vessels of the destroyed temple in a triumphal procession, including the menorah, the sacred seven-branched candelabrum found within the sanctuary (Josephus, *War* 5:216–17, 7:158–62).

Credit: American Numismatic Society, public domain.

Credit: Beth Ha-Shalom, CC BY 3.0, unchanged, https://creativecommons.org/licenses/by/3.0/deed.en.

as the Pharisees more successfully adapted to the new context. The increasing profile of their leadership contributed heavily to the eventual emergence of Rabbinic Judaism. Revolutionary zeal persisted in some circles as well, anticipating the eventual Bar Kochba Revolt against Rome (132–135 CE). The theological problems of the Revolt and its aftermath remained acute for the authors of *4 Ezra*, *2 Baruch*, and *Apocalypse of Abraham*. What had happened to the covenant, its promises, and laws amid the catastrophe? How does divine justice work amid the recurrent frailties of human sin? Why did God allow Jerusalem to fall? What would the future hold for the nation?

4 Ezra and 2 Baruch

The apocalypses of *4 Ezra* and *2 Baruch* share many literary and theological strategies as they address these monumental challenges. They appear to have been written in Palestine near the end of the first century CE. Both interpret the aftermath of the Revolt through the literary context of the Babylonian Exile. Ezra and Baruch had helped to preserve and redirect the Jewish community after the exile (*4 Ezra* 5:17–18, 12:40–51; *2 Baruch* 2:1, 44:1–46:7). By attributing their revelations to these figures, the apocalypses represent analogous attempts to sustain and reform the Jewish community after 70 CE.

They include apocalyptic visions familiar to the genre, as well as extended dialogues. These **dialogue apocalypses** explore questions of theodicy, Israel's destiny, and the role of the law in the present crisis—questions paramount to the Jewish community at the end of the first century. The dialogues further advance the apocalyptic genre as a medium of intellectual debate, inquiry, and deliberation, a distinct development beyond earlier apocalypses. Both works further interpret Rome as the "fourth kingdom" of Daniel, an evil world dominion that the Messiah's advent will destroy (*4 Ezra* 12:11–12; *2 Baruch* 39:5). They also locate the origins of evil within humans' own internal nature rather than in supernatural demonic entities, a surprising contrast to other apocalypses.

With these shared features, the two books are often interpreted together. The question of their relationship is intriguing. Some commentators favor *4 Ezra* as the earlier composition. If so, then *2 Baruch* may reflect an attempt to provide greater assurance of the reasonability of divine justice than its more vexed predecessor. Perhaps *2 Baruch* also sought to instruct the totality of the Jewish community (*2 Baruch* 46:4) (Henze 2011), even as *4 Ezra* addressed more specialized esoteric knowledges to "the wise" (*4 Ezra* 14:26, 45–48). On the other hand, if *2 Baruch* was earlier, then perhaps *4 Ezra* took a more critical, restless view of apocalyptic theologies found in its predecessor. While this question remains insoluble, the two contemporary apocalypses can be meaningfully compared as diverse apocalyptic responses to a critical moment within human history.

4 Ezra

Modern editions of *4 Ezra* often depend upon the complete Latin version, which was translated from Greek, and the Greek from an original Hebrew (or Aramaic) composition. Syriac, Ethiopic, and other versions are also preserved. Chapters 1–2 and 15–16 (often entitled 5 and 6 Ezra) in the Latin version represent later Christian additions to an earlier Jewish apocalypse (chs. 3–14).

Structure

Much of the meaning of *4 Ezra* is concentrated into a carefully ordered, sevenfold structure (3:1–5:20, 5:21–6:35, 6:36–9:26, 9:27–10:59, 11:1–12:51, 13:1–58, 14:1–48) (see Box 3.4). After extensive dialogue between Ezra and the angel Uriel, the fourth unit charts a transition in which Ezra receives three visions. The dialogue units typically begin with Ezra's prayer, fasting, and lamentation over the fallen nation (5:20, 6:35–37). Yet in the fourth unit, Ezra is commanded to fast no more, but rather to eat the flowers of the field (9:23–27). This transformation from dialogue to vision—from fasting to flowers—inaugurates three final revelations. The work concludes with a narrative in which Ezra instructs his contemporaries to prepare for the age to come by keeping the law.

> **Box 3.4 Structure of *4 Ezra*/2 Esdras**
>
> Christian Additions (2 Esdras 1–2/5 *Ezra*)
> chs. 1–2 Oracles against Israel
> Jewish Apocalypse (*4 Ezra*)
> 3:1–5:20 Dialogue 1: Questioning the Past
> 5:21–6:35 Dialogue 2: Interpreting Israel's Election
> 6:36–9:26 Dialogue 3: Mysteries of Creation
> 9:27–10:59 Vision 1: A Woman Weeping
> 11:1–12:51 Vision 2: The Eagle and the Lion
> 13:1–58 Vision 3: The Man from the Sea
> 14:1–48 Conclusion: Writing the Law
> Christian Additions (2 Esdras 15–16/6 *Ezra*)
> chs. 15–16 Oracles against the Nations

Dialogues

Ezra's revelatory dialogues vigorously lament the historical situation of Israel's fall to "Babylon" and incisively question the deity's justice amid these dire circumstances. The angel faithfully answers Ezra's "anxious words" (3:3; cf. 5:34), often from perspectives familiar to apocalyptic theologies. Yet Ezra remains unsatisfied, as each angelic discourse leads only to a deeper conundrum. Chapter 7 offers a vivid illustration. When Ezra questions whether humans will be punished immediately after death or later, at the final judgment (7:75), the angel offers an entire discourse "on death." It provides one of the most resplendent descriptions of the afterlife in early Jewish literature (7:78–101). Despite the angel's magisterial answer, however, Ezra can only lament its deeper implications: very few will enjoy a blessed afterlife, so great is the pervasiveness of evil among humans (7:116–26).

Due to its complexity, there are different ways to interpret the impressive dialogue of the book. Whose voice best represents the author's viewpoint: Ezra's, the angel's, both, neither? The angel mediates divine answers to human questions, and yet the answers themselves only raise further problems. On the other hand, Ezra is repeatedly vindicated for speaking righteously (6:30–34, 8:37; cf. Job 42:7–8), even if he still reasons from within the finite boundaries of human experience, a limitation of which the angel warns from the beginning (4:1–12, 5:31–40). Life within the present, evil age involves the limitation of human understanding, even for such a noble figure as Ezra (7:62–74). The author seems more invested in the total encounter between Ezra and the angel than in too easily resolving legitimate tensions between human experience and divine revelation.

Another feature of the dialogue involves the interaction between national and universal concerns. Ezra questions God's overwhelming justice upon Israel through the Roman destruction: What meaning does the national tradition of God's covenant with Israel now have in light of this devastating event? And yet the problem is not only the triumph of Rome but the universal prevalence of the "evil heart" that God has allowed to flourish since Adam (3:20; 4:30; 7:48, 66–70, 92). Israel's national transgression only reveals the evil heart that tragically leads all humans toward sin. Thus, Ezra grievously laments, "O Adam, what have you done? For though it was you who sinned, the fall was not yours alone, but ours also who are your descendants" (7:118).[5]

The extent of Ezra's desperation is highlighted through comparison with *2 Baruch*, whose dialogues are typically shorter and reach a more confident sense of resolution. Moreover, Baruch's dialogues transpire directly with the deity, unmediated by angels. While *2 Baruch* is aware of the consequences of Adam's sin (*2 Baruch* 54:15–19, 56:5–15), they primarily concern mortality. Humans possess the power to choose good, and "each of us has been the Adam of his own soul" (54:19; cf. Sir 15:11–20).[6] The law and covenant thus offer a more immediate and optimistic path to redemption. Yet for *4 Ezra* the way forward is not so easy.

There are also different ways to interpret the dialogue's conclusion. As Ezra continually despairs the plight of Israel and the prevalence of the evil heart, he boldly intercedes for divine mercy, which alone can resolve the human condition (8:35–36, 45; cf. 7:132–40, 12:48). Perhaps Ezra's journey leads beyond retributive notions of justice to a revelation of divine mercy. Another way to read the conclusion is to recognize the eternality of the law itself. Even in his angst, Ezra discovers that "the law does not perish but remains in its glory" (9:32–37).[7] The survival of the law, even beyond the temple's destruction and human frailty, demonstrates that divine justice remains at work in the world (cf. 3:20; 7:72, 94). The book's concluding scene will, in fact, emphasize Ezra's role in receiving the law by revelation and teaching it to the nation (14:19–22). The book may encourage its contemporaries to follow Ezra's journey "from someone full of despair . . . into someone who is ready to receive the Torah once more" (Najman 2014, 66). Such strong emphasis upon the law accords well with the theologies of emerging rabbinic leaders, even if 4 Ezra has its own distinctly apocalyptic and esoteric manner of advancing this message.

Visions

The transition between dialogue and vision also develops an epistemological theme. As the dialogue concludes, Ezra no longer fasts and laments, but eats the flowers that grow in the field of Ardat (9:23–27, 12:46–51). Three visionary episodes then unfold. The transition emphasizes how Ezra's noble, yet insufficient, attempts to understand divine justice now give way to a more transcendent plane in which God's ways become knowable through revealed visions (5:36–40, 10:25–37, 13:53–58, 14:38–48). If there are answers to Ezra's questions, they ultimately lie beyond the boundaries of ordinary human knowledge (3:31) (Hogan 2008).

Ezra's first vision is a masterpiece (9:38–10:59). He sees a woman weeping. She mourns because her only son died on the very day he entered his wedding chamber. As he speaks to her, Ezra surprisingly shifts roles from mourner to comforter (Stone 1990). With dramatic irony, he consoles her that her personal grief is no greater than that of the nation, which now laments the downfall of Zion. Suddenly, the face of the mysterious woman gleams like lightning, and she screams with a terrible cry. She disappears, and in her place Ezra sees a powerful city being built upon vast foundations. The experience deprives Ezra of all understanding, and the angel returns to interpret. The woman is Zion, and the great city is the city of the Most High, the heavenly Jerusalem that God preserves forever. The mysterious vision encourages Ezra to believe that Jerusalem remains with God on a transcendent plane, despite its earthly destruction. Ezra's entrance into the transcendent city then gives way to two more revelations.

In his second vision, a three-headed eagle with twelve wings ascends from the sea to rule the earth. The eagle (Latin: *aquila*) was a conspicuous symbol within Roman iconography, often featured upon the sacred military standards that Roman troops carried into battle. The vision in *4 Ezra* co-opts this prominent imperial symbol. The three heads depict the Flavian emperors (Vespasian, Titus, Domitian) in the generation after the Revolt. The vision further equates the great eagle with "the fourth kingdom which appeared in a vision to your brother Daniel" (12:11–12; cf. *2 Baruch* 39:5).[8] *4 Ezra* thus applies to Rome the status that the Greek Empire held in Daniel 7. The reign of the eagle is ultimately brought to its end by a lion, the figure of the messiah. The messiah offers a prophetic indictment against Rome's cruelty, then destroys its rulers and redeems the righteous remnant of Israel. God currently preserves the messiah until the end of days, and he will arise from the posterity of David.

In the final vision, a man rises from the sea and flies with the clouds of heaven to a mountain, where all nations make war against him. The man breathes a stream of fire, destroying them without a single weapon. Angelic interpretation identifies the man as the messiah, who will stand against the nations on a renewed Mount Zion. The fire that he breathes will be the law of God that judges the nations. Elsewhere, the angel explains that the messiah's earthly kingdom will eventually end. The messiah will die, after which the present structures of creation will cease and only the glory of the Most High will remain (7:26–44).

The book's conclusion reaffirms Ezra's experience of revelation. He drinks a mysterious drink, like water and fire, given to him by God, which fills his soul with understanding. He then dictates the twenty-four books of what is apparently the Hebrew Bible, as well as seventy additional books of esoteric knowledge shared only among the wise. Perhaps this is how the author expected his own apocalypse to be interpreted, as a document of specialized, revealed wisdom for select audiences only.

2 Baruch

Modern translations of *2 Baruch* depend upon the only complete Syriac manuscript found within Codex Ambrosianus. Yet the heading of the Syriac version reports that it has been translated from Greek. It is possible that the Greek version, in turn, depended upon a Hebrew or Aramaic original. Chapters 1–77 preserve an apocalypse, appended in chapters 78–87 by an Epistle that consoles the nation after the Babylonian conquest. Codex Ambrosianus numbered the book among other scriptural texts; otherwise *2 Baruch* is typically accounted among the Pseudepigrapha.

Like *4 Ezra*, the apocalypse of *2 Baruch* utilizes narratives, dialogues, and visions. Yet *2 Baruch* lacks the strict structure of *4 Ezra*. Instead, narratives, dialogues, and visions are more typically integrated throughout the entire book. The author skillfully utilizes these materials to lead the reader on a journey from despair to consolation (Sayler 1984). More fully than *4 Ezra*, *2 Baruch* is filled with poetic interludes in which Baruch laments, prays, and worships, offering a liturgical approach to the trauma of its time (chs. 5, 10–12, 14, 21, 35, 48, 54, 75).

Lamenting the Temple

The fate of the temple occupies an important role early in the book. As Baruch laments the coming destruction of Jerusalem, God consoles him with the certainty that the earthly city, which is about to be destroyed, should not to be confused with the heavenly city that God prepared from the creation of the world (4:2–7). Differing somewhat from this presentation, Baruch also sees an angel take the sacred vessels from the temple and commit them to the earth, saying, "[G]uard them until the last times" (6:8); "and the earth opened its mouth and swallowed them up" (6:10).[9] Safely preserved within the earth, they will presumably be restored at the end time, not unlike the resurrection, when the earth shall also give back the dead (23:4–6, 50:2). Both passages, despite their differences, emphasize the supernatural survival of the temple in the aftermath of its present collapse.

This is poignantly expressed as Baruch travels to the ruins of the Holy of Holies and weeps there in words inspired by the lamentations of Jeremiah: "O, that my eyes were springs, and my eyelids a fountain of tears. For how will I lament for Zion, and how will I mourn over Jerusalem?" (35:2–3; cf. Jer 9:1).[10] As Baruch laments the fallen temple, he falls asleep and enters into a visionary state. Lamentation over the fallen temple now opens into revelations of future redemption. Deliverance will be achieved in a future age beyond the corrupting realities of sin and death that dominate the present world.

The Cedar and the Vine

Baruch sees a vine and fountain, surrounded by a forest of cedars. As the water pours forth from the fountain, it washes away the cedar forest. One final cedar is then brought before the vine. The vine speaks, indicting the cedar for its cruel domination of the land, after which the cedar is burned to ashes and the land is restored to paradisiac conditions (chs. 36–37). The interpretation of this "landscape apocalypse" reveals that the cedars represent "four kingdoms" that will rule the world. Babylon's conquest over Israel is succeeded by other world empires, now ending in Rome. The fountain and the vine represent "my anointed one," who will wash away the great forest and bring its final ruler to Mount Zion, where the messiah will convict him of his crimes and execute him. Then the messiah will reign in Jerusalem until "the world of corruption has ended" (40:3).

Apocalypse of the Cloud

Baruch's final vision is a temporal apocalypse, in which world history is portrayed through a cloud that pours forth dark and bright waters. Through this image, *2 Baruch* portrays earlier scriptural history as radically alternating twelve times between good and evil eras, although dark waters were always more abundant than bright (53:6). As the black waters pour forth, they bring great destruction, followed by brief attempts to heal the world through bright waters that succeed them. For example, the reign of the wicked Judaean king Manasseh represents the dark waters that immediately precede the bright, healing reforms of King Josiah (64:1–66:8). Yet the entire structure of the vision insists upon the prevalence of evil, despite the intermittent flourishing of righteousness.

After these twelve ages, the vision embarks upon the eschatological future. One final cascade of dark waters will bring bewilderment upon all nations. As chaos disrupts the social structures of the present world, wars will escalate—and "everyone who saves himself from the war will die in an earthquake, and he who saves himself from the earthquake will be burned by fire, and he who saves himself from the fire will perish by famine" (70:8).[11] Anyone left will then fall into the hands of the anointed one for final judgment (70:10). The nations that harmed Israel will fall beneath his sword. Other nations will live peacefully within a messianic reign (72:1–5). The curses of Genesis 3:16–19 will be reversed. Women will no longer suffer pain in childbirth, and the earth will easily yield its fruits (73:7–74:4). Isaiah's royal prophecies regarding the house of Jesse (Isa 11:1–9) will be fulfilled in the peaceful, earthly kingdom of the messiah (73:6).

Apocalypse of Abraham

The *Apocalypse of Abraham* (*ApAbr*) survives in medieval Slavonic manuscripts. The Slavonic witnesses reflect a translation from Greek, which, in turn, depended upon an original Hebrew (or perhaps Aramaic) composition. Commentators have frequently interpreted the book as filled with later Christian interpolations,[12] yet more recent studies have demonstrated the originally Jewish nature of the apocalypse (Kulik 2004). From this perspective, *Apocalypse of Abraham* offers yet another instance of apocalypse writing in the crucial generation after the temple's destruction, an issue with which it is deeply concerned (ch. 27). It registers interesting commonalities and contrasts with *4 Ezra* and *2 Baruch*. Along with *2 Enoch*, it further serves as an important transitional link between apocalypticism and the rise of early Jewish mysticism.

Opening Narrative

The work opens with an entertaining narrative (chs. 1-8) in which Abraham describes how he originally came to repudiate the idols of his father to serve the one, true, living God. While serving his father, Terah, an idol-maker, the unlucky Abraham accidentally destroys his father's idols, thereby proving that they are no true gods. Abraham even challenges his father, "You are a god to them, since you have made them ... and their power is vain."[13] The narrative concludes, as lightning burns down the house of his father, destroying Terah and his idols. God, however, delivers Abraham from the fiery conflagration.

Apocalypse

This narrative introduction transitions into a literary apocalypse (chs. 9-31). The occasion of the revelations is Abraham's sacrifice and mysterious covenant encounter with God, described in Genesis 15 (*ApAbr* 9-14). The belief that Abraham entered into revelatory consciousness in this episode is attested in other ancient sources (cf. *4 Ezra* 3:13-14, *2 Baruch* 4:4).[14] The *Apocalypse of Abraham* heightens the intensity of the encounter with accents of the revelation to Moses on Mount Horeb (Exod 3:1, Deut 4:10; cf. *ApAbr* 12:3). Through the covenant sacrifice, Abraham, who has repudiated the idols of his ancestors, now encounters revelations from the living God.

As Abraham prepares the sacrifice, he enters into a revelatory state and encounters the powerful angel Yahoel, in whom God "put together his names" (10:8). Yahoel serves a harmonizing role that maintains cosmic order and destroys the false worship that destabilizes creation (cf. 18:8-11). It was thus Yahoel who destroyed Terah's idolatrous house (10:9-14). Where Abraham chases away the "birds of prey" that have come to consume his sacrifice (Gen 15:11), *ApAbr* interprets them as Azazel, the evil demonic entity known from the Enoch literature. Yahoel instructs Abraham to rebuke Azazel, exhorting him to "be bold and have power" (14:3). The angel concedes that without Abraham's righteous human agency, his own powers to counteract Azazel will be limited (14:4). After this conflict, Yahoel and Abraham, together, ride the wings of the sacrificial birds (Gen 15:9) majestically into the heavenly world (*ApAbr* 15:1–3).

The apocalypse aims to disclose both the ages of history (9:9–10), as well as the mysteries of the created universe (12:10), blending aspects of temporal and cosmic revelations. Abraham witnesses the sound of the divine presence and the deity's chariot-throne but cannot behold the "Eternal Mighty One," who is enshrouded in flame (16:3, 18:13–19:2). As the revelations unfold, Abraham beholds a multifaceted "picture" that portrays God's preordained design for human existence (chs. 21–29). The picture is highly dualistic, presenting Abraham's offspring to one side and other nations on the other. A striking claim of the vision is that God's own people, Israel, will repeatedly struggle against Azazel throughout their history, according to the divine plan (22:5). The belief that God has set antagonizing supernatural powers over the chosen people is familiar from the "seventy shepherds" of Enoch's Dream Visions (chs. 89–90), yet it is equally perplexing to Abraham, who enters into an extended dialogue with God concerning the mysteries of this dualistic plan.

Like *2 Baruch*, the dialogue transpires directly with God, unmediated by angels; like *2 Baruch*, questions provoke further visionary revelations; and like *2 Baruch*, divine answers remain relatively clear and knowable, offering consolation within the present age of evil. Abraham raises four specific questions: (1) Why did God invest the divine plan into the hands of Azazel (20:7, 23:12)? (2) Why did God allow humans to desire evil in their heart (23:14)? (3) Why ordain the sins that led to the temple's destruction (26:1)? (4) How much time will pass between the temple's fall and final redemption (ch. 29)? Abraham's questions are reminiscent of those asked in *4 Ezra*, especially those concerning the nature of sin, the power of the "evil heart," and the timing of redemption.

The deity faithfully addresses each question. On the nature of sin, God emphasizes the cooperative interplay between the influence of Azazel and the complicity of human free will (23:12–13). The vitality of human responsibility is even illustrated in Terah's idolatry: "[A]s the will of your father is in him, so your will is in you, so also the will desired by me is inevitable" (26:5).[15] Like Terah, the idolatrous transgressions of Israel brought about the temple destruction (chs. 25–27). On the timing of final redemption, twelve periods remain (29:2).

In the twelfth, the *Apocalypse of Abraham* appears to include an anti-Christian polemic against a man "shamed and struck, worshipped by the heathen and Azazel" (29:7).[16] If, indeed, this is an allusion to Jesus, the *Apocalypse* extends its critique of false worship to the veneration of Jesus, who will lead the Gentiles astray and tempt Abraham's own descendants (29:12–13).

The final redemptive scenario of the book emphasizes an interplay of human and divine agency, not unlike its earlier treatment of the will. At the end of the twelfth hour, God sends forth ten devastating plagues upon the nations, paralleling the Exodus from Egypt (29:14–15, 30:1–8; Cf. Rev 16). Amid the plagues, God will yet preserve a righteous remnant who will perform true worship. These shall rise up and "destroy those who have destroyed them" (*ApAbr* 29:19). Thus, righteous human agency, fortified by God's help, will overthrow those who have destroyed the temple. Yahoel's earlier counsel to Abraham resonates in the power of the righteous: "Be bold and have power" (14:3). Only through courageous acts of righteousness will final redemption dawn (cf. *1 Enoch* 90:13–15).

As Abraham returns to the earth, the vision of final redemption is interpreted more fully, this time with a stronger emphasis on heavenly, messianic intervention. After the ten plagues, God promises, "I shall sound the trumpet from the sky, and I shall send my Chosen One, having in him one measure of all my power" (31:1).[17] The designation for the messiah as God's "Chosen" is reminiscent of the Parables of *1 Enoch*. The *Apocalypse*'s final emphasis upon the combined forces of human and messianic agency offers an interesting contrast with *4 Ezra*, which emphasizes divine, rather than human, intervention (4:33–43). Scholars have thus found within the *Apocalypse of Abraham* a more activist, even militant apocalypticism in the aftermath of the temple destruction, perhaps a reflection of the growing revolutionary environment that would later contribute to the Bar Kokhba Revolt (132–135 CE) (Mueller 1982).

Apocalypticism in the New Testament

The interrelationships between Early Judaism and the nascent church are perhaps nowhere more evident than in the prominence of apocalypticism within New Testament literature. Theories about the historical emergence of Christian origins have frequently asserted that it developed precisely from circles in which apocalypticism had already played a prominent role. Earlier apocalyptic beliefs regarding messianism and resurrection took on new meanings as they came to be reinterpreted in light of Jesus's life and the experiences of the early church communities. Given the prevalence of apocalyptic discourse in multiple genres that derived from different circles within the church, it has hardly proven an overstatement to regard apocalypticism as "the mother of all Christian theology" (Käsemann 1969, 102). As we have seen, however, the varieties within ancient Jewish apocalypticism were profound, raising ongoing questions about the diverse qualities and functions of apocalyptic thought in particular New Testament writings.

The Gospel of Mark

The eschatological nature of Jesus's teaching and activity comprise a major theme in Mark. While it did not utilize the Q traditions, Mark pursues its own distinct interpretation of Jesus's teaching and activity, one in which apocalypticism plays a pervasive role. For Mark, Jesus's own teaching and activity transpire within the context of latter day sufferings that precede final redemption.

Preaching the Kingdom

The first words of Jesus in Mark concern the advent of the reign of God: "The time is fulfilled, and the kingdom of God has come near; repent, and believe in the good news" (1:15).[18] This brief opening declaration positions the kingdom as an imminent, impending dominion, soon to be established within the present world. This "good news" of coming redemption demands immediate repentance, a turning away from present behaviors and customs, if one is to "enter the kingdom" (9:47; cf. 10:13–27, 12:33–34). The imminence and urgency of the kingdom's advent resound in Jesus's later revelation to his disciples: "Truly I tell you, there are some standing here who will not taste death until they see that the kingdom of God has come with power" (9:1).

The expectation that God's dominion will yet be established throughout the present, corrupted world is a ubiquitous feature of apocalyptic discourse. The Book of Watchers anticipates the establishment of God's own sovereign throne upon the earth (*1 Enoch* 25:3–4).[19] As God's rule is fully established, the righteous will experience eschatological life within the presence of a restored temple. The hope of a restored, righteous dominion throughout the earth resounds in Daniel, where "kingship and dominion . . . shall be given to the people of the Holy Ones of the Most High" (Dan 7:27). Daniel invests God's coming, everlasting dominion into a collective company of righteous human and angelic agents who mediate divine rule. In the Parables of Enoch, the present rulers of the earth will be dethroned, as God's "Elect One" sits upon "the throne of glory" (55:4).[20] *Fourth Ezra* and *2 Baruch* anticipate a coming messianic reign that ends Rome's current kingship over the earth.

Little Apocalypse (Mark 13)

The apocalypses, however, differ on what God's reign may look like and how it might be actualized. Mark, too, has its own distinct treatment of the kingdom, one that emphasizes the faithful suffering that must take place before its powerful advent. This is especially the case in Jesus's last extended teaching in Mark, often known as the "Little Apocalypse" (ch. 13). Just prior to his own impending suffering, Jesus forecasts the social turmoil that would irrupt upon the next generation in the Great Jewish Revolt and the temple's destruction. In this way, Mark's "Little Apocalypse" shares rhetorical features of literary **testaments**. The testamentary features of the Epistle of Enoch offer meaningful comparison. Like Enoch, Jesus admonishes future generations concerning the evils of the latter days; he further encourages the righteous to persevere with assurances of ultimate redemption.

The discourse paints the bleakest possible portrait of the sufferings and woes that precede final redemption. The temple's destruction and universal warfare mark only the beginning of the darkest moment in human existence:

> When you hear of wars and rumors of wars, do not be alarmed; this must take place, but the end is still to come. For nation will rise against nation, and kingdom against kingdom; there will be earthquakes in various places; there will be famines. This is but the beginning of birth pangs. (Mark 13:7–8)

The emphasis upon catastrophic wars that precede God's final intervention is widespread among apocalypses. *Fourth Ezra* anticipates that the whole earth "shall make war against one another, city against city, place against place, people against people, and kingdom against kingdom" (*4 Ezra* 14:31; cf. 9:1–5, *2 Baruch* 70:6–10).[21] Wars further abound throughout Daniel's final revelation (Dan 11:2–45).

Indeed, Daniel exerts a strong influence throughout the "Little Apocalypse." Where Mark regards this era as a time of "suffering such as has not been from the beginning of the creation" (Mark 13:19), Daniel views its own context as "a time of anguish, such as has never occurred since nations first came into existence" (Dan 12:1). Yet another commonality with Daniel involves Mark's call to martyrdom and faithful suffering, while proclaiming the good news (Mark 13:9–13). Daniel positions the wise teachers of its own community as being refined through suffering, as they teach the multitudes in righteousness in the present age of wickedness (Dan 11:33–35).

Jesus's discourse even directly alludes to Daniel, suggesting that an intensive reinterpretation of the earlier apocalypse deeply inspired Mark's presentation. Mark appears to equate the "desolating sacrilege" against the temple in Daniel with Rome's later aggression in the Great Revolt (Mark 13:14; cf. Dan 11:31). Thus, Mark shares with post-70 CE Jewish apocalypses the tendency to apply Daniel's prophecies concerning the terrors of the Greek Empire to Rome's devastation of Jerusalem and the temple (*4 Ezra* 12:10–12; *2 Baruch* 39:5).

The hope of final redemption featured in the "Little Apocalypse" also bears the strong influence of Daniel in its final prophecy concerning the "the Son of Man":

Then they will see "the Son of Man coming in clouds" with great power and glory. Then he will send out the angels, and gather his elect from the four winds, from the ends of the earth to the ends of heaven. (Mark 13:26–27)

Mark's discourse envisions coming redemption through the advent of the heavenly Son of Man "coming in clouds," like the vision of Daniel (7:13). Yet here, Daniel's simile ("one like a son of man") has become a more confident designation for a singular messianic redeemer. Mark shares this understanding of the "Son of Man" figure with the Parables of Enoch, where "that Son of Man" will execute God's final judgment and redeem "the righteous and elect" (*1 Enoch* 62:13–14). The discourse concludes, as Jesus reminds readers for the second time in the book, that "this generation will not pass away until all these things have taken place" (Mark 13:30; cf. 9:1).

The omens and signs that surround Jesus's death imply that the messiah's suffering has set into motion the larger apocalyptic drama that now engulfs Mark's own context. As Jesus dies, darkness covers the earth for three hours, and the veil of the temple is torn apart (15:33, 38). These ominous signs, especially the tearing of the temple veil, link Jesus's death to the later temple destruction and the ensuing catastrophes prophesied in the "Little Apocalypse." In this sense, the messiah himself participates in the latter day afflictions that extend into Mark's own time. It is possible that Mark interpreted Jesus's faithful suffering as the catalyst that set the final apocalyptic drama into motion.

In spite of these dark realities, Mark encourages his community through Jesus's faithful suffering. Perhaps Mark would have agreed with the *Apocalypse of Abraham*'s exhortation to "be bold and have power" (14:3) in the face of pressing evil. The work inspires bold action within the present crisis by preaching the good news of the kingdom, as Jesus did, and by remaining vigilant until the promised advent of "the Son of Man." As its narrative ends, the story of the empty tomb encourages Mark's community even in its terror, astonishment, and fear that they shall yet see the resurrected Jesus, "just as he told you" (16:1–8).

Pauline Apocalypticism

Motivating Paul's polemic against idolatry and polytheism (see Chapter 2) stands an impending awareness of God's coming wrath upon the world. As Paul reveals in his earliest letter, 1 Thessalonians, the "Day of the Lord," a concept established in earlier prophetic literature,[22] will bring final redemption to the "children of light"—yet for those "of darkness," "sudden destruction" will soon fall upon them, with no escape (5:1–11). Christ's second advent, also known as the *Parousia* in Paul's letters, will unleash God's final judicial reckoning upon human sin, including those who say "peace and security," a possible allusion to the Roman imperial propaganda of his day.

For those "in Christ," however, Paul's apocalypticism takes a consolatory tone (4:18, 5:11), as believers await final reunion with the messiah. Even deceased believers will participate in this final advent, as the dead "in Christ" will be resurrected together to meet him "in the air" (4:17–18). Paul expects these events to transpire soon, within his own lifetime (4:15), attesting to the urgency in which he interprets his own apostolic role within an unfolding apocalyptic drama.

Paul's apocalypticism, however, is not simply future expectation. The very events of the messiah's cross and resurrection have inaugurated the final progression of creation and history, so that the "end time" has already begun and is hastening toward consummation. Paul shares with many of his apocalyptic contemporaries this urgent awareness of being swept up into the midst of the last things. Standing within the midst of the coming transformation, Paul's theology exhibits its own dynamic tension between the idea that redemption has "already" joyously begun in Christ and the awareness that it has "not yet" reached finality.

Already and Not Yet

In 1 Thessalonians, Paul calms anxiety regarding those who have died prior to Christ's return (4:13–18) and clarifies "the times and seasons" that are yet to come (5:1–11). The letter reveals how fully the church, even at a very early stage, became troubled over the delay of the *Parousia*, a problem that would intensify in later generations (e.g., Mark 13:32–37; Acts 1:6–8; 2 Pet 3:1–13). Paul addresses this challenge by explaining how believers now stand between the resurrection of Christ, in which redemption has already dawned, and the final advent, in which "the dead in Christ" shall also be resurrected. In the meantime, Paul's ethics encourage sexual purity, love, hard work, and autonomy from external powers (1 Thess 4:3–12, 5:12–22).

The future, unrealized dimensions of redemption take precedence in 1 Corinthians. Paul chastises the "arrogant" at Corinth for their presumption (1 Cor 4:8–13) concerning human wisdom (3:18–23), sexual practices (5:1–8), banqueting (10:14–33, 11:17–22), worship (12:1–14:33), and disregard for resurrection (15:1–58). While the underlying theologies that motivate such Corinthian attitudes are far from certain, it is clear that Paul advocates a more humble recognition of the limitations of human knowledge, the weakness of present embodiment, and the continuing power of "the last enemy," death (15:26). In light of these realities, Paul concludes with a rousing argument that believers still await final transformation at the end of the age, when "we shall all be changed, in a moment, in the twinkling of an eye, at the last trumpet" (15:21–22).

Paul can also emphasize the present realities of redemption that have already dawned in Christ. Through the powerful triumph of the cross, the resurrection, and the Holy Spirit, redemption has tangibly begun (Beker 1980). The eschatological "joy" that arises from the experience of salvation thus meets the reader throughout Paul's letters (1 Thess 1:6; 2 Cor 8:2; Gal 5:22; Rom 14:17; Phil 1:25). In Galatians, Paul emphasizes the new, prevalent "freedom" from the powers of "this present evil age" that now dawns in the life of believers (1:4, 2:4, 3:28, 4:21–31, 5:1–13). In one of the most radically realized expressions of his theology, Paul claims that the very structures of presently embodied life have dissolved through a new, spiritual unity "in Christ" (3:27–28). Believers are nothing less than "a new creation" (6:15; cf. 2 Cor 5:17). Paul thus severely repudiates circumcision for the Gentiles as a falling away from the powers of redemption that already operate in their midst.

Like the Jewish apocalypticism of his day, Paul shares the assumption that final redemption will comprise an extended progression, one within which the faithful will suffer affliction until the moment of God's final victory. The dynamics of suffering and hope comprise a prominent strand within his apocalypticism in Romans, which emphasizes the present suffering of humanity, as well as the entire physical creation, under the annihilating powers of sin and death (Rom 1:18–3:20, 8:19–23) (Keck 1988). God's powerful "righteousness" to deliver humanity is unleashed in the cross and resurrection, apocalyptic acts of redemption that break the cosmic dominion of these forces. Paul ecstatically concludes that present sufferings will fade within the divine glory to be revealed at the end of the age, as God's final victory becomes complete (8:38–39). He thus exhorts the Romans, in spite of the sufferings of the present life, to clothe themselves in an "armor of light" with "the hope of salvation" and advance toward the impending day with vigilant joy (13:11–14).

Paul among the Apocalypses

The dynamics of Paul's apocalypticism are thus vibrant, adaptive, multifaceted—so much so that contemporary scholars continue to deliberate how they hold together (Blackwell, Goodrich, and Maston 2016). Paul himself offers distinct evidence for the possibilities of ancient apocalypticism, since his letters leave behind multiple applications to differing contextual scenarios—all from the same generative mind. To no one's surprise, Paul achieved his own creative synthesis among the apocalyptic traditions of his time.

Paul's apocalypticism is evident in the subsequent confusions that it raised within the very churches he founded. In 1 Thessalonians (4:13–5:11) and 1 Corinthians (15:20–28, 42–57), he repeatedly addresses uncertainties concerning the timing, sequence, and logistics of future redemption. Such vexing problems concerning the fate of the dead and the timing of final redemption were common among earlier and later apocalyptic thinkers (Dan 7:25, 8:14, 9:24–27, 12:5–13; *4 Ezra* 4:33–6:34, 7:26–44; *2 Baruch* 21:19, 26:1, 56:1–3; *ApAbr* 29:1–2). That Paul's letters must so repeatedly resolve doubt, confusion, and anxiety over these issues reveals how fully they had been an integral feature of his teaching among the churches.

Revelatory encounters comprise a significant aspect of Paul's own mystical experiences, as he describes his translation into the heavens to hear transcendent mysteries (2 Cor 12:1-10; cf. 5:16-17), like the sages of the apocalypses. Most important, Paul insists that his "gospel" to the Gentiles is itself the revelation of a divine mystery (Gal 1:11-17), spiritually empowered to play a decisive role in the redemption of the world (1 Cor 1:17-25, 2:1-13, 4:1, 15:51; Rom 1:16-17, 11:25-36). While the redemption of the Gentiles is not a frequent subject among the apocalypses, the utopian, universal eschatology of the Enoch literature (*1 Enoch* 10:20-22, 90:37-40) incorporates the Gentiles into final salvation, as the human itself is liberated from the powers of primal transgressions and evil cosmic forces. Such precedents become radically intensified in Paul's apocalypticism, as the righteousness of God redeems the human, both Jew and Greek, from the cosmic powers of sin and death (Rom 1:16-17).

Paul's apocalypticism embraces both judicial and cosmic understandings of the end (de Boer 2020). The imminent advent of God's justice upon human wickedness (1 Thess 5:1-11; 2 Cor 5:10; Rom 2:1-16) shares in the expectations of the great judgment day repeatedly anticipated in the apocalypses. Paul labors among the churches that they may be found "blameless" upon that day (1 Thess 3:13, 5:23; 1 Cor 1:8; Phil 1:10, 2:15). Yet more than this, Paul's apocalypticism possesses cosmic, dualistic assumptions, in which "the rulers of this age" are being destroyed through the victory that has dawned in Christ (1 Cor 2:6-8; cf. 1 Thess 2:18; 1 Cor 3:18, 5:5, 10:20-21; 15:24-28, 54-57; 2 Cor 2:11, 4:4, 11:14, 12:7; Gal 1:4, 3:22, 4:1-11; Rom 6:1-14, 8:18-39, 12:2). In such cases, Paul imagines a cosmos pervaded by rebellious forces that annihilate the created world and drive humanity toward destruction, like the authors of the Enoch literature. His desperation over the cosmic power of sin further anticipates *4 Ezra*'s angst over the universal "evil heart."

The final cosmic victory over "the last enemy" of death (1 Cor 15:26) still awaits realization upon the future horizon of Paul's thought. It is perhaps in his thinking on resurrection that Paul is at his most classically apocalyptic, especially since resurrection and redemption from death comprise a recurrent emphasis among the major early Jewish apocalypses. In 1 Thessalonians, he anticipates resurrection as a spatial transference "to meet the Lord in the air" (4:17). This assumption about resurrection may be compared with Daniel (12:1–3) and the Epistle of Enoch (102:4–104:4), where the righteous will be exalted from the realm of the dead into a celestial existence among the angelic hosts.

In 1 Corinthians, Paul emphasizes the transformative nature of resurrection, as the earthly body, subject to sin and death, will be "changed" into a "spiritual body," a new form of existence configured upon the messiah's own transcendent, resurrected embodiment (1 Cor 15:42–57; cf. Phil 3:21). Paul's emphasis upon transformation is shared especially with *4 Ezra* (7:26–42) and *2 Baruch* (49:1–51:16), which describe resurrection within the context of a larger cosmic renewal. In this case, Paul's apocalypticism seems to embark upon a fully transcendent horizon rather than simply a restoration of the world as it has been in the past. The coming redemption remains a "mystery" (1 Cor 15:51; Rom 11:25–36), a transformation of reality into a new creation in which "God will be all in all" (1 Cor 15:28).

Apocalypse of John

The New Testament concludes with a monumental specimen of the apocalyptic literary genre, the book of Revelation, also known as the Apocalypse of John. The Apocalypse emerges within the context of the late first century CE. Like its contemporaries, *4 Ezra* and *2 Baruch*, it utilizes "Babylon" as a literary context for interpreting Rome's power and predetermined destruction (Rev chs. 17–18). The events of the late first century are experienced in a distinctive way by "John," an early church leader of Jewish heritage who instructs a group of churches in Asia Minor. John writes late in the history of the apocalyptic genre, allowing a vantage from which he utilizes earlier conventions with perception and skill (Blackwell et al. 2019). As he does so, he shows himself a master of ancient apocalyptic discourse. The result is an apocalypse that strikes clear continuities with other specimens of the genre. Ironically, however, the world's most famous ancient apocalypse is also far from typical. It offers radical innovations within apocalyptic literary conventions. The work thus presents itself as an apocalypse that is at once traditional and strange.

Revelation

This is immediately apparent in how the Apocalypse presents itself as a revelation. While other apocalypses attribute revelations to figures of the past, the visionary recipient of the book of Revelation is simply "John," a recognized contemporary and "brother" of those to whom he writes (1:9). The Apocalypse represents a more immediate revelation concerning what "must *soon* take place" (1:1, cf. 1:3; 2:16; 3:11; 22:7, 10, 12, 20). Unlike Daniel (12:4, 9), John is even prohibited from sealing the written revelation for a later time (Rev 22:9–10): The present is both the time of revelation and urgent fulfillment. In this way, the work utilizes the literary features of an apocalypse, yet also presents itself as an even more immediate, urgent word of "prophecy" written directly to the churches (1:3, 10:11, 19:10, 22:6–10).

Apocalyptic Letters

The first major unit of the book contains apocalyptic epistles, revelatory letters written to seven churches of Asia Minor (1:4–3:22). Epistles may initially seem out of place within the apocalyptic genre. Nevertheless, there are precedents for John's revelatory letters. The Epistle of Enoch, for example, presents itself as a revealed composition that Enoch writes to Methuselah and later descendants (92:1, 93:1, 100:6). The missive encourages future generations to endure the injustices that will come upon them with the hope of everlasting salvation. As 2 Baruch concludes, Baruch sends two written epistles to the scattered tribes of Israel (77:11–26; cf. Jer 29). These comprise a "letter of instruction and a scroll of hope" (77:12), that may "strengthen" the exiles in their despair.[23] The rhetorical features of exhortation and comfort found in Enoch's Epistle and in 2 *Baruch*'s letter may be compared with John's letters. They, too, encourage the churches to persevere with hope during evil times (Rev 2:2–3, 10, 19; 3:10–11) and to avoid false teaching (2:2, 6, 9, 14–15, 20–21; 3:9)—thus, "overcoming" or "conquering" (2:7, 11, 17, 26–29; 3:5, 12, 21) in their present hour of tribulation.

Celestial Documents

As he encourages the troubled churches, John repeatedly reminds them that their names have been written in "the book of life of the lamb." John draws upon a classic apocalyptic motif, "the heavenly book" or "heavenly tablets." The final revelation of Daniel concludes with the promise that "your people" will be delivered at the end of the age, "all who are found written in the book" (Dan 12:1). For Daniel, the heavenly book appears to contain a preordained record of the righteous and wicked, whom God will faithfully judge (cf. 7:9–11). Enoch recounts the Apocalypse of Weeks directly from heavenly tablets, as they reveal the predetermined course of human history (*1 Enoch* 93:1–3). In the Epistle of Enoch, the sage faithfully testifies from the heavenly tablets (*1 Enoch* 103:2–3), which already foretell salvation for the suffering righteous and punishment for the wicked (see also *Jubilees* 6:34–36, 30:21–23; *4 Ezra* 6:20; *2 Baruch* 24:1). Predeterminism is a frequent assumption among traditions about the heavenly book, since the course of creation, history, and final redemption has already been inscribed in the heavens.

John also appeals to celestial documents, which he witnesses in the heavenly world. John sees a scroll, written upon both sides and sealed with seven seals, in the right hand of God. As each seal is opened, violent devastation is unleashed upon the earthly realm, suggesting that the two-sided scroll contains a predetermined sentence of divine judgments (Rev 5:1–5). In other contexts, John encourages the churches to persevere, knowing that their names have been written "in the book of life from the foundation of the world" (17:8; cf. 3:5, 13:8). The predestined nature of their redemption grants assurance that no present evil can threaten the reality of their salvation (21:27; cf. 20:12–15). Thus, the heavenly book tradition features in a consolatory way, encouraging readers in their affliction and reaffirming the reliability of future judgment.

The Thousand Years

One of the more controversial passages of Revelation concerns the earthly reign of the messiah for one thousand years (20:1–6). To participate in this epochal reign, the righteous martyrs of John's community would be resurrected in a "first resurrection" (20:5). At the conclusion of this millennium, John turns to the final, conclusive events of his eschatology: Satan will be destroyed (20:7–10), all the dead will be raised for final judgment (20:11–15), and the celestial Jerusalem will descend from heaven to a purified earth (21:1–22:5). Since the messiah's millennial reign occurs just before these ultimate events, it is sometimes called an "interim" messianic kingdom. Later Christians would struggle to understand John's one thousand years and offered different ways of interpreting its relationship to human history. In John's context, however, the presentation of the messiah's epochal reign upon earth is a feature that can be identified in contemporary apocalypses. The interim messianic reign immediately anticipates the final transformation of the cosmos, as it also does in *4 Ezra* and *2 Baruch*.

The messiah will enjoy a reign of "four hundred years" in *4 Ezra* (7:28), a number perhaps inspired by Israel's original oppression in Egypt (cf. Gen 15:13) (Stone 1990). A similar number appears in the Babylonian Talmud (*Sanhedrin* 99a). This will be a time of joy for all those who have survived the evils of the last days. At the end of the four hundred years, the messiah will die. The final transformation of the cosmos will ensue, and the dead will be raised (*4 Ezra* 7:31–35, cf. 12:32–34). In *2 Baruch*, paradisiac conditions will prevail during the messiah's reign (29–30). The curses of Genesis 3:16–19 will be reversed (*2 Baruch* 73:7–74:4), and Isaiah's royal prophecies regarding the house of Jesse (Isa 11:1–9) will be fulfilled in the messianic kingdom (*2 Baruch* 73:6). While *2 Baruch* offers no specific chronology, portions of the book imply that the messiah's reign will endure until the end of the structures of the present, corruptible world (74:2–4). In these cases, *4 Ezra* and *2 Baruch* balance hopes for an earthly political restoration of messianic rule with a more universal transformation of the entire cosmos.

Fourth Ezra and *2 Baruch* help to place John's millennium in its contemporary context. Like *4 Ezra* and *2 Baruch*, John presents the thousand years as the era just prior to the final consummation of the present world. Where *4 Ezra* assigns a chronology of four hundred years, John assigns a one-thousand-year chronology to this era—one that is more expanded, more glorious. Later deliberations on the length of the messiah's reign in the Babylonian Talmud range from forty to as many as seven thousand years (*Sanhedrin* 99a). John positions resurrection in relationship to the messianic age, a tendency also found in *4 Ezra* (7:31–35) and *2 Baruch* (30:1–5). As in *4 Ezra*, a final resurrection of all the dead will take place for divine judgment just after the messiah's reign. John, however, also innovates by framing the millennium with two resurrections. In the "first resurrection," the fallen martyrs of John's own community will be raised from the dead to a position of rule within the messianic era.

John thus consistently contours more widespread apocalyptic traditions to address the very endangered churches to whom he writes. The revelation of the book has been unveiled for them; their names have been written in the heavenly book; and their destiny, whether living or dead, is to reign with the messiah in a world that realizes the deity's purpose for a blessed creation.

4
Rewriting Scripture

Amid their shared interests and differences, wisdom and apocalyptic writings pursue their aims by creatively recasting earlier scriptural traditions. Ben Sira's "Praise of the Ancestors," Wisdom's retelling of the exodus, the reinterpretation of earlier prophecies in the apocalypses—all attest to the crucial role of interpretation. Beyond these examples, interpretation comprised an urgent necessity across many sectors of Early Judaism. The interpretation of Israel's law proved essential to defining religious practices, including ritual and worship in the Jerusalem temple. It further pervaded questions of cultural, familial, moral, and political order. With such profound issues at stake, interpretation raised questions of authority and contributed to the formation of rival movements. Amid the many competing religious claims within ancient Judaism, who ultimately possessed the insight, the inspiration, to interpret scriptures faithfully? While interpretation may be found within many different literary genres, entirely new literary works also emerged through the reinterpretation of earlier scriptures. This chapter explores the ingenious interpretive culture of Early Judaism through two masterworks of ancient scriptural interpretation: *Jubilees* and the *Book of Biblical Antiquities*.

Explicit Interpretation

Attempts to classify the diverse arts of ancient interpreters inevitably fall short of their creativity. Their skills may be compared to those of musical improvisation. At first glance, they appear to compose scriptural interpretation spontaneously through intuitive genius, as they respond to their immediate contexts. A closer look, however, reveals that they also operate from a vast, internalized repertoire of ancient knowledges and carefully disciplined techniques. They are often interested in resolving perceived problems or mysteries within the text, even as they advance their own interpretive agendas. In assessing the variety of their arts, it is helpful to distinguish between explicit and implicit styles of interpretation.

With **explicit** interpretation, a commentator quotes a passage from a scripture text, then interprets it. A delineation between scripture and commentary becomes apparent. Among the Dead Sea Scrolls, a passage from the *Rule of the Community* offers a vivid example of explicit interpretation of Isaiah 40:3:

> [T]hey shall separate from the habitation of unjust men and shall go into the wilderness to prepare there the way of Him; as it is written, *"Prepare in the wilderness the way of [the* LORD*], make straight in the desert a path for our God"* (Isa 40:3). This is the study of the law, which he commanded by the hand of Moses, that they may do according to all that has been revealed from age to age, and as the prophets have revealed by his holy spirit. (VIII 14–15)[1]

This passage explains the rationale that motivated the author's community to separate from other Jews in the Judaean wilderness. The phrase "as it is written" introduces a citation of Isaiah 40:3 that identifies the community's separation "in the wilderness" as a literal fulfillment of scriptural prophecy. In the ensuing commentary ("This is . . ."), the prophet's vocation to "prepare the way of the LORD" is now embodied in the community's devotion to the Torah, which they pursue along a "straight" path of total obedience. The prophecies of the past contain a mystery that finds living realization within the interpreter's current religious experience.

Explicit exegesis would become the most frequently encountered style of interpretation in New Testament and Rabbinic literature, especially as the contours of a scriptural canon began to develop. Explicit exegesis assumes the primacy of an earlier scriptural writing. While the commentator may possess a unique authority, expertise, or inspiration, explicit exegesis typically proceeds with the assumption that interpretation extends from the primary authority of earlier scriptures.

Implicit Interpretation

With **implicit exegesis**, a scripture is represented with interpretive alterations interwoven into the fabric of an earlier text. The lines between scripture and commentary diminish as interpretation becomes ingrained within the very content of a modified scriptural passage. Where "scripture" ends and "interpretation" begins is, thus, not immediately apparent (Crawford 2008). Implicit interpretation may be identified within the Hebrew Bible, as Deuteronomy refashions earlier laws and as Chronicles rewrites portions of Samuel and Kings. Varied methods are utilized for modifying and implicitly reinterpreting scriptural passages.

A scriptural text may be recast through **harmonization**, as disparate texts on compatible subjects merge into a single, new version. Harmonization helped ancient interpreters reduce the complexity of multiple versions of narratives and laws. Among the Dead Sea Scrolls, harmonization is frequent within the *Temple Scroll*, a vast legal work that rewrites scriptural laws. In one example, the *Temple Scroll* merges laws on sexual immorality in Deuteronomy (22:13–30) with similar laws found in Leviticus (18:10, 15; 20:12, 17, 19, 21). The Deuteronomic and Levitical texts are initially linked by similar prohibitions against adultery and incest (Deut 22:22, 30; Lev 20:10–11). As the author harmonizes the two passages, the result is a more extensive treatment of sexual laws in which both sources now speak in a common Deuteronomic voice (*11QTemple^a* LXV 7–LXVI; *4QTemple^b* frgs. 15–20).

Implicit interpretation may also proceed by omission and expansion. Omission of scriptural content may reduce tensions among multiple versions of a tradition or avoid negligible (possibly embarrassing) subject matter. Entirely new content may also be added. On a smaller scale, mere phrases or sentences may be interwoven. For example, as the *Temple Scroll* harmonizes laws on adultery and incest, it seamlessly interweaves a new prohibition against niece-marriage: "A man is not to take the daughter of his brother or the daughter of his sister because it is an abomination" (LXVI 16–17).[2]

This may seem a surprising maneuver to contemporary readers. How can one add new legal material to a purportedly authoritative religious text? What motivates such interventions into earlier scriptures? The answers to such questions vary widely, including attempts to contemporize, renew, correct, or expand earlier traditions (Zahn 2012). In the present case, the *Temple Scroll* extends the scriptural prohibition against incest with aunts (Lev 18:12–14, 20:19–20) to the analogous case of marrying a niece. Thus, there is some warrant for the addition within the existing scriptural passage. Since niece-marriage was otherwise practiced within this era (e.g., Josephus, *Antiquities* 20:145; cf. Gen 11:29; Josh 15:16–17), the author's rewriting of scripture audaciously challenged existing legal and cultural assumptions. To rewrite a scriptural text was a bold move with profound ramifications.

Rewritten Scriptures

On a larger scale, extensive new content units may also be added. This often results in the creation of new literary works that become distinguishable from their scriptural sources. Geza Vermes (1973) once classified such newly formed compositions as "Rewritten Bible," a "narrative genre" closely attached to some book in the Hebrew Bible, which then recasts the scriptural text by rearranging, conflating, or supplementing its contents. Such works included *Jubilees*, the *Book of Biblical Antiquities*, the *Genesis Apocryphon*, and Josephus's *Jewish Antiquities*. The Dead Sea Scrolls have subsequently revealed that rewriting exceeds the boundaries of Vermes's "narrative genre," including nonnarrative legal (e.g., *Temple Scroll*) and prophetic rewritings (*Pseudo-Ezekiel*) (Zahn 2012). The interpretive practices of these works have been compared with the targums and midrashim of later Judaism. Indeed, they often attest continuities (and contradictions) with the **halakhic** and **aggadic** traditions of Rabbinic Judaism (see Box 4.1).

In addition to recasting known scriptural books, rewritings frequently incorporated sources unknown among later canons, creating their own expansive synthesis of authoritative traditions. Thus, they operated from a basis of authoritative sources that far exceeds the writings of the later Hebrew Bible alone. For this reason, the term

> **Box 4.1 Targum and Midrash**
>
> A Targum is a "translation" or "interpretation" (Hebrew: *targûm*) of the Hebrew scriptures into Aramaic that also interweaves paraphrases and interpretive expansions. Midrash (Hebrew: *dāraš*, "to pursue, study, inquire") is an attempt to interpret a perceived problem within a scriptural text. Answers may be found by looking elsewhere among the Hebrew scriptures, by creatively utilizing extrascriptural legends, or by offering logical arguments. Halakhic midrashim (pl.) interpret legal texts within the Torah, typically in the attempt to resolve questions of legal practice. Aggadic midrashim focus on nonlegal traditions and are frequently concerned with ethical, theological, and spiritual themes.

"rewritten scriptures" (rather than "Bible") is utilized in this chapter. Since the arts of rewriting flourished centuries prior to the closure of the biblical canon, some authors may have presented their newly created compositions as extensions of scriptural revelation, not merely secondary works of interpretation. Rewritings like the *Temple Scroll* and *Jubilees* even claim to transmit a divine revelation. The popularity of these works among the Dead Sea Scrolls implies that such claims could be well received among early audiences.

The question persists as to the survival of rewritings beyond the context of Early Judaism. On one hand, the New Testament, the Mishnah, and Talmud preserve no further large-scale endeavors to rewrite scriptural books. This would suggest that rewritings gradually decelerated in popularity in the early church and Rabbinic Judaism, especially as a more selective canon of scriptural documents emerged. On the other hand, manuscript discoveries beyond the New Testament reveal glimpses into literary circles in which rewritings persisted. Such works as the *Syriac History of Joseph*, the *Cave of Treasures*, and the *Palaea Historia* demonstrate how early Jewish strategies of rewriting lived on within later Christian historical works (Bauckham, Davila, Panayotov 2013–). Many of the interpretive traditions in rewritten scriptural narratives can also be identified within the colorful "Tales of the Prophets" (*Qiṣaṣ al-Anbiyā'*) that later became popular within Islam.

Jubilees

Since its modern rediscovery, *Jubilees* has been esteemed among the most important writings for the study of ancient Judaism. Indeed, the book represents one of the most formidable works of legal interpretation from this historical era. *Jubilees* continuously recounts scriptural narratives from creation to the revelation of Israel's law on Mount Sinai (Gen 1–50; Exod 1–24). One can appreciate its arts of interpretation by comparing it carefully with corresponding passages of Genesis and Exodus.

For centuries, *Jubilees* was known among Western scholars only in Greek and Latin citations. Yet in the nineteenth century, missionaries recovered a complete Ethiopic translation. Like *1 Enoch*, the book survived as a canonical document within the Ethiopian church. Copies of *Jubilees* among the Dead Sea Scrolls demonstrate that it had already been written in Hebrew sometime prior to 125–100 BCE. Its ancient title among the scrolls appears to have been "The Book of the Divisions of the Times according to Their Jubilees and Their Weeks" (*Damascus Document* XVI 1–4). Its original date of composition remains unknown.

Internal details could reflect the historical circumstances of the Hellenistic Reform and Maccabean Revolt. *Jubilees* envisions a time of evil, when circumcision is abandoned and the temple defiled—not unlike the experiences of the Revolt (*Jubilees* 1:7–14, 15:33–34, 23:16–23; cf. 1 Macc 1; Dan 11). *Jubilees* certainly takes a critical stance toward the religious climate of its day, insisting that the law has not been properly observed. In critically addressing its context, the book reminds readers of the fundamental story of the covenant, a covenant that remains eternally viable despite recurrent cycles of legal transgression. *Jubilees* has traditionally been viewed as the work of a single author, yet recent scholarship has considered whether a later hand reinterpreted and expanded select episodes (Kugel 2012; Segal 2007).

Angelic Narration

Where Genesis tells its story through anonymous, third-person narration, *Jubilees* makes a decisive change. It pervasively rewrites its scriptural sources as a first-person angelic narration to Moses at Mount Sinai. The book opens with a preface, in which God directly reveals an overview of the narrative (1:1-26), then commissions the "Angel of the Presence" to dictate its fuller details from seven heavenly tablets (1:27-29, 30:20-22). The angel continually reminds Moses that the revelation derives from these celestial tablets, further claiming to have been an eyewitness participant in crucial episodes of Genesis and Exodus (2:3, 30; 3:1, 9-15; 4:5-7, 23; 5:23; 6:22; 10:9-14, 23; 12:26-27; 14:20; 16:1-28; 18:9-12; 19:3; 30:20-21; 41:24; 48:1-19).

Since the angel appears to reference the Torah as "the first law" (2:24, 6:22), this may imply that *Jubilees* represents a second law that completes the revelation at Sinai. The phrase "the law and the testimony" (title; 1:4, 25-29; 2:24, 33; 3:14; cf. Isa 8:16-20) may also suggest that the book offers an authoritative, angelic testimony to Israel's law. As angelic disclosure, second law, and legal testimony, *Jubilees* presents itself as a divinely revealed religious authority.

Chronology and Calendar

Scriptural stories are also rewritten according to a particular world chronology that is preordained within the heavenly tablets (1:29; see also title; 1:4, 26; 50:13). Based upon the laws of Leviticus 25, the book interprets a "jubilee" as a forty-nine-year epoch that consists of seven divisions of seven years, called "weeks" of years. Forty-nine jubilees and nine years pass from Adam to Sinai (*Jubilees* 50:2-4). Thus, the exodus and Sinai revelation transpire within the fiftieth jubilee (48:1), which will conclude forty years later with the entrance into the promised land.

This chronology is further calculated according to a 364-day solar calendar (6:17-38; cf. 2:9-10). *Jubilees* coordinates the religious festivals of Judaism with specific days in this calendar (see Box 4.2), including religious observances not mentioned within the Torah. While the 364-day solar calendar presents these festivals on consistent days of the week, following lunar calculations would lead to irregular observance days, making "a day of testimony a reproach and a profane day a festival" (6:37).[3] Thus, the author adamantly rejects the use of

Box 4.2 The Solar Calendar in *Jubilees*

Religious Observances	Month-Day	*Jubilees*
Day of Remembrance	1-1	5:30, 6:23-31, 7:1-6, 13:8-9, 24:22, 27:19, 28:14; cf. 29:16
Passover	1-14	17:15-18:3, 49:1-23
Festival of Unleavened Bread	1-15 to 21	49:22-23; cf. 18:18-19, 29:5
Festival of Weeks/ Oaths/First Fruits	3-15	1:1, 6:17-22, 14:10-20, 15:1, 16:13, 22:1, 28:15, 29:5-7, 44:1-5
Day of Remembrance	4-1	3:32, 5:29, 6:23-31, 16:1, 28:24, 45:1; cf. 29:16
Day of Remembrance	7-1	5:29, 6:23-31, 12:16, 31:3; cf. 29:16
Day of Atonement	7-10	34:12-19
Festival of Tabernacles	7-15 to 21	16:20-31
Day of Addition	7-22	32:16-29
Day of Remembrance	10-1	5:30, 6:23-31, 7:1-6, 33:1; cf. 29:16 (See further VanderKam 2001)

lunar-based calendars that prevailed during his time. By comparison, calendrical notices in Genesis and Exodus are often cryptic and few, yet the author of *Jubilees* invests remarkable mathematical ingenuity in interpreting them to align with a legally normative world chronology.

Law and Narrative

Jubilees also interweaves legal traditions into appropriate moments of the story—even prior to the revelation at Sinai. Consequently, extensive laws from the Torah (and other sources) are retrojected back into Genesis (see Box 4.3). By frontloading the Genesis narrative with extensive legal materials, the book advances its interpretation of some of the most contentious legal issues of the Second Temple era.

This recasting of scripture also conveys the message that Israel's law was not newly revealed to Moses. It had existed eternally from creation and was gradually revealed to the ancestors, who practiced it long before the Sinai revelation. Thus, ancestors such as Enoch, Noah, Abraham, and Jacob offer no precedent for a Jewish way of life beyond legal observance. They, too, observed the laws of the timeless, eternal covenant that remained immutable for the author's own generation. Neither the legal transgressions of Israel's earlier history nor the more recent Hellenistic Reform could nullify the covenant. Amid recurrent experiences of national failure and legal transgression, the law and testimony would stand for all time, offering continual hope of renewal.

Abraham (chs. 11–23)

Jubilees' extensive rewriting ultimately created a compelling, coherent literary narrative in its own right, a remarkable achievement by its authorship. The book's presentation of Abra(ha)m offers an accessible way to appreciate its compositional arts in action. A frequently expanded aspect of the Abraham story in later Judaism, Christianity, and Islam was the creation of an entire "prehistory" of his life prior to Genesis 12. Such prehistories were likely inspired by Joshua 24:2–3. In this passage, Abraham's ancestors lived beyond the river and "served other gods." How did Abraham come to forsake these deities and worship God? Genesis offers no solution. Ancient interpreters, however, searched the scriptures (and other sources) for clues that would supply the "missing" details. *Jubilees* represents the earliest known attempt to create such a prehistory (VanderKam 2018).

The prehistory in *Jubilees* remains linked to the scriptural story by interpreting the names of Abraham's ancestors (Gen 11:20–32). For the author, such names contain hints of Abraham's formative background, which are then elaborated with creative details. The birth of Serug (11:20–22), for example, whose name implies "turning away" (cf. Hebrew: *sûr*), marks a distinct moment in *Jubilees*' interpretation of history (*Jubilees* 6:17–19), when the descendants of Noah "*turned*

Box 4.3 Law and Narrative in *Jubilees*

Legal Topic	Jubilees	Narrative Context
Sabbath laws	2:17–33	Creation
Purification after childbirth	3:8–14	Eve
Nakedness	3:30–31, 7:20	Adam/Noah
Violence/murder	4:2–6	Cain
Precise retaliation	4:31–32	Cain
Blood/diet	6:12–14, 7:26–33; cf. 21:6	Noah
Festival of Weeks/Oaths/First Fruits	6:15–22; cf. 14:10–20, 15:1–16, 16:13, 22:1–9	Noah
Four Remembrance Days	6:23–31	Noah
364-Day solar calendar	6:32–38	Noah
Winemaking/fruits	7:1–6, 35–37	Noah
Priestly tithes	13:25–27	Abraham
Circumcision	15:25–34; cf. 20:3	Abraham
Incest	16:7–9	Lot and his daughters
Festival of Tabernacles	16:20–31	Abraham
Festival of Weaning	17:1	Abraham
Festival of Unleavened Bread	18:17–19	Abraham
Sexual immorality, intermarriage	20:4–6; cf. 7:20–25, 25:1–10, 39:6–7	Abraham
Idolatry	20:7–8; cf. 12:1–5, 21:1–5	Abraham
Blood and sacrifice	21:6–20	Abraham
Marry the elder first	28:6–8	Jacob
Intermarriage	30:7–17	Dinah and Shechem
Second tithe	32:2–15	Jacob and Levi
Day of Addition	32:27–29	Jacob

Legal Topic	Jubilees	Narrative Context
Incest	33:9–20	Reuben and Bilhah
Day of Atonement	34:12–19; cf. 5:18	Joseph
Incest	41:16–28	Judah and Tamar
Passover	49:1–23	Moses
Sabbath	50:1–13	Moses

back to commit all sin and transgression" (11:6). They intermarry with the Chaldeans, eating blood and practicing violence, idolatry, and slavery (11:1–5).

Standing behind this "turning away" is Prince Mastema, a demonic chieftain who proliferates transgression and punishment among humans. Although God had imprisoned 90 percent of the Watchers' offspring at the time of the Flood, Mastema, also called *satan*, retained command of 10 percent, to mislead humans and punish them for evil (*Jubilees* 10:1–9). In this way, the theodicy of *Jubilees* emphasizes God's preordained control of the world, while accounting for the continuing presence of evil. Through such creative etymologies, *Jubilees* supplies missing details about Abraham's background, while also recasting the story within a dualistic drama of good and evil.

At a young age, Abraham rejects the idolatry and ritual pollution of the Chaldeans. He zealously burns their idolatrous shrine (12:12–14). Studying the stars, he concludes that only one true God rules creation. He prays for deliverance from evil spirits, for the faithfulness of future generations, and for direction about where to travel next (12:16–21). In response, the Angel of the Presence reveals the divine promises (cf. Gen 12:1). The promises emerge, then, as Abraham is already seeking God, a departure from Genesis, where God more suddenly, mysteriously calls him.

The angel then teaches Abraham Hebrew, "the tongue of creation" (*Jubilees* 12:26–27) and the apparent language of the heavenly tablets (3:26–31), details found nowhere in Genesis. This allows Abraham to study "the books of his fathers," a body of priestly lore transmitted from Enoch and Noah (12:27, 21:10). To judge from other contexts, these "books" contain detailed accounts of legal observance related to calendar and sacrifice (4:17–19, 6:1–38, 7:20–39, 16:20–31, 21:1–20). Such priestly books offer yet another strand of continuity that unifies the religion practiced by the ancestors. Through this prehistory, Abraham thus passes gradually from his idolatrous surroundings "beyond the river" to become a faithful priest and intercessor for his people.

Once Abraham receives the promise, Genesis relates the story in which he conceals the full identity of Sarah from the Egyptians (Gen 12:12–13). The embarrassing moral ambiguities of Abraham's deception are omitted in *Jubilees*, where Pharaoh takes Sarah entirely by force and justly suffers divine wrath (*Jubilees* 13:13–15). Israel's ancestors in *Jubilees* typically embody faithful legal devotion (10:17, 19:13, 27:17, 35:12, 36:23–24). Their imperfections in Genesis are often minimized and even apologetically explained (41:23–28). At his death, the angel declares, "Abraham was perfect in all of his actions" (23:10).

The stories of Genesis 15 and 17 comprise crucial episodes in *Jubilees*' interpretation of the covenant. The Torah presents covenants with Noah (Gen 9:1–17), Abraham (chs. 15, 17), and Israel (Exod chs. 19ff.), yet their relationships are not fully explained. Through its arts of rewriting, *Jubilees* repeatedly emphasizes the harmony and continuity of a single eternal covenant, which is renewed with Abraham after the descendants of Noah have "turned away."

Calendar creates a powerful correspondence among these covenants. They coincide with the Festival of Weeks—in the middle of the third month (3-15) (*Jubilees* 14:1, 10): "And *on that day* we made a covenant with Abram, just as we had made a covenant *in that month* with Noah" (14:20; cf. 6:17–22).[4] It is also just after this day that God has called Moses himself to Sinai to receive the revelation (1:1). The angels of heaven, Noah, Abraham, and Moses all keep this festival and renew the same covenant that God established eternally from creation. In each case, observance of the Festival of Weeks further inaugurates an event of divine revelation. Calendar becomes a vehicle of profound religious meaning that synchronizes the continuity of a single, eternal covenant as it is gradually revealed to the ancestors throughout time.

The covenant of Genesis 17 coincides yet again with the festival in the middle of the third month (*Jubilees* 15:1–2), as God reveals

> **Box 4.4 On the Eighth Day**
>
> | Genesis 17:14 | Jubilees 15:14 |
> |---|---|
> | "Any uncircumcised male who is not circumcised in the flesh of his foreskin shall be cut off from his people; he has broken my covenant." (NRSV) | "And the uncircumcised male who is not circumcised in the flesh of his foreskin *on the eighth day*, that soul shall be cut off from his people, for he has broken my covenant." (trans. Charles) |

the commandment of circumcision. The command follows Genesis 17:10–14 closely, yet with apparent revision (see Box 4.4).

Genesis certainly indicates that circumcision should occur when the child is eight days old (17:12), yet this permits certain ambiguities. For such reasons, the Mishnah allows a range between the eighth and twelfth days (*Sabbath* 19:5). *Jubilees* insists no true circumcision can occur other than "on the eighth day" (15:25–32). There will be "no circumcising of days" from this command (15:25). Anyone violating this law will belong "not to the children of the covenant . . . but to the children of destruction" (15:26).[5] *Jubilees'* rewriting thus clarifies and intensifies Genesis.

The Angel of the Presence further explains how even the angels themselves were created circumcised (15:27). In this surprising disclosure, *Jubilees* again affirms that the covenant was eternally established at creation and practiced by angels. Over all other nations, God has appointed evil spirits who lead them astray. Yet through the covenant, Israel has been uniquely elected to stand united with the angels under God's direct rule (15:27–32; cf. 2:17–22), keeping the law and celebrating the feasts in synchronicity with the heavenly hosts. The angel warns Abraham that future generations will abandon this law— setting the stage, yet again, for the great renewal of the covenant under Moses (15:33–34; cf. 6:17–19).

As the angel recounts the episodes of Genesis 18, he describes how "we" foretold the birth of Isaac, whose very name was inscribed in the heavenly tablets (*Jubilees* 16:1-4). The narrative otherwise omits Abraham's remarkable intercession for the innocent (Gen 18:16-33). The predetermined divine plan needs no such human persuasion in *Jubilees*. Sodom's destruction has been recast to warn against sexual immorality (*Jubilees* 16:5-9), a frequent tendency elsewhere (30:5-23, 33:9-20, 39:5-8, 41:23-28; cf. 20:1-6). Isaac's birth (Gen 21) transpires at the Festival of Weeks (3-15), the very day in which the covenant promises were originally revealed. Abraham circumcises Isaac—"on the eighth day," of course—"the first that was circumcised according to the covenant" (*Jubilees* 16:14).[6]

The dismissal of Hagar and Ishmael displays dramatic accents (Gen 21:9-21; *Jubilees* 17:4-14): Abraham joyously celebrates the fulfillment of the promises, as Ishmael dances before him. Sarah becomes jealous at the festive scene. Abraham grieves for both Ishmael *and Hagar*, as they are driven out. Amid the pathos, however, *Jubilees* reaffirms that all has transpired according to the divine plan (17:6-8).

Jubilees then treats one of the greatest stories among scriptural narratives: the sacrifice of Isaac (Gen 22:1-19), also known as the *Aqedah* (the "binding" of Isaac) in later Judaism. The rewriting of the story begins on a heavenly plane, as it introduces a rationale for the otherwise mysterious trial. On the twelfth of the first month (1-12), Prince Mastema demands a trial of Abraham, after "words came in heaven" regarding his faithfulness (*Jubilees* 17:15-16). God immediately expresses total confidence in Abraham, since he has already prevailed through a series of earlier trials (17:17-18). *Jubilees* even reworks the conclusion of the story, so that the trial reveals what God already knows about Abraham's "faithfulness" from the very beginning (see Box 4.5).

Genesis, however, permits the interpretation that God suddenly, mysteriously tests Abraham—and the outcome remains in suspense until the end: "*Now I know.*"

In creating this preface to the trial, *Jubilees* apparently turns to Job 1-2, whose plot has been transposed into the story. The connection between the two stories may initially seem arbitrary, yet the characterization of Abraham as one who "fears God" (Gen 22:12; *Jubilees* 18:9, 11) is also applied four times to Job (1:1, 8-9; 2:3). Both stories deal with the death of offspring, and sacrifice features prominently. The

> **Box 4.5 I Have Now Shown**
>
> | Genesis 22:12 | Jubilees 18:11 |
> |---|---|
> | "*Now I know* that you fear God, because you have not withheld from me your son, your only son." (NRSV) | "*I have now shown* that you are one who fears the Lord." (trans. VanderKam 2018) |

apparent connection with Job casts entirely new shades of meaning upon the *Aqedah*. *Jubilees* now renders a more dualistic account, as Mastema takes on the role of Satan, the true originator of the terrible trial. God's own direct responsibility is correspondingly diminished. In the end, Abraham's faithfulness will shame Prince Mastema to his face (*Jubilees* 18:12), further exemplifying how faithfulness to the law will banish evil from Israel.

After this expanded introduction, the story follows Genesis closely, yet with significant additions. Abraham and Isaac reach the mountain "on the third day" (Gen 22:4). *Jubilees* exploits this chronological detail to emphasize its calendar. The conclusion to the story will explain how the days of the trial anticipate the seven-day Festival of Unleavened Bread (*Jubilees* 18:18–19). The actual date of the sacrifice itself appears to correspond with the Passover sacrifice (1-14), "on the third day" after the trial began (1-12) in heaven (18:4). As Abraham names "the mountain of the Lord," the angel clarifies, "It is Mount Zion" (18:14), the future site of the Jerusalem temple (1:27–28, 4:26). By adding these calendrical and geographical accents, *Jubilees* recasts the story as an anticipation of Passover (and Unleavened Bread), which will later be celebrated with sacrifices at the Jerusalem temple (49:18–21). Abraham, once again, takes on a priestly characterization.[7] The story also foreshadows the final plague of the exodus, where the Passover sacrifice will, once again, deliver the firstborn of Israel from Mastema (49:1–6).

As the momentous story concludes, the angel explains how the narrative has transpired according to the schema of "ten trials," in which Abraham is repeatedly found "faithful" (19:3, 8–9). These have included going to a strange land, famine, wealth, endangerment of Sarah, circumcision, dismissal of Hagar and Ishmael, the *Aqedah*, death of Sarah and buying a burial plot (17:17-18). The tradition of Abraham's "ten trials" remained popular in later Judaism,[8] where the *Aqedah* typically features as the final trial. *Jubilees* appears to enumerate the great trial as the seventh, perhaps attesting an earlier stage in the development of this tradition.

Additional expansions of the scriptural narrative surround the last days of Abraham, as he offers final testament to his heirs. Abraham lives to see the birth of Jacob, his grandson, establishing him as his successor upon the earth (19:26-29, 22:10-30). He further blesses Rebekah and instructs her concerning Jacob's unique role (19:15-25). These colorful expansions to Genesis support the continuity of the religion practiced by the ancestors. So close are Abraham and Jacob that the ancestor spends his final night asleep with his grandson, whom he blesses and kisses seven times before peacefully departing this life (chs. 22-23). It is then Jacob who becomes the most significant ancestor throughout the remainder of the book.

Abraham's death provokes commentary on the larger course of history. While *Jubilees* does not delve deeply into eschatology, two digressions (1:7-29, 23:11-32) reveal that the jubilees and divisions of the times extend into a future horizon. The angel foretells a time of future wickedness when Israel will forsake the covenant and come under the rule of the Gentiles. The harrowing description of this national collapse likely anticipates the perceived violence and legal transgression of the author's own time.

The book ultimately takes an inspiring, consolatory view of this bleak forecast. In the very midst of this wickedness, the youths will search the law anew (23:26-32). As they return to the law, they will be liberated from their enemies and their lifespans will increase to antediluvian proportions. The author may have believed that he stood at the threshold of these events and wrote to inspire this last great renewal of the eternal covenant. Through this eschatological renewal, God's own righteousness would be vindicated for all time, fulfilling a stated purpose of the entire book: "[W]rite them in a book so that their generations might see that I have not abandoned them on account of all the evil which they have done in transgressing the covenant . . . and they will know that I have truly been with them" (1:5-6).[9]

Biblical Antiquities (*Liber Antiquitatum Biblicarum*)

The *Book of Biblical Antiquities* (*Liber Antiquitatum Biblicarum*, *LAB*) demonstrates that the methods of scriptural rewriting continued well into the first century CE. Like *Jubilees*, *LAB* begins with Genesis-Exodus. Yet *LAB* extends into episodes of Numbers, Deuteronomy, Joshua, Judges, and Samuel, finally concluding with the death of Saul (1 Sam 31–2 Sam 1). Since *LAB* foreshadows the rise of David (chs. 59–60), the original ending may have been lost or never completed. On the other hand, the tragic demise of Saul's leadership and the unfulfilled longing for David's kingdom offer a meaningful conclusion in their own right. Hope amid historical despair represents a major concern of *LAB*'s rewriting of scriptural traditions.

Medieval editions titled the work *Philonis Antiquitatum Liber* since it circulated with Latin translations of Philo's works. Attribution to Philo, however, has been conclusively disproven. The unknown author is sometimes called Pseudo-Philo, although pseudonymous authorship in Philo's name is used nowhere. Early modern editions began to title the work *Liber Antiquitatum* (some adding *Biblicarum*). Hebrew was probably the original language, from which it was further translated into Greek and from Greek into Latin. *LAB* is not known to have featured among later canons. Nevertheless, its arts of interpretation attest abundant affinities with the interpretive practices of the early church and Rabbinic Judaism.

LAB was likely written in Palestine sometime in the first century CE. Among the only internal hints to its original setting, *LAB* reports that sacrifices continue to be practiced in the Jerusalem temple "even unto this day" (22:8–9). Nowhere does it acknowledge the temple's destruction in the Great Revolt. A setting prior to 70 CE may thus be possible. Unlike *Jubilees*, the book makes no explicit claim to transmit a divine revelation. Instead, *LAB* compiles and reinterprets Israel's historical traditions in a unified way that was relevant to its first-century setting.

Rewriting Scripture in LAB

LAB utilizes the Pentateuch, as well the historical books of the Hebrew Bible (Samuel, Kings, Chronicles), as a unified narrative. The perceived harmony within this total story allows *LAB* to improvise sophisticated relationships between otherwise disparate scriptural texts, coloring particular episodes with creative new shades of meaning. The theological interpretation of history found in the book of Deuteronomy pervades the work. This "Deuteronomistic" interpretive paradigm explains how Israel's history was the direct result of its covenant with God—a covenant whose laws its leaders broke, invoking God's righteous judgment in the Babylonian Exile and other this-worldly historical disasters. While God desired to bless Israel through the covenant, it also contained curses upon transgressors. *LAB* frequently reinterprets and modifies this theodicy. Deuteronomic laws on worship, idolatry, and intermarriage also feature among its major legal concerns.

Further complementing these Deuteronomistic tendencies, the book draws upon prophetic literature and Psalms, accenting the narrative with literary and theological pathos. Otherwise unknown sources also appear to have been included. The extended narrative of Kenaz (chs. 25–28), for example, tells the story of the first of the judges to have served after the death of Joshua. Since this figure is only briefly mentioned among scriptural books (Josh 15:17; Judg 1:13; 1 Chron 4:13), *LAB* appears to have incorporated otherwise unknown sources to tell his heroic story.

In four instances, *LAB* directly imitates the phraseology of Kings and Chronicles when redirecting readers to its sources (*LAB* 35:7, 43:4, 56:7, 63:5): "Are they not written in the book of Judges?" (35:7; cf. 1 Kings 14:19; 2 Chron 27:7).[10] These imitative formulae may reveal the attempt to compose a chronicle, modeled upon the books of Kings and Chronicles. Like Chronicles, in fact, *LAB* opens with substantial genealogies, starting with Adam. Genealogies vastly condense most of the material found in Genesis, allowing more expanded narratives of the flood and the tower of Babel.

The Flood (ch. 3)

The flood story follows Genesis closely, while offering interpretive revisions. When God limits the human lifespan (Gen 6:3), *LAB* observes, "For them he set the limits of life, but the crimes done by their hands did not cease" (*LAB* 3:2).[11] For *LAB*, limiting the human lifespan proves an insufficient measure against sin. Where God declares to Noah, "I will establish my covenant with you" (Gen 6:18), *LAB* adds "to destroy all those inhabiting the earth" (*LAB* 3:4; cf. 11:1).[12] The story's conclusion will reiterate this dual feature of the covenant: to save and to destroy. God's benign promise in Genesis (8:21) never again to curse the earth applies only to the flood waters in *LAB*. Famine, sword, fire, death, earthquakes, and dispersion will otherwise provide future instruments of retribution (*LAB* 3:9). These alterations render a more Deuteronomistic flood story, in which God's covenant foretells both blessing and curse.

In Genesis, God unreservedly promises that the seasons will never again cease "throughout all the days of the earth" (Gen 8:22). For *LAB*, however, this order will endure only "until" the transformation of the present world, as the dead are raised for final judgment (*LAB* 3:9–10). *LAB* thus fortifies its Deuteronomistic interpretation of history even further by emphasizing eschatological justice, a tendency repeated throughout the book (16:3; 19:4, 12–15; 23:13; 33:2–3). Such hopes ensure the inevitability of divine justice amid otherwise excruciating episodes in Israel's history.

The Tower of Babel (chs. 6–7)

An expanded rendition of the Tower of Babel (Gen 11:1–9) surprisingly places Abraham at its construction, forming a prehistory not unlike *Jubilees*. In this remarkable innovation, Abraham resists the plan to build the tower and endures the threat of martyrdom. How could *LAB* have taken such dramatic liberties with the Genesis narrative? In the first case, the author transposes the plotline of Daniel 3 into the action. God thus saves Abraham from the fiery furnace of the Babylonians, like Shadrach, Meshach, and Abed-Nego. The transposition of elements from one scriptural source into another is a favorite technique of *LAB*. The rationale for linking the two disparate stories may initially seem arbitrary. Closer examination reveals that this interpretive maneuver arises from a carefully devised textual correlation between the two narratives.

Some ancient interpreters read Genesis 15:7 as indicating that God brought Abraham out of "the *flame* (Hebrew: *m'wr*) of the Chaldeans," rather than out of the city "*Ur* (*m'wr*) of the Chaldeans."[13] *LAB* repeatedly emphasizes that God literally saved Abraham "from the flame" of the Chaldeans' fiery furnace (6:15–18; 23:5, 32:1), like the heroes of Daniel 3. "Babel" in Genesis merges with "Babylon" in Daniel (cf. "Shinar" in Gen 11:2 and Dan 1:2); the tower's bricks are baked (Gen 11:3) in none other than Nebuchadnezzar's fiery furnace (Dan 3:6);[14] and the construction of the tower with its "top in the heavens" parallels the lofty "height" of the king's golden idol (Dan 3:1; cf. *LAB* 12:3). The correlation with Daniel transforms the available meanings of the Genesis story: the construction of the tower now equates to false worship and idolatry.

Abraham in LAB

Like the heroes of Daniel, Abraham is willing to suffer martyrdom, yet God delivers him from the furnace. God's blessings upon Abraham are, in fact, foretold at the very moment in which the tower is being built (7:3–4). The implicit contrast between Babel and Abraham in Genesis (cf. Gen 11:4, 12:2) becomes unmistakable in *LAB*. Although a genealogy (*LAB* 8:1–14) otherwise condenses most of Genesis 12–50, the covenant promises to Abraham remain alive as later characters reflect upon his life. In this artful way, the covenant with Abraham takes on expanded meanings, as it echoes through later contexts of Israel's story.

The prophecies of Balaam (Num 22–24), for example, memorialize Abraham (*LAB* 18:4–6), even though he is mentioned nowhere in the underlying scriptural narrative. In a daring interpretive maneuver, *LAB* recasts the *Aqedah* through God's own first-person perspective. While Isaac suffers no literal harm, God regards the offering as a genuine blood sacrifice due to the mutual obedience of Abraham and Isaac. The sacrifice marks the definitive moment of God's everlasting election of Israel: "[F]or his blood did I choose this people" (18:5).[15]

LAB returns to Abraham as it presents Joshua's renewal of the covenant (*LAB* 23; Josh 24). Where Joshua briefly memorializes Abraham (Josh 24:2–4), *LAB* creates an expanded alternative by substituting the comforting exhortation of Isaiah 51. Abraham and Sarah are "the rock from which you were hewn, and the quarry from which you were dug" (Isa 51:2).[16] Joshua further recounts the mysterious covenant ceremony of Genesis 15. The "deep sleep" and "terrifying darkness" that fell upon Abraham (Gen 15:12) have become an apocalyptic tour of the cosmos (*LAB* 23:6; cf. *ApAbr*). Symbolic interpretation of Abraham's sacrifice ensues: the young dove (Gen 15:9) is Abraham; the turtle dove represents Israel's future prophets, and the ram, its sages; the she-goat stands for the mothers of Israel (*LAB* 23:7). God regards the ceremony as an everlasting witness that "I will not transgress my words" (23:7).[17]

The "Song of Deborah" (Judg 5) reflects again upon the *Aqedah*, a feature found nowhere in the scriptural poem. It was because angels envied Abraham that God required the sacrifice (*LAB* 32:1-2; cf. *Jubilees* 17:15-16).[18] Contrary to Genesis, Abraham informs Isaac that he will be sacrificed. In response, Isaac wonders how a human can be sacrificed, like a lamb, as a sin offering (*LAB* 32:3), yet he is equally willing to be offered (cf. 40:1-4). Due to the obedience of Abraham and Isaac, God vows, "[Y]our memory shall remain before me forever" (32:4). Once again, the *Aqedah* confirms God's everlasting election of Israel. In these episodes, reminiscence upon Abraham shines a bright ray of hope amid agonizing failures within Israel's history.

Deborah

Deborah's song highlights *LAB*'s larger concern with female characters (cf. 9:5-10, 31:3-9, 40:1-9, 42:1-7, 50:1-51:7, 64:1-9). She is among the most significant figures in the book: "a mother in Israel" (Judg 5:7), a "woman of God," a "holy one who exercised rule" and "strengthened a fence about her generation" (*LAB* 33:1, 6). She further ranks in a succession of leaders (30:2, 5) who restore Israel to the covenant after repeated transgressions. Deborah offers a remarkable interpretation of such failures: as iron becomes soft when cast into fire but hardens when taken out, so Israel has been obedient during the lifetime of righteous leaders yet has turned away from the covenant after their deaths (30:6). In spite of this recurrent pattern, however, God will faithfully keep the covenant: "For our fathers are dead, but the God who established the covenant with them is life" (30:7).[19] Hope in the living God amid failed national leadership addresses one of the major concerns of the book (Murphy 1993).

Moses and Sinai (chs. 11–13)

The author's assumptions about the covenant especially shine through in *LAB*'s account of the Sinai revelation. Deuteronomistic themes of proper worship and sexual purity preoccupy its treatment of law. The laws of the tabernacle prepare a proper dwelling place for God (*LAB* 13:1–2; cf. Exod 25–31), until the eventual construction of the Jerusalem temple (*LAB* 22:1–9). This allows the festivals of Leviticus 23 to be continually practiced (*LAB* 13:4–7). This order of law, temple, and festival observance, however, is threatened by the interrelated transgressions of idolatry, intermarriage with Gentiles, and magic.

The concern with idolatry in the creative retelling of the Babel episode is thus sustained throughout subsequent narratives (11:6, 12:1–10, 19:6–7, 25:7–13; 44:1–7; cf. 2:9–10). Intermarriage with Gentiles is forbidden in several colorful episodes (9:1, 5; 18:13; 21:1; 30:1; 43:5; 44:7; 45:3). Perhaps the most striking case rationalizes the union of Tamar with her father-in-law, Judah (Gen 38), precisely as an attempt to avoid intercourse with the Gentiles (9:5): Even incest becomes preferable to intermarriage. The arts of magic, originally taught to humans by fallen angels (34:2–3), further seduce Israel into these sins (25:10–12, 34:1–5). Concerns with idolatry, intermarriage, and magic are interwoven even into scriptural contexts where they were not originally apparent (Murphy 1993).

As Moses enters the darkness of Sinai (Exod 20:21), he beholds visions like an apocalyptic seer. Indeed, the entire context of the Sinai revelation is described in the vivid imagery of a cosmic, apocalyptic event (*LAB* 32:7–8). Moses beholds the tree of life, preserved with God in the heavens. *LAB* explains that it was a branch from the very tree of life that was cast into the bitter waters of Marah to nourish Israel on its journey to Sinai (e.g., Exod 15:22–25). The miraculously sweetened waters then "followed them in the wilderness forty years"

(*LAB* 11:15),[20] providing Israel with a continuous water supply in the desert.

The golden calf (Exod 32) reveals one of *LAB*'s fullest expressions of how God deals with Israel as a covenant partner. As the people build the calf, the episode becomes a direct fulfillment of God's earlier words at Babel: "[T]hey will adventure all that they aspire to do and worse" (cf. Gen 11:6; *LAB* 12:3; cf. 7:2). Again, the author draws a remarkable correspondence among disparate scriptural stories, as the calf now replicates the earlier sin of the idolatrous tower. Yet now it is not the Chaldeans who transgress, but Israel. The aftermath deeply psychologizes the deity's despair over Israel's transgression (cf. Exod 32:7–10): surely if Israel has already turned to idolatry, their sin will only escalate in the promised land.

Forecasting a desperate future, the deity's pathos over the history of Israel is poignantly conveyed. Near the point of despair, God painfully wonders, "Are the promises at an end which I made to their fathers?" (*LAB* 12:4).[21] In a flourish of conflicted emotional turbulence, the deity vows to forsake Israel, only to make peace with them again and build a sanctuary—"a house that will be destroyed because they will sin against me. And the race of men will be to me like a drop from a pitcher and will be reckoned like spittle" (12:4; cf. 7:3; Isa 40:15).[22] Here, *LAB* interweaves the poetry of Isaiah 40, which hails God's infinite superiority over the nations and their idols (cf. *4 Ezra* 6:56). If Israel, God's final link to humanity, cannot be trusted, the deity vows to disregard humans altogether. The passage crystallizes *LAB*'s pessimism over whether Israel will keep faith with God. Even more than this, it implies that the fate of the entire human race also rests somehow with the viability of the covenant with Israel.

Moses intercedes with God, comparing Israel poetically to a vine that has lost its fruit (*LAB* 12:8–10). The metaphor of the vine/vineyard (cf. Ps 80:8–19; Isa 5:1–7) resounds elsewhere in *LAB* to express Israel's unique relationship with God (*LAB* 18:10–11, 23:11–12, 28:4, 30:4, 39:7). Moses urges God to relent, lest all has been done "in vain" (cf. 9:4, 18:11, 28:5, 40:5): "For even if you plant another vine, this one will not trust you, because you have destroyed the former one" (12:9).[23] Amid the tensions between justice and mercy, hope and historical despair, *LAB* encourages its contemporaries that the integrity of the covenant will ultimately rest upon the assurance of divine faithfulness (cf. 13:10, 15:7, 21:2-6). The golden calf episode leads onward to the construction of the tabernacle and God's ultimate promise never to forsake Israel: "for I am faithful in my ways" (13:10).[24]

Scriptural Interpretation in the New Testament

No New Testament document endeavored to rewrite continuous portions of scriptural books on the scale of *Jubilees* and *LAB*. Nevertheless, shorter units retell scriptural stories, such as the exhortation on faith in Hebrews 11 and Stephen's speech in Acts (7:1-53). Such rhetorical units frequently exhibit, on a smaller scale, methods of implicit interpretation found within *Jubilees* and *LAB*. Scholars have further compared the editorial tendencies of the gospel writers to specimens of "rewritten scripture." As the gospel writers edit and implicitly reinterpret their sources, they, too, harmonize, rearrange, omit, and add both smaller and larger expansions.

The Rock That Followed

A focused example of Paul's exegesis (1 Cor 10:1-11) reveals how scriptural interpretation in New Testament literature often reflects interpretive assumptions found in works like *Jubilees* and *LAB*. In his lengthy admonition against eating foods sacrificed to idols (1 Cor 8-10), Paul turns to the scriptural context of Exodus through Numbers, as he interprets a series of provocations between God and Israel. These narratives serve as "types" or "examples" (1 Cor 10:6, 11) that warn the Corinthians amid their present controversy over eating meats sacrificed to idols:

1. The Red Sea (Exod 13:17-15:21)
2. The provision of manna (Exod 16:1-36)
3. The provision of water (Exod 17:1-7; cf. 15:22-27; Num 20:1-13, 21:16-18)
4. The golden calf (Exod 32:1-35)

5. Fornication with Moab and Midian (Num 25:1–9)
6. The bronze serpent (Num 21:4–9)
7. Complaints against Moses and God (Exod 16:2–3; Num 14:2).

Paul carefully collects and structures episodes from disparate contexts to make his case. The first three sequential episodes illustrate God's faithful, life-giving provision. Yet with an explicit citation of Exodus 32:6, the golden calf turns to the dangers of idolatrous feasts, sexual immorality, and divine judgment: "The people ate and drank and rose up to play." The final three examples demonstrate God's subsequent, death-dealing judgments upon the ancestors, fortifying Paul's stern admonition.

As Paul interprets these carefully structured episodes, he fuses the identities of Israel and the Corinthians. The Corinthians become interrelated with Israel, "our ancestors," who were "baptized into Moses in the cloud and at the sea" (1 Cor 10:1–2), even as the Corinthians have been baptized into Christ. As "spiritual" food and drink, the wilderness manna and water anticipate the Eucharist. The rock from which water flowed becomes Christ himself (10:3–4).

In taking these liberties, Paul acknowledges that he interprets in a nonliteral fashion. He uses the term "spiritual" (10:3–4) to express the inherent message within earlier scriptures that now speaks to the Corinthians. In mysterious ways (cf. 2:9–16), this "spiritual" quality within scripture transcends its own immediate contexts as an "example" or "type" (*typos*) to future generations. The examples of Israel, spiritually interpreted, now address the Corinthians, "on whom the ends of the ages have come" (10:11).[25] Eschatological awareness that the Gentiles have been incorporated into the promises to Israel (cf. Rom 11:11–32) further underlies Paul's "spiritual" reading of the scriptural narratives.

Paul also reveals that he is the heir of interpretive traditions that arose from within his ancient Jewish context. In the wilderness, Israel "drank from the spiritual rock that followed them, and the rock was Christ" (1 Cor 10:4). How did Paul imagine that a rock, flowing with water, "followed" Israel in the wilderness? He was not alone in this assumption. As we have seen, *LAB* describes how Moses purifies the bitter waters of Marah (Exod 15:22–27) with a branch from the tree of life. The sweetened waters then "followed them in the wilderness forty years, and went up with them into the hills and went down with them into the plain" (*LAB* 11:15).[26] Paul and *LAB* both assume that a miraculous supply of waters literally "followed" Israel. Yet how did they arrive at this understanding?

Within the Torah, four separate narratives describe a miraculous supply of water (Exod 15:22–27, 17:1–7; Num 20:1–13, 21:16–18). None of them literally claims that a rock or waters followed Israel. Yet the relationships among these accounts provoked ancient interpreters. Since the waters of Meribah (Exod 17:1–7) are mentioned a second time in a different location in Numbers (20:1–13), some ancient readers imagined that they must have followed Israel throughout their wilderness journey. Another rationale rests with a particular reading of Numbers 21:17–20 in which it was not Israel but rather "the well" (vv18–20) that traveled throughout the hills and valleys to Moab. Thus, a well of water came to follow Israel (Fisk 2001). *LAB* appears to harmonize the stories of Numbers 21 and Exodus 15, referencing "the well [Num 21] of the water of Marah [Exod 15]" (*LAB* 20:8).

Other ancient interpreters equated the stone "well" of Numbers 21 with the "rock" from which water flowed in Exodus 17 and Numbers 20. A physical description of the envisioned stone well survives in the Tosefta:

> And so the well which was with the Israelites in the wilderness was a rock, the size of a large round vessel ... rising with them up onto the mountains, and going down with them into the valleys. (*Sukkah* 3.11)[27]

Paul's reference to "the rock that followed them" appears to be focused on the story of Exodus 17. His reference is so incidental, so subconscious, that some scholars suggest Paul could not have imagined the scriptural story any other way (Enns 1996). The interpretive tradition of "the rock that followed" became part of the very fiber of the scriptural story for Paul. At the same time, its function within the passage is not coincidental. For Paul, the miraculous character of the rock shows that it was, indeed, "spiritual" and points to a transcendent reality: "the rock was Christ."

Even in this interpretive leap, Paul may be compared with contemporary interpreters who assigned a mystical, transcendent, or divine character to the supply of water. *LAB* identifies the branch of Exodus 15, which purified the waters, with the heavenly tree of life in Paradise. Philo of Alexandria likewise associates the branch with the tree of life and the promise of immortality (*Migration* 36–37). As for the water of Exodus 17, Philo identifies the rock with "the wisdom of God," from which divine knowledge pours into the repentant soul (*Allegorical Laws* 2:86; cf. *Drunkenness* 112; *Worse Attacks Better* 118). Paul's claim that "the rock was Christ" may be viewed in broad continuity with the interpretive practices of his time, which imagined the sacred and transcendent features of the waters that God graciously provided in the wilderness.

Hebrews and the Aqedah

Among the most prolific interpreters of scripture in the New Testament is the unknown author of the book of Hebrews, often known as the Hebraist. The Hebraist's hermeneutical sophistication, as well as his deep immersion within the interpretive culture of ancient Judaism, are well illustrated in the book's rendition of the sacrifice of Isaac:

> By faith, Abraham, when he was tested, brought forth Isaac. And he who received the promises was bringing forth his only son, of whom it was said, "In Isaac shall your seed be called" [Gen 21:12], having reasoned that God was powerful to raise him even from the dead, whence he also received him back, in a parable. (Heb 11:17–19)[28]

Hebrews' rendition of the story transpires within the book's majestic exhortation on faith (11:1–12:13), which recounts examples of faithfulness from the creation of the world to the activities of Israel's kings, prophets, and martyrs. Abraham's faith plays a paradigmatic role within the larger exhortation, in this case highlighted by his hope in God's power to raise the dead.

The structure of the passage offers two parallel claims that surround a brief citation of the promise of offspring found in Genesis 21:12: "In

Isaac shall your seed be called." The first set of parallel claims describes Abraham himself as one whose faith in the divine promises is tested (Heb 11:17); the second psychologizes his internal hope that God would even raise Isaac from the dead in order to keep the promise (11:19). As compared with Genesis 22, therefore, the Hebraist offers two major expansions or revisions: (1) the faith of Abraham has become his defining virtue, not simply the "fear of God" (cf. Gen 22:12); (2) belief in resurrection inspired Abraham to face the grievous trial with hope.

These are indeed sweeping revisions of the Genesis story. For these reasons, interpreters have accentuated the Hebraist's extraneous impositions upon the narratives of the Hebrew Bible (Attridge 1989). From a historical-developmental viewpoint, such recognition is valuable. Faith is not an explicit concern of Genesis 22, nor is Abraham's hope in resurrection. Indeed, a great deal of interpretive tradition had developed historically between the composition of Genesis 22 and the Hebraist, traditions that are now interwoven back into the fabric of the story. The Hebraist, however, was far from alone in these enhancements to the scriptural story. Contemporary sources reveal the extent to which ancient interpreters viewed the monumental Genesis story through layers of enhanced meaning that included Abraham's "faithfulness" and his hope in the afterlife.

Faith

For Hebrews, it was "by faith" that Abraham resolved the paradox between two contradictory divine words: the earlier promise of offspring through Isaac (Gen 21:12) and the current command to sacrifice him (22:1–2). While "faith" is mentioned nowhere in the Genesis account, other ancient interpreters insisted together with Hebrews that "faith" was specifically the virtue demonstrated within the trial.

In *Jubilees*' rendition, Abraham was "faithful" throughout the earlier trials he experienced: "And in everything in which [God] tested him, he was found faithful. And his soul was not impatient. And he was not slow to act because he was faithful and a lover of the Lord" (17:18).[29] In the conclusion to the trial, *Jubilees* reiterates faithfulness by interweaving this quality into the divine word to Abraham (Gen 22:15–18), even where it was not explicitly found: "And I have made known to all that you are faithful to me in everything which I say to you" (*Jubilees* 18:16).³⁰ Within *Jubilees*' schema of ten trials, Abraham is repeatedly "found faithful" (19:9).

A comparable version of the story is found in a Dead Sea Scroll strongly influenced by *Jubilees*. In *Pseudo-Jubilees*ᵃ, Abraham's faith is again centrally highlighted. By prefacing the episode with Genesis 15:2–6, *Pseudo-Jubilees*ᵃ emphasizes that Abraham "believed" God (Gen 15:6). With the outcome hanging in the balance, the trial fundamentally concerns "[whether] he would be found false and whether he would not be found faithful" (*Pseudo-Jubilees*ᵃ frg. 2 II 7–8).³¹

Other writings briefly accentuate Abraham's faithfulness, as though this characteristic had become synonymous with the trial. First Maccabees glorifies Abraham's faith: "Was not Abraham found faithful in trial, and it was reckoned to him as righteousness?" (2:52). Ben Sira likewise remarks, "[I]n trial, he was found faithful" (44:20; cf. Neh 9:8). In these cases, Abraham's "faith" has become a virtually subliminal association with the trial, even though this quality is mentioned nowhere within Genesis 22. In this sense, Hebrews does not superimpose "faith" externally upon the scriptural episode so much as it views the story through the interpretive preconceptions of its time.

Nor was the Hebraist the first within the New Testament to associate Abraham so intensively with faith. Paul's exegesis in Galatians 3:6–29 and Romans 4:1–25 insists upon "faith" as the defining characteristic of Abraham's relationship with God. Paul is much more focused on the faith of Abraham prior to his circumcision in Genesis 17, rather than on the *Aqedah* (esp. Gen 15:1–6 and 12:1–7; Rom 4:10). Nevertheless, both early church authors stand within a larger current of interpretive tradition that found in Abraham the essence of human faithfulness.

Afterlife

The psychologizing of Abraham (and Isaac) is a repeated technique among ancient interpreters of the trial. The minimalist storyline of Genesis leaves behind suggestive hints of Abraham's obedient state of mind, Isaac's innocence, the hope of provision, and the promise of return. Ancient interpreters remained only further intrigued, psychologizing Abraham, Isaac, even the deity. Hebrews, too, psychologizes Abraham. It was through his premeditated faith in resurrection that Abraham endured the great trial. Abraham had "reasoned within himself" that God would keep the promise—even if only by the extreme measure of resurrecting Isaac from the dead.

Hebrews further comments that "in a similitude," "in a parable," "in a manner of speaking," Abraham did "receive" Isaac back from the dead, as the trial relented. At least "in a parable," Hebrews shares with some ancient sources that it was *as though* death had been encountered and overcome in the trial. As we have seen, *LAB* insists that God regarded the trial as though it were a genuine sacrifice, going so far as to claim, "[F]or his blood did I choose them [e.g., Israel]" (*LAB* 18:5).[32] While literal death did not occur, it was as though obedience in the offering had shed blood. As Abraham had fully intended to give Isaac to God, God recounts, "I gave him back to his father" (18:5). In Hebrews, too, Abraham receives his son back again, as though it were from death itself, a "parable" of resurrection. Faith in the divine promises resonates throughout the larger exhortation, as the ancestors transcend death "by faith" (Heb 11:4–5, 13, 21–22, 26, 35).

Other ancient interpreters found faith in the afterlife exemplified in the trial. As Josephus recasts the episode, Abraham reveals directly to Isaac that his sacrifice will guarantee an everlasting divine favor. Abraham anticipates how God will receive Isaac as an acceptable sacrifice into immortality within the divine presence: "Amid prayers and sacrifice, he shall favorably accept your soul and hold it fast unto himself" (*Antiquities* 1:231). Josephus's language for Isaac's soul or life as a sacrifice is also reflected in *LAB* (32:2–3; cf. 40:3), where Isaac expresses wonder that "the Lord has made the soul of a man worthy to be a sacrifice" (32:3). As in Josephus, *LAB* imagines the sacrifice as Isaac's entrance into "life without limit and time without measure" (32:3).[33] Hebrews takes its own analogous approach to psychologizing Abraham, who faces the agony of the trial through hope in resurrection.

Isaac's own miraculous birth from Abraham's "mortified" body (Heb 11:12) had already represented a triumph over death for the Hebraist. Perhaps it is on this basis that Abraham faces the trial with such daring hope in resurrection. Paul's exegesis in Romans 4 also offers precedent for associating Isaac's birth with the hope in resurrection. Against all hope, against his own body "as good as dead," against the barrenness of Sarah, Abraham believed the promise of the God "who gives life to the dead and calls into existence the things that are not" (Rom 4:17–21). In Paul's case, Abraham's hope in resurrection is applied to his faith in the initial promise of offspring rather than the *Aqedah*. Hebrews appears to extend Abraham's hope in resurrection even further, to the critical moment of the great trial itself.

By psychologizing Abraham's faith in resurrection, Hebrews joins Josephus and *LAB* as first-century witnesses that found hope in the afterlife in the agony of the trial, a relationship more elaborately developed among later aggadic midrashim.[34] The Hebraist's deep immersion within the interpretive cultures of ancient Judaism thus becomes apparent by comparing his version of the trial story with contemporary renditions.

Other "Interpretive Traditions"

Paul and Hebrews reveal select instances of a much larger phenomenon in which New Testament authors reflect scripture as it was mediated through the interpretive traditions of Early Judaism. Readers of the New Testament today, therefore, need not be surprised to learn that "Moses was instructed in all the wisdom of the Egyptians" (Acts 7:22), a claim found nowhere in Exodus yet popular among early Jewish authors (Philo, *Moses* 1:21–24). Was Israel's law "ordained by angels" (Gal 3:19; cf. Acts 7:38, 53; Heb 2:2), as Paul suggests? The claim is more compatible with passages of Philo (*Dreams* 1:141–43) and Josephus (*Antiquities* 15:136; cf. *Jubilees* 14:20) than with Exodus. Who are Jannes and Jambres (2 Tim 3:8)? Pharaoh's magicians, of course—anonymous in Exodus, yet named in the *Damascus Document* (V 17–19). Was Noah a "preacher of righteousness" before the flood (2 Pet 2:5)? Not so much in Genesis as in Josephus (*Antiquities* 1:73–75) and the *Sibylline Oracles* (1:150–95). A rock surely followed the church in its ongoing journey with scripture, one hewn out of the interpretive imagination of its early Jewish context.

5

In the Wilderness

As new manuscripts of early Jewish writings became available in the nineteenth and early twentieth centuries, a startling discovery dramatically expanded the range of literature available to modern scholars in 1947. This initial discovery of Dead Sea Scrolls from Cave 1, near an ancient ruin called "Qumran" in the Judaean wilderness, unveiled remarkably preserved Hebrew and Aramaic scrolls originally copied in the Hellenistic and Roman eras. Cave 1 further inaugurated a decade of discovery (1947–56) in which eleven caves would yield approximately nine hundred ancient manuscripts. The magnitude of these discoveries for the study of the Bible, Judaism, and Christianity cannot be overstated. They offer the earliest available manuscripts of scriptural texts, dating prior to the origins of Rabbinic Judaism and the church. Previously unknown compositions further opened vast, new reservoirs for understanding the diversity of Judaism within this crucial era of history.

The Community of the Dead Sea Scrolls

An ongoing mystery since the discovery has been the identity of those responsible for this monumental collection. Since the scrolls were copied within the Hellenistic and Roman eras up until the Great Jewish Revolt, scholars have sought their original proprietors within this historical context (ca. 250 BCE–68 CE). Approximately 25 percent of the scrolls comprise **biblical manuscripts**, early copies of books that would appear in the Hebrew Bible. This immediately reveals the scripturally focused character of the movement that preserved the scrolls. They were concerned with living out the heritage of Israel's law and prophets in their own time.

The remaining **nonbiblical manuscripts** offer further revelations. The *Rule of the Community*, among the first scrolls discovered in Cave 1, advances a disciplinary code for a *yaḥad*. This "union" or "community" separates from other Jews to pursue its distinct interpretation of Israel's law under priestly leadership. The community forms a highly structured society, with an extended novitiate prior to full membership and a disciplinary code for errant members. Such regulations preserve the community's purity in matters of food, drink, and bodily conduct. Since ordinances for women are absent, the *Rule* appears to have addressed an exclusively or predominantly male order. Viewing themselves dualistically as "Sons of Light" within the context of an apocalyptic age of "darkness," the *yaḥad* defines its role within the Judaean wilderness as a living fulfillment of Isaiah 40:3. Through their sanctity and adherence to Israel's law, they were preparing "*in the wilderness* the way of [the LORD]" (VIII 14).

One approach to the movement that preserved the Dead Sea Scrolls has been to associate it with the *yaḥad* described in the *Rule*. If so, the community represented an apocalyptic sectarian movement that voluntarily separated from other Jews and took refuge in the Judaean wilderness. There, they aspired to live out their practice of Israel's law in priestly holiness within the context of an intentionally organized society. Other scrolls that resemble the religious ideology found in the *Rule* are often classified as **sectarian literature**. These writings are believed to have been composed or edited within the same sectarian religious movement.

Righteous Teacher

Several sectarian writings unveil at the center of the community's identity a previously unknown religious leader, the "Righteous Teacher" (or "Teacher of Righteousness"). The Teacher, who is never explicitly named, powerfully embodies the roles of priest, scribe, and recipient of divine revelation. The *Damascus Document* describes the advent of the Teacher to a struggling group of penitents sometime after 177 BCE. In their moment of crisis and failure, God "raised for them a Righteous Teacher to guide them in the way of his heart" (*Damascus* I 10–11). His death is also referenced, implying that the Teacher deceased prior to ca. 100 BCE, by which time *Damascus* had likely been composed. The Teacher emerges as the gracious act of God to redirect a struggling religious movement in the "righteous statutes" of Israel's law.

Several commentaries highlight the Teacher's activity as a fulfillment of scriptural prophecy. The *Commentary on Habakkuk* interprets Habakkuk 2:1–4 as fulfilled in the advent of the Teacher, "to whom God made known all the mysteries of the words of his servants the prophets" (VII 3–5).[1] The description hails the Teacher as a recipient of divine revelation, not unlike an apocalyptic seer. The Teacher's revealed interpretation of Israel's law brings him into conflict with a "Wicked Priest." This epithet appears to ridicule the prevailing high priests of the Hasmonean Dynasty, who ruled from 152 to 63 BCE. In search of the Teacher's identity, some scholars propose that he may originally have served as a temple priest, perhaps even a high priest, prior to the Hasmoneans. Yet the story of the Teacher has been so heavily mythologized within the complex language of prophetic oracles that his historical identity remains elusive. What is clear is that his memory powerfully shaped the community's identity as the heirs of his definitive, yet rejected, revelation.

Legal Conflicts

Additional sectarian writings attest the community's legal conflicts with other Jews. *Some Works of the Torah* enumerates over twenty points of legal practice that explain why "we have separated ourselves from the multitudes of the people." Legal issues regarding purity stand at the heart of their concern. The work concludes with a diplomatic address that pleads with the Jerusalem priesthood to accept its legal claims, admonishing that to err in these matters will "lead the people astray," defiling the temple. The exhortation strongly indicates that disputation over specific legal practices concerning purity represented the decisive factor in the community's self-definition and separation from other Jews.

Tensions

In spite of the intriguing insights they provide, tensions and inconsistencies remain among the sectarian writings. The *Rule of the Community* (VI 13–24) and *Damascus Document* (XV 5–16), for example, exhibit discrepancies on precisely how one entered the community. *Damascus* also offers legal disciplines for men and women, including marriage (VII 4–15), issues absent from the *Rule*. Thus, it remains in question how both rules could have been directed toward the same group. These differences are indicative of a larger range of tensions within the sectarian literature. Such tensions may reflect phases within the historical progression of a movement that existed for some two centuries. On the other hand, they may also indicate that the movement standing behind the Dead Sea Scrolls was itself internally diverse, as individual collectives practiced its disciplines with moderate variations (Collins 2009). *Rule*, for example, may have served a more specialized stratum of priestly elites in the Judaean wilderness, even as *Damascus* addressed a broader movement in cities and camps throughout the land.

Ancient Historians

Was the community ever referenced by contemporary writers? Within the same historical and geographical environment, the Roman historian Pliny the Elder (d. 79 CE) utilizes earlier sources describing an isolated "tribe of the Essenes." In this somewhat derisive account, Essenes live in celibate poverty "on the west side of the Dead Sea" just beyond the coast, with palm trees, rather than women, as their only companions (*Natural History* V xvii). Since Pliny locates an "Essene" settlement near the location of the scrolls and alludes to their celibacy (a possible feature of the *Rule*), the community may have represented a branch of the larger Essene movement. This **Essene Hypothesis** gains further momentum from other ancient authors, who identify Essenes as pure religious communalists who pursued a specialized form of Jewish devotion renowned for its organization, egalitarianism, and discipline. While these authors were outsiders to the Essene movement, their accounts nevertheless share meaningful intersections with the *Rule* and other sectarian writings.

Josephus, for example (*War* 2:119–60; *Antiquities* 18:11, 18–22), describes the Essenes as celibate communalists, who disdain wealth and "devote their property to the order" (*War* 2:122). The *Rule* stipulates that the property of those entering the community must be officially registered. Its purity must be ensured before it can intermingle among the community's possessions (VI 13–24). Josephus reports that Essenes require a three-year initiation. The *Rule* describes a prolonged two-year novitiate after an initial examination period. Josephus's Essenes share with the *Rule* a predeterministic theology (*Rule* III 15–17; Josephus, *Antiquities* 18:18). Josephus agrees with Pliny on Essene celibacy, yet clarifies that branches of the movement do practice marriage. Such diverse marital practices could be reflected in the apparent divergences between the *Rule* and *Damascus*. Although Josephus does not perfectly replicate the internal content of the scrolls, the breadth and consistency of their correspondence have made the Essene Hypothesis a traditionally appealing approach to understanding the community of the scrolls.

Archaeology

Archaeology, too, may offer evidence for the community's activity. Nearby Caves 4–10 stands a site, called in Arabic Khirbet Qumrān, the "Ruin of Qumran" (see Box 5.1). The ruin stands upon one of the elevated terraces overlooking the northwest coast of the Dead Sea. Cave 4, which offered the most voluminous manuscript finds, stands just west of the ruin. Caves 1–3 and 11 extend upon a north-south axis from Qumran. Although no scrolls were discovered directly at the ruin, coins from the second century BCE demonstrate that the site was utilized in the Hellenistic era. On this basis, the earliest possible date for Hellenistic occupation would begin sometime after ca. 140 BCE (de Vaux 1973). More recent assessments favor a later date, after ca. 100 BCE (Magness 2021). Portions of the site were destroyed and occupied by the Romans during the Great Revolt, ca. 68 CE. The ancient

Box 5.1

Qumran, Dead Sea.
Credit: Ondřej Žváček, CC BY 3.0, https://creativecommons.org/licenses/by-sa/3.0/deed.en.

Assembly Hall at Qumran.
Credit: Teqoah, CC BY 3.0, https://creativecommons.org/licenses/by-sa/3.0/deed.en.

occupation of the site thus transpires within the same era in which many scrolls were copied.

Some relationship between Qumran and the Dead Sea Scrolls has been a traditional interpretation of the evidence. Qumran preserves fragments of the same style of cylindrical pottery in which several Cave 1 scrolls were contained, thus perhaps linking the ruin to the caves and the scrolls themselves. The architectural design of Qumran provides a reasonable environment for the communal disciplines of the *Rule*. Approximately ten stepped bathing pools, or *miqva'ot*, offer accommodation for ritual lustrations (Magness 2021). Such lustrations were necessary for practicing the purification laws of the Torah and are repeatedly emphasized in the *Rule*. Several of these surround a narrow room (22m long), with an accompanying chamber containing over one thousand pottery vessels, a suitable facility for pure communal meals and assemblies. A cemetery outside the walls of the site further accommodates eleven hundred graves, many of which date from the Second Temple era. Among the limited number of graves excavated, the predominance of adult male remains may suggest that these were not family burials, but those of a larger, primarily male community. The date and architecture of Qumran suggest that it would have provided an appropriate communal headquarters for the *yaḥad*, as it prepared "in the wilderness the way of the LORD."

Scriptural Manuscripts and Their Interpretation

The Dead Sea Scrolls preserve the earliest known copies of scriptural books, dating centuries earlier than previously known medieval copies. These manuscripts raise important questions about the history of scriptural books, as well as the nature of "scripture" in Early Judaism prior to the closure of the canonical process. Just over two hundred manuscripts preserve copies of the same books found within the Hebrew Bible, with the possible exception of Esther. The community further preserved copies of writings later numbered among Deuterocanonical Books and Pseudepigrapha.

Textual Plurality

The scrolls attest different versions of individual scriptural books, a phenomenon known as **textual plurality**. The most frequently preserved version is the "proto-Masoretic"/"proto-Rabbinic" type, which represents the kind of text that would ultimately feature as Judaism's official version, the Masoretic Text (MT). The eventual preference for the MT was thus already gaining momentum. The scrolls, however, supply other versions. Scriptural versions akin to the Samaritan Pentateuch are attested. Others resemble the underlying Hebrew text that formed the basis for the Septuagint (LXX). Still others resemble none of these types (Tov 2001). Many scriptural books, therefore, were likely studied in more than a single version within the community. For example, the book of Jeremiah is one-eighth shorter (2,700 words) in the LXX and preserves a different arrangement of materials after 25:13, when compared with the MT. Among the scrolls, Jeremiah appears in Hebrew texts closer to the longer MT (e.g., *4QJeremiah*$^{a,\ c,\ e}$), as well as the shorter LXX version (*4QJeremiah*$^{b,\ d}$). The scrolls may further imply that textual plurality prevailed within broader sectors of ancient Judaism.

Great Isaiah

As the earliest complete copy of a scriptural book (ca. 125 BCE), the *Great Isaiah Scroll* from Cave 1 offers a wealth of evidence for understanding scriptural texts. The completeness of the scroll allows for a full, revealing look at how scribes copied, preserved, and corrected ancient manuscripts. Even as it generally resembles the MT, *Great Isaiah* registers over 2,600 variants, an unusually large number resulting in extensive corrections by later scribes (Ulrich and Flint 2011). In fact, the very scribe who copied the *Rule of the Community* from Cave 1 offered his own corrections to *Great Isaiah* by consulting other manuscripts. This indicates that *Great Isaiah* was carefully studied and revised within the sectarian community. Over time, the scroll was even repaired by stitching separated sheets of parchment together again.

In select cases, *Great Isaiah* may preserve a shorter, earlier version of particular passages prior to later expansion. In Isaiah 2:9–11, for example, the MT preserves a longer text. After declaring that humanity will be humbled and brought low (2:9a), the MT suddenly breaks in, "Do not forgive/raise them" (2:9b) and commands the wicked to hide themselves from the coming terror of the Lord (2:10). The LXX further adds, "when he arises to shatter the earth." As Eugene Ulrich explains, *Great Isaiah* does not attest the somewhat apocalyptic content of 2:9b–10 but moves more swiftly in concise parallel structures:

> So humanity is humbled,
> and everyone is brought low.
> The proud eyes of humanity will be brought low,
> and the arrogance of humans shall be humbled.
> (2:9a, 11) (Ulrich and Flint 2011).

Further revealing is that two additional copies of Isaiah (*4QIsaiah^{a,b}*) preserve the longer reading of the passage in contrast to *Great Isaiah*. As in the case of Jeremiah, the prophetic voice of Isaiah appears to have been heard in a plurality of forms within the community of the scrolls.

Authoritative Literature

The scrolls preserve especially strong attestation of books of the Torah and Prophets, as well as a smaller collection of the Writings (the three major divisions of the later Hebrew Bible). Yet the community appears to have operated with a much broader understanding of authoritative literature than would prevail at the closure of the canonical process. Writings not included in the Hebrew Bible feature so prominently that they may have been revered with a level of authority equal to that of later canonical books. The fourteen (or fifteen) copies of *Jubilees* outnumber most books in the Hebrew Bible, surpassed only by Genesis, Exodus, Deuteronomy, Isaiah, and passages of Psalms. *Jubilees* is also referenced as an authoritative writing that explains the content of the written Torah in the *Damascus Document* (XVI 1–5). The eleven copies of portions of *1 Enoch* raise similar possibilities. Tobit, later featured in Greek among the Apocrypha, makes an appearance among the scrolls in portions of one Aramaic and four Hebrew copies. These manuscripts demonstrate the originally ancient and Jewish context of these writings, long prior to their later transmission in Christian circles. They also reveal that the sectarian community actively adopted, studied, and valued writings that originated within their broader Jewish context. There was thus an expansive variety of ancient Jewish traditions that informed the identity of the community and its more specialized sectarian ideology.

Reshaping Scripture

Scriptural texts appear in modified forms, including rewritings, anthologies, and targums. The popularity of rewritten scriptures, like *Jubilees*, is reflected in the *Temple Scroll* and *Reworked Pentateuch*, vast legal documents formed through the arts of rewriting the laws of the Torah. Scripture is modified and implicitly interpreted in **anthologies** that select disparate passages that illumine a common theme. The *Testimonia*, for example, anthologizes scriptures dealing with messianic figures and eschatological antagonists. The *Consolations* select citations from Isaiah that offer "comfort" (Isa 40:1) to the suffering righteous. The scrolls further attest early specimens of targumic translation of scriptural texts from Hebrew into Aramaic (*Targum of Leviticus, Targum of Job*).

Sectarian Hermeneutics

As it searched the scriptures, the community developed its own distinct methods of interpretation. The *Pesharim* ("Commentaries") comprise a series of seventeen explicit commentaries on continuous passages of the minor prophets, Isaiah, and Psalms. The term *pesher* and its cognates are used in Genesis (ch. 40) and Daniel (ch. 4) in reference to unloosening or resolving the mysteries of revelatory dreams. The *Pesharim* take a comparable approach to interpreting cryptic mysteries of divine revelation hidden away in prophecy. Their methods thus resemble interpretations of revealed visions in apocalypses. A possible implication of this hermeneutical approach is that the *Pesharim* comprise inspired, authoritative interpretations, in which the community heard the living voice of prophecy speaking in its midst (Lim 2013). *Pesher* interpretation may even surpass the knowledge of the ancient prophets themselves (*Commentary on Habakkuk* VII 3–5).

After explicitly citing the scriptural text, the commentator declares its *pesher*. This interpretive art unveils the story of the Righteous Teacher, the rise of the *Kittim* (a probable reference to the Romans), and the community's future salvation. Competing parties are a frequent concern of interpretations, often expressed through encoded epithets that utilize wordplay. The "Wicked Priest" (Hebrew: *ha-côhēn hā-rāšāʿ*), for example, likely maligns the "high priest" (*ha-côhēn hā-rōʾš*) of Jerusalem. Those who "seek smooth things" (*dôršēy haḥălāqôt*) rather than the fundaments of Israel's "law" (*hălākôt*) probably references the Pharisees (*Commentary on Nahum*). The community's hermeneutics thus emphasize that its precarious struggle for righteousness now lives out the fulfillment of mysteries spoken long ago by Israel's prophets. *Pesher* hermeneutics are also employed in a wider range of compositions that thematically interpret collections of eschatological prophecies (*Melchizedek, Florilegium, Catena A*).

Rule Documents

The term "rule" (*serek*) is utilized in several sectarian writings as a designation for communal norms governing a particular scenario. This title is written on the outside of the great *Rule of the Community* scroll from Cave 1. Two additional rules, dealing with different circumstances, are also found within the same scroll (*Rule of the Congregation, Rule of Blessings*). The *Damascus Document* and *War Scroll* reveal how the community utilized a broader range of rules that stipulated proper communal order in varied contexts. Taken together, the community's rules demonstrate the intensity of its devotion to structuring a pure way of life before God, both in the present moment of its agonizing affliction and in the future time of its predestined salvation.

Rule of the Community

The *Rule of the Community* establishes a disciplinary code for a group of Jewish males who enter into a covenant community structured by a strict process of initiation, pure meals, liturgical observances, and dualistic theological teachings. The internal social world of the *Rule* reveals the interplay of hierarchal offices and functions that order the community's social life, including a "council of the community" (VIII 1–7), "priests" (II 19–20, VI 3–5, etc.), an "examiner" (VI 12–20), an "instructor" (III 13), and the general assembly of the "many" (VI 17–25). Its thirteen copies range in date from ca. 125–100 to 30 BCE. The *Rule* exhibits structural divisions that may suggest it emerged from earlier compositional units (see Box 5.2). Variations among the existing manuscripts demonstrate that the *Rule* was a living document revised to meet the community's immediate needs.

The Cave 1 *Rule* opens with a Preamble (I 1–15), declaring the community's mission to serve God by practicing the Torah "with the whole heart," language inspired by the laws of Deuteronomy (cf. 6:5). Instructions are then given for a renewal of the covenant (I 16–III 12), in which priests lead members in rituals of repentance, blessings upon the community, and curses upon those outside. The principal

---

Box 5.2 Major Units of the *Rule*

I 1–15	Preamble
I 16–III 12	The Covenant and Its Renewal
III 13–IV 26	Dualistic Treatise
V 1–VII 25	Communal Disciplines
VIII 1–X 4	The Holy Congregation
X 5–XI 22	Hymn of Praise

theological awareness of the *Rule* emerges in a dualistic teaching that every member must be taught (III 13–IV 26). The explicit demand implies that this "Dualistic Treatise" expresses the community's core sectarian theology. The community interprets its vocation as "Sons of Light," called to live out a preordained role within a world divided between two cosmic entities, the "Spirit of Truth" (the "Prince of Light") and the "Spirit of Falsehood" (the "Angel of Darkness"). The community suffers affliction and refinement within this dualistic scenario, until God's final judgment. The treatise reveals the community's radical commitment to one of the most highly intensified expressions of dualistic theology within ancient Judaism.

Columns 5–7 declare the daily norms that shape the community's life as an "assembly of holiness" (V 20). Norms include entrance requirements, pure meals, ritual lustrations, examinations, and disciplinary measures. These columns express the supreme priority of purity within the community, since only after prospective members endure thorough initiation may they have access to its pure food and drink.

Rules for "a holy congregation" (VIII 1–X 4) may supply the earliest historical nucleus of the *Rule*. These columns describe a community of twelve men and three priests who fulfill the vocation of atoning for the land of Israel through their faithful legal observance. The striking claim reveals that the *yaḥad* considers itself—and not the temple priesthood—as performing the divinely ordained rites for atoning for sins. The community envisions its way of life as a kind of wilderness priesthood, a living alternative to the corrupted Jerusalem temple service during the present age of falsehood. Concluding the *Rule* is a moving hymn that praises the deity's transcendence, mercy, and holiness (X 5–XI 22). In spite of humanity's impurity, the community finds itself graciously enlightened in heavenly wisdom and welcomed into the divine presence, as they worship together with the angelic hosts.

The large Cave 1 scroll contains two additional rules. While the *Rule of the Community* addresses the present dualistic age of affliction, the *Rule of the Congregation* (1QSa) concerns the realization of the messianic era, "when [God] brings forth the messiah with them." The *Rule of Blessings* (1QSb) likewise presents a series of benedictions upon leaders who will emerge during the time of salvation. These rules affirm an ideal portrait of social organization and legitimate rule, offering a critical contrast to the current order of their time.

Damascus Document

Present in ten copies, the *Damascus Document* contains a disciplinary rule for righteous Jews, both men and women. These have devoted themselves to a "new covenant" (CD VI 5, 19) codified in "Damascus," a term that may symbolize the community's self-imposed exile from other Jews (cf. Amos 5:27). *Damascus* opens with an exhortation (I-VIII, XIX 33-XX) that introduces an extended legal exposition (XV-XVI, IX-XIV). The exhortation bewails the transgressions that have repeatedly ensnared Israel throughout its history, especially the "three nets" of fornication, wicked wealth, and defilement of the temple. The legal exposition stipulates norms for oaths, offerings, legal testimony, Sabbath, ritual lustrations, and dietary laws. Adherence to these laws now offers the promise of a "new" (or "renewed") "covenant," turning the tide from the disastrous transgressions of Israel's past.

A "rule" of communal organization further addresses men and women dwelling "in camps" and "assemblies" (XII 22-XIV 21) as they practice these laws among non-Jews. Priests advise each camp in legal matters, as an Instructor teaches the community's disciplines and beliefs. Since a version of *Damascus* was discovered within a cache of ancient manuscripts in Cairo, it appears to have enjoyed broader circulation beyond the Judaean wilderness. The implied setting of *Damascus* as a rule for men and women living among Gentiles may indicate that it served broader social contexts beyond the immediate environs of Qumran.

War Scroll

The *War Scroll* stipulates a legal military code for the last days, when Israel and the nations will clash in an apocalyptic holy war. Legal practice in warfare represents a topic of concern within the Torah (e.g., Deut 20) and other writings (e.g., 1 Macc 2:27-48; *Temple Scroll* LVIII). The

War Scroll stipulates an idealized, ceremonial conflict, as priests dictate the legally proper methods of warfare and preserve Israel's purity. Although human agency plays a vital role in the warfare, it ultimately reaches a stalemate between good and evil. In the seventh part of the war, God alone must resolve the conflict after human faithfulness has reached its limits. The scroll's frequent references to the *Kittim* reveal how apocalyptic circles envisioned a sacred warfare against the Roman Empire in the generations prior to the Great Revolt.

Legal Writings

The rules reveal the community's aspiration to practice the Torah's laws in purity under direct instruction from priestly leadership. Writings completely devoted to legal interpretation also flourish within the collection. Alongside the rules and copies of *Jubilees*, they offer crucial insights into the interpretation of law in ancient Judaism. Two extensive examples include the *Temple Scroll* and *Some Works of the Torah*.

Temple Scroll

The *Temple Scroll* primarily concerns the temple and its environs. Its earliest manuscript witness dates to ca. 150–125 BCE, yet the time of its original composition remains unknown. The scroll begins by describing sacred artifacts and altars (III 1–XIII 8), then proceeds to annual feasts (XIII 9–XXIX 8), the architecture of the temple complex (XXIX 8–XLV 7), and purity rules (XLV 7–LI 10). Its remaining columns conclude with a rewriting of Deuteronomy 12–26 (LI 11–LXVI 17) dedicated to political and social laws. The scroll thus begins with the scriptural context of Exodus and ends near the conclusion of Deuteronomy, mirroring the major legal content of the Torah. While the Torah is the primary source for these laws, unknown legal sources also appear to have been utilized. As it rewrites its legal sources, the scroll recasts laws as a divine first-person discourse: it is God who directly speaks within the scroll, not simply Moses or an angel (cf. *Jubilees*). An important implication of this alteration is that the scroll not only mirrors the content of the Torah but aspires to stand alongside it—perhaps above it—as a divine revelation of Israel's law.

The architecture of the temple court is massive, encompassing an area the size of the entire city of Jerusalem. Its magnitude may express the conviction that the entire city of Jerusalem must maintain an appropriate level of purification. Purity laws safeguard the sanctity of this vast temple, governing issues of bodily fluids, corpses, leprosy, unclean birds, animal hides, and diet. Latrines may be located only three thousand cubits outside of the complex; sexual intercourse is prohibited within the city (XLV 11–12). The temple complex is even separated from the city by a trench, one hundred cubits wide, to guard its purity (XLVI 9–11), "so that they may not come suddenly into my temple and desecrate it."[2] Certain fantastic or utopian features challenge the constraints of realism, but they equally express the supreme priority of the temple's holiness. The idealized architecture offers an implicit criticism of the actual structure of the temple in ancient times.

The scroll's annual festivals include observances not found within the Torah, including the feasts of new wine, oil, and wood (XIX–XXV). Its authors appear to have practiced additional festivals beyond those observed by other Jews. Their dates are reckoned according to a 364-day solar calendar (cf. *Jubilees*). The civil-political laws of Deuteronomy 12–26 demand that Israel's king (cf. Deut 17:14–20) remain separate from the priesthood and obediently follow priestly counsel. Such a view of kingship would have conflicted with the practices of the Hasmonean Dynasty, which governed both priestly and civil matters. The divergences between the ideal vision of the scroll and the practical realities of the Hellenistic era suggest that the scroll represented a kind of reformist, eschatological Torah that Israel would follow in a new era, when God would "create my sanctuary, establishing it for myself for all time" (XXIX 9–10).[3]

Some Works of the Torah

"These are some of our words" (B1; cf. Deut 1:1). With this declaration, *Some Works of the Torah* treats over twenty points of law. The "words" of the authors clarify their views on legal issues ranging from sacrifices to diet, foreigners, the disabled, liquid streams, corpses, and priestly marriages. Most of their judgments are prohibitive: they admonish that disputed or currently unobserved practices constitute violations of Israel's law. For example, the authors understand impurity as traveling through liquid streams. If one pours a liquid from a pure vessel into an impure one, impurity travels through the stream and both are defiled (B55–58). Other Jews were less concerned with this problem. Later rabbinic writings, in fact, attribute an opposite opinion to the Pharisees (Mishnah, *Yadayim* 4:7). Yet for these authors, the matter was one of many crucial points of law in which "the priests ought to keep watch... lest they lead the people into sin" (B12–13, 25–27, 80–82).

The concluding unit of the work comprises a diplomatic address persuading an anonymous recipient to accept the authors' rulings (C10). The authors appeal to the promises of Deuteronomy 30:1–8 as a hopeful invitation that the reader may return to the true practice of the law. Now is the urgent moment—"This is the latter days"—when the promise will be fulfilled (cf. *Jubilees* 1:7–25, 23:11–32; Lev 26:40–45). With such hopes of reconciliation, the authors insist upon their sincerity. Their separation from the multitudes is not motivated by sedition. They write civilly to one, moreover, who has "intellect and knowledge of the law," all the more reason that he, like David, should turn and be forgiven. It is possible that the address represents a diplomatic attempt by the community's leaders—perhaps even by the Righteous Teacher—to persuade Jerusalem's high priest to adopt their legal judgments. Whatever its original context, the six copies of this work (penned in the first century BCE) demonstrate that it continued to inform the community's stance on legal controversies and how it interpreted its origins.

Other Works

Additional legal writings span an abundant range of topics, including Sabbath, liability, diet, marriages, waste (*4QHalakah A–C*); gleaning wheat, slavery, the temple tax, accusing a virgin (*4QOrdinances*); and the transfer of impurity (*Tohorot*). While occasional exceptions may be identified, the larger trajectory of the legal literature expresses the view that contemporary Judaism and its leaders have become negligent in legal observance, especially in matters related to purity (Harrington 2004). Such tendencies only reinforce the urgency of the community's vocation as a "holy house for Israel" (*Rule* VIII 5).

Psalms, Hymns, Prayers

The concluding hymn of the *Rule* vows that the *yaḥad* will regularly bless the Lord "at the beginning of the months of the seasons and on holy days" (X 5–8). Larger collections of hymns, prayers, and psalms flourish among the scrolls, revealing the community's self-awareness as a sacred assembly of perpetual worship.

Great Psalms Scroll

Passages of Psalms feature in a variety of compositions among the scrolls that include thirty-six manuscripts. The *Great Psalms Scroll* from Cave 11 (*11QPsalm^a*) presents portions of Psalms 101 and following. Yet its order and contents differ surprisingly from other known versions. Intermingled within the collection are psalms not included in the MT yet found within the Syriac Psalter (Psalms 154, 155, and 151A, B). The erotic wisdom poem of Ben Sira 51 appears. Several previously unknown compositions are also interspersed. A "Plea for Deliverance" prays for divine mercy, forgiveness of sins, and deliverance from evil spirits:

> Forgive my sin, O LORD, and cleanse me from my iniquity.
> Bestow on me a spirit of faith and knowledge.
> Let me not stumble in transgression.
> Let not Satan rule over me, nor an evil spirit. (XIX 13–15)[4]

A poem celebrates Mount Zion ("Apostrophe to Zion") and envisions its future glory among all nations (XXII; cf. Isa 2:1–5). A "Hymn to the Creator" praises the deity for the wisdom manifest throughout creation (XXVI).

David's role in the composition of the Psalms becomes a point of emphasis as the collection concludes (XXVII). David's final prayer of 2 Samuel 23:7 appears, as does the previously unknown "Compositions of David," which describes how he received 4,050 songs by prophetic revelation. The songs are further subdivided into liturgical categories, to be performed in conjunction with a 364-day solar calendar. This emphasis upon the solar calendar implies that the scroll may have comprised a version of Psalms specifically edited for sectarian purposes by the *yaḥad*. The substantial differences between the *Psalms Scroll* and other ancient versions reveal how portions of Psalms (esp. chapters 90–150) could be collected in substantially different forms as late as the first century CE, when the scroll appears to have been penned (ca. 30–50 CE). Additional scroll manuscripts further exhibit the fluidity and variety in which passages of the Psalms were collected.[5]

Thanksgiving Hymns

The *Thanksgiving Hymns*, surviving in eight copies, offer one of the most sophisticated poetic compositions of this era. Major units of the collection begin with the formula "I thank you, O Lord, because . . ." or "Blessed are you, O Lord, because . . ." The speaker then praises the deity for a variety of salvific benefits, including deliverance from enemies, sanctification from impurity, and enlightenment in the mysteries of wisdom. In some cases, the speaker even enjoys the presence of eschatological life, as though elevated from the abyss of death into an everlasting, angelic existence (XI 19–36).

The *Hymns* feature a number of continuities with the sectarian literature and likely reflect the spiritual devotion of the *yaḥad*. The work expresses the voice of those who "have gathered ourselves in community [*yaḥad*]" (VII 7; cf. VI 18, XI 23, XII 24). Some scholars have imagined that portions of the work comprise "Hymns of the Teacher" (esp. cols. X–XVI) that were either composed by the Righteous Teacher or reflect upon his experiences. Supporting this identification is the possibly autobiographical character of several hymns that describe the speaker's turmoil and vindication.

Whether or not such an identification can be sustained, it is clear that for the sectarian community, enlightenment in the divine mysteries involved the deepest agonies of rejection and opposition within the present age. In a storm of turbulent poetic images, the speaker gives expression to the community's tribulation while reaffirming its identity as God's chosen recipients of divine mercy and knowledge. Through the depths of affliction, God vindicates the speaker, bringing him through the crucible like gold, wrought in fire—like purified silver, refined seven times (XIII 16).

Other Works

Other liturgical writings include the *Angelic Liturgy* (or *Songs of the Sabbath Sacrifice*), a sequence of songs to be performed with the offering of the Sabbath sacrifice according to the solar calendar. As humans perform the sacrifice on earth, their observance synchronizes with the transcendent worship of the angelic hosts. *Bless, O My Soul* praises the deity for having mercy upon the destitute and atoning for sin. *Words of the Luminaries* takes a more historical approach to worship, offering daily prayers through reminiscence upon Israel's past. Together, these works offer insight into the devotional life of the community and the riches of early Jewish prayer and spirituality.

Wisdom and Apocalypticism

Previously unknown sapiential and apocalyptic traditions abound among the scrolls. The scrolls demonstrate how these two originally distinct traditions could be well integrated with one another by the Hellenistic and Roman eras. The community's apocalyptic awareness was concerned with the unique revelation of divine wisdom in its midst, a wisdom that allowed the community to understand and practice the Torah correctly in an evil age. Moreover, several previously unknown wisdom instructions anticipate final judgment upon wisdom and folly, which have been interpreted within a dualistic, eschatological paradigm.

Wisdom Writings

In seven copies, *Instruction for a Student* (*4QInstruction*) presents a formal wisdom instruction in which an experienced sage offers counsel to a "poor" novice. In practical matters, the sage reminds students of their poverty and the need to rely on God as the source of life. The student must maintain financial integrity, avoiding greed and quickly repaying loans. Such practical instructions are set within a larger cosmic context. The sage speaks of "the mystery that is yet to be": "Gaze upon the mystery that is yet to be/come, and understand the birth-time of salvation, and who is to inherit glory and trouble."[6] The precise meaning of the "mystery" eludes immediate definition. It clearly places wisdom within the context of a revealed mystery. The "mystery" involves clear discernment between good and evil and the eschatological consequences that await them. Like the Wisdom of Solomon, the *Instruction* exhibits the adaptation of future eschatological hopes into reflection on wisdom.

Lady Wisdom appears within several compositions. Faced with the impending realities of mortality and the final judgment, *Sapiential Work* sternly instructs "the simple" to "seek the way to life." God has freely given Lady Wisdom as a gift to all Israel. Holding fast to her results in a prosperous, righteous existence. *Beatitudes* pronounces poetic blessings (e.g., "beatitudes") upon those who pursue Lady Wisdom, especially when confronted with the harsh lessons she teaches. This work shares with Ben Sira the conviction that wisdom is to be found in the law: "Blessed is the one who attains wisdom and walks in the law of the Most High."[7] Lady Wisdom's evil counterpart, *Lady Folly*, is also the subject of a skillful poem on the seductress who leads the foolish to destruction (cf. Proverbs 7).

Apocalypticism

The community clearly valued the heritage of Israel's wisdom. Yet it was crucial to the community that the mysteries of wisdom had been uniquely revealed within its own midst during a time of eschatological crisis. As chosen recipients of an urgent revelation, the community defined its identity through an apocalyptic self-understanding. The *Rule* characterizes the *yaḥad* as "Sons of Light" who practice the Torah within a dualistic cosmos divided between Light and Darkness, Truth and Falsehood (*Rule* III 13–IV 26). The community's ardent legal concerns were thus intensified by the apocalyptic awareness that the true practice of the Torah had been exclusively revealed to them, even as their contemporaries remained blinded by the Spirit of Falsehood. The community presently lives in an era of dualistic struggle: the "Spirit of Truth" aids them in the pursuit of righteousness, even as the "Angel of Darkness" opposes, tempts, and frustrates their vocation (III 17–IV 18). At the end of the age, God would destroy the Spirit of Falsehood forever, purifying humans and restoring them to the glory in which they were originally created (IV 20–23).

The community also shared in the messianic hopes found in apocalyptic circles. In the *Rule*, the community must pursue its original norms "until the coming of the Prophet, and the Messiahs of Aaron and Israel" (IX 11). A similar formulation appears in the *Damascus Document* (XII 23–XIII 1). With dual messiahs presiding over priestly (i.e., Aaron) and civil (i.e., Israel) affairs, these writings anticipate an eschatological restoration of legitimate rule. Since this "diarchal" messianism (i.e., "two" rulers) appears in major sectarian writings, it may represent a distinctive adaptation of messianic expectation within the *yaḥad*. Other writings presuppose more diverse assumptions about messianism (e.g., *Rule of the Congregation*, *Rule of Blessings*, *Commentary on Genesis A*, *Messianic Apocalypse*, *Aramaic Apocalypse*). Nevertheless, they indicate that messianic hope found a stable reception among the community's eschatological expectations.

No new literary apocalypses were discovered among the scrolls. Only *New Jerusalem* shares generic features of literary apocalypses, as the architecture of an eschatological Jerusalem is revealed to a chosen recipient (cf. Ezek 40–48). Nevertheless, several compositions have contributed important new specimens of apocalyptic thought. The *Messianic Apocalypse* addresses itself as an exhortation to "those who seek" God, even when they receive no immediate rewards. In consoling the righteous, the work forecasts the blessings of the messianic era, when "heaven and earth shall hearken unto his Messiah."

These blessings, modeled upon earlier prophecies (Isa 51, 61) and psalms (Ps 147), further envision "wondrous things that have not existed," including the hope of resurrection. Other fragments exhibit an interest in cosmic realms of punishment and reward reminiscent of apocalyptic tours.

The influence of Daniel 7–12 upon later compositions is evident in the *Aramaic Apocalypse*. Like the vision of Daniel 11, the work foretells a conflict between the King of Egypt (cf. Daniel's "King of the South") and the King of Assyria ("King of the North"). Within this crisis emerges one who "will be called [gr]eat, and will be designated by his name. He will be called 'Son of God,' and they will call him 'Son of the Most High.'"[8] In the immediate context, it remains uncertain whether the text envisions an apocalyptic enemy (like Antiochus IV in Daniel) or a messianic deliverer. The concluding lines of the fragment, however, envision a messianic figure, as violence ceases and God's kingdom is established forever: "[God] will wage war for him; he will place the peoples in his hand and cast them all away before him. His rule will be an eternal rule."[9] The one called "Son of God" thus emerges as a messianic ruler who will administer justice at the time God's reign is fully established.

The Dead Sea Scrolls and the New Testament

The scrolls offer immediate, firsthand insights into the character of at least one sector of Palestinian Judaism during the time of Jesus and the origins of the church. One of the most pervasive results of the discovery has been an unprecedented awareness of the diversity of ancient Judaism. For approximately two centuries, the community of the Dead Sea Scrolls comprised a religious movement that rejected Jerusalem's priestly temple leadership, as well as popular movements like the Pharisees. Their Judaism was defined neither by temple priests nor by Pharisees, revealing that a diverse proliferation of religious movements prevailed in Palestine during the era of the church's origins. Jesus and his earliest followers also emerged from within this variegated religious context; like the community, they also defined their identity in conflict with priestly and Pharisaic leadership.

Some proposals have more boldly identified the community as an actual ancestor to the early church, as though Jesus and his earliest followers had rather directly emerged from the *yahad* or the broader Essene movement. Indeed, select historical scholars had identified Jesus as "Essene" even before the scrolls were known (Kohler 1918); their actual discovery only further provoked this possibility. Such approaches, however, have typically overestimated isolated comparisons, while diminishing important differences. Direct historical links between the two remain elusive. No New Testament person or writing appears among the scrolls. Nor are there direct references to the *yahad* or "Essenes" in the New Testament.

A superior approach, articulated by Lawrence Schiffman (1995), is to recognize, first, what the scrolls reveal about the breadth and diversity of Early Judaism. Within this context, one may then consider how the nascent church and the authors of the scrolls offered their own distinct visions of how to live out the heritage of Israel's religion within the first-century Palestinian environment that both shared. With this understanding, three categories have inspired the most ardent focus when discussing the scrolls and the New Testament: actual persons, communal structures, and religious ideas.

John the Baptist

The actual person exhibiting the most promising commonalities with Qumran and the Essenes would likely be John the Baptist. John and the community appear to have been active in the same time and region (Matt 3:1; Josephus, *Antiquities* 18:116–19). Both emphasize that rituals of purification in water must further be accompanied by a repentant life of moral behavior (*Rule* III 8–9; Josephus, *Antiquities* 18:117; Mark 1:4; Luke 3:7–14). Both fulfill the explicit prophecy of Isaiah 40:1–3 "in the wilderness" (*Rule* VIII 13–16; Mark 1:1–4). Both anticipate the eschatological cleansing of the human by a "Holy Spirit" (*Rule* IV 20–22; Mark 1:8). Both criticize their contemporaries for permissive matrimonial practices (*Damascus* IV 15–V 2; cf. *Temple Scroll* LVII 15–19; Mark 6:17–18). The conspicuous alignment of these factors has led some scholars to conclude that John the Baptist could have had a historical relationship to Qumran or the Essene movement. If so, then Jesus himself stood that much closer to the community's thought and activity.

At the same time, differences between John and the community are apparent. For the *yaḥad*, the Jordan River offered no specialized meaning, yet John's baptism in the Jordan symbolized a new entrance into the land, an eschatological renewal of Israel (cf. Josh 3). Rituals of immersion in water were a regular expression of the community's observance of purity. Yet John's baptism appears to have represented a unique event, a final purification for eschatological judgment. The sociological features of the two also diverge. John is not associated with the incorporation of property, nor with a novitiate. His wilderness preaching was so public that it provoked the opposition of Herod Antipas, the participation of Jesus, and the historical memory of Josephus. The *yaḥad*'s more introverted devotion, however, left behind few clues to its internal beliefs and practices until the modern discovery of the scrolls. Some scholars favoring a relationship between John and Qumran thus suggest that the Baptist must ultimately have broken away from any earlier associations with the community to forge his own path. Perhaps such comparisons ultimately reveal how the wilderness region became a religious setting of renewal that attracted many otherwise diverse religious impulses, including the community, John, and Jesus himself.

Communal Structures

The social organization of the community has often been compared with communal structures in the early church. The book of Acts, for example, reports that in the Jerusalem church, "all who believed were together and had all things in common; they would sell their possessions and goods and distribute the proceeds to all, as any had need" (2:44-45).[10] Since Acts describes this phenomenon originally among Jewish believers in Jerusalem (cf. 4:32-37), the account has frequently been compared with contemporary precedents among the scrolls.

The *Rule* describes how an initiate's property gradually enters among the purified possessions of the *yaḥad* (VI 14-25). Property is initially submitted to administrators, although it remains the owner's possession, segregated from the community. Nor may an initiate prematurely utilize the community's purified possessions. Only after achieving full membership would one's property be fully incorporated. This is not precisely the same practice described in Acts. Purity, not charity, motivates these norms. Acts may, nevertheless, be more closely compared with the *Damascus Document*, which offers a "rule" by which the sectarian community will care for its disadvantaged by contributing two days' wages per month. They will continue according to this norm until the advent of the messianic era (XIV 12–22). Josephus's description of the Essenes also hails their disdain for wealth, as they intermingle their resources and share possessions among brothers (Josephus, *War* 2:122). Luke's own idealizing characterization of the early believers may appeal to the renown of religious societies, like the Essenes, so highly acclaimed by Josephus for their egalitarianism.

The disciplines of the Matthean community also offer comparison with those of the *yaḥad*. The fourth extended discourse in Matthew centers on communal order, as Jesus teaches the habits of mind and behavior that should characterize the "church" (ch. 18). Humility and forgiveness are predominant values, even as Jesus sternly admonishes against offending weaker members. To reconcile conflicts, Matthew includes a disciplinary code for confronting and reconciling those who sin. Two or three witnesses are demanded amid such confrontations, in accordance with the law of Deuteronomy 19:15. If an offender still defies correction, the matter comes before the whole church. The code includes the possibility of ostracism for one who will not heed the admonitions of the church.

The *Rule of the Community* and the *Damascus Document* also preserve their own regulations for admonishing errant members. Matthew, the *Rule*, and *Damascus* all demand witnesses (cf. Deut 19:15): "A man shall not bring a matter against his companion before the Many, unless it is with admonition in the presence of witnesses" (*Rule* VI 1; cf. *Damascus* IX 1–X 4). Matthew and the *Rule* stipulate an initial admonition with witnesses prior to accusing anyone before the entire community. Like Matthew, the scrolls further encourage the values of humility and compassion toward associates

(*Rule* II 24–25, IV 2–7), as well as the responsibility "for each man to admonish his neighbor in truth and humility and steadfast love" (V 24–25; *Damascus* IX 9; cf. Lev 19:17). The scrolls demonstrate how Matthew's communal norms had precedents among contemporary sectarian movements.

Religious Ideas

It is in the realm of religious ideas that the scrolls make their most substantive contributions to New Testament studies. The scrolls repeatedly demonstrate the extent to which the New Testament authors reinterpreted religious traditions that had their earlier origins in Palestinian Judaism. This is an important recognition, since prior to the discovery of the scrolls it was more commonly assumed that the early church rapidly adapted to Hellenism, which offered the predominant conceptual environment in which the theology of the New Testament writings developed (Bultmann 1997). The scrolls, however, have demanded a corrective to this tendency and a more complex recognition of how New Testament literature reflects an ongoing interconnectedness with the religious traditions of Palestinian Judaism, even as the church adapted to its broader Mediterranean environments.

The scrolls reveal, for example, how Jewish messianism played important roles in the church's interpretation of Jesus. One immediate example may be observed in the *Messianic Apocalypse*, which offers a description of the messianic era that coincides remarkably with the Q tradition preserved in Luke 7:18–23 and Matthew 11:2–6 (Tabor and Wise 1995). Both sources envision events that will transpire when the messiah is revealed (see Box 5.3).

The unusual commonalities may be explained by mutual reliance upon the prophecy of Isaiah 61 (see also Isa 51; Ps 146). Surprisingly, however, both sources also interject the resurrection of the dead among these expectations, even though it is not apparent in Isaiah 61. Thus, both sources work not only from Isaiah but from a common interpretive tradition that expanded the prophetic text with apocalyptic hopes, like resurrection. The scrolls confirm, in this instance, how the

> **Box 5.3 Signs of the Messianic Era**
>
> | Luke 7:22 | *Messianic Apocalypse* |
> |---|---|
> | "[T]he blind receive their sight; the lame walk; those with a skin disease are cleansed; the deaf hear; the dead are raised; the poor have good news brought to them." (NRSV) | "For he shall glorify the pious upon a throne of kingship forever, liberating prisoners, restoring sight to the blind, comforting the down[trodden].... For he will heal the slain, and the dead he will cause to live, to the poor he will bring glad tidings." (frgs. 2 II + 4) |

gospel traditions reinterpret messianic expectations from their formative Palestinian environment.

The dualism of the community's sectarian ideology has proven useful for understanding the conceptual and sociological features of dualistic theology in the New Testament. This includes, especially, the dualistic, "light-darkness" paradigm of the Fourth Gospel. The "Farewell Discourse" of John (chs. 14–17) foretells the "Spirit of Truth," which is already present among the disciples and will soon dwell within them, guiding them in their ongoing life within the darkness of the present world. The Spirit plays an important epistemological role, teaching the disciples "all things" and renewing their understanding of all that Jesus has said (14:26). It is unknown to the world. Yet the Spirit unites the disciples with Jesus and the Father (14:15–21). The Spirit's work is defined in dualistic terms. It will convict the world of coming judgment, "since the Prince of this world now stands condemned" (16:8–11). Through the Spirit, John's community receives a unique epistemological awareness that marks a strong boundary between its own identity and "the world," which stands under the rule of Satan.

The *Rule* also uses the term "Spirit of Truth" within its dualistic theology. For the community, the Spirit of Truth (Prince of Lights) was created by God as the dualistic counterpart to the Spirit of Falsehood (Angel of Darkness). The Spirit of Truth aids the "Sons of Light"/"Sons of Truth" amid their struggles within the present world, liberating the community from conceptual falsehood and making it possible to discern and practice the Torah faithfully. The Spirit produces ethical and epistemological qualities that serve "to enlighten the heart... to make straight... all the paths of true righteousness." Those who "walk in" the Spirit of Truth will likewise inherit endless joy in everlasting life (*Rule* IV 2–8).

Such conceptual affinities have raised the possibility that John's community originally emerged from sectors of Palestinian Judaism that interpreted reality in such strongly dualistic terms. Some have even ventured the possibility that the theology of the Fourth Gospel may have been shaped in a decisive way by the Qumran community or broader currents of Essenism. At the same time, it remains important to account for differences. For John, the "light of the world" was Jesus himself, an identification that radically reinterpreted any earlier dualistic influences. Moreover, the Johannine community appears to have lived out its dualism sociologically in a different way than did the *yaḥad*. John's dualistic language galvanized a mixed community of Jews, Gentiles, and Samaritans. Such differences highlight the distinctiveness of John's dualism, even as it draws upon theologies that were popular within sectors of Palestinian Judaism.

In these and many other examples, the scrolls help readers of the New Testament to understand how its authors continuously reinterpreted earlier Palestinian traditions, as the church adapted to broader social environments. It is thus far less certain today precisely how one should draw the conceptual lines that distinguish the church's emerging theologies from those that flourished within its Palestinian Jewish context.

6
Jews, Greeks, and Romans

Philo of Alexandria and Flavius Josephus (Yosef ben Matitiyahu) composed extensive literary works that conscientiously interacted with Hellenistic thought and sought to establish a place for Judaism within Graeco-Roman culture. Both emerged from aristocratic circles. Both defended Jews against false charges in formal literary **apologies**. Their writings survived primarily within Christianity, even as Rabbinic Judaism found them less useful. The two also pose revealing contrasts. Philo's works are primarily exegetical and philosophical; Josephus writes as an historian. Philo died prior to the Great Revolt; Josephus experienced it as a defeated revolutionary general. Philo's career transpired in the Alexandrian Diaspora; Josephus was a proud Judaean and controversial public figure who spent his final days in Rome. In what they share, as well as how they differ, they open expansive windows into the interactions between Jews, Greeks, and Romans in the first century.

Philo of Alexandria

Philo (ca. 20 BCE–ca. 50 CE) appears to have invested his life in painstaking philosophical exegesis of the Torah. Less is known about his biography. His enculturation into the Hellenized Jewish aristocracy of Alexandria is apparent in his writings, which reveal his formation in Greek **encyclical paideia**, a liberal arts education in grammar, music, geometry, and logic that prepared elites for professional life (*Preliminary Studies* 15–18). He reports visiting Jerusalem for prayer and sacrifices in the temple (*Providence* 2:64). His illustrious family was well connected to the Roman and Herodian courts. His brother Alexander the Alabarch had a prolific economic and political career (Josephus, *War* 5:205; *Antiquities* 18:159–65, 19:276). Alexander's son (Philo's nephew) Tiberius Julius Alexander became Roman procurator of Judaea, then prefect of Egypt. Ironically, he would serve Rome as "commander of the entire military campaign" at Titus's siege of Jerusalem (Josephus, *War* 2:309, 490-97; 5:45-46; 6:236-43; *Antiquities* 20:100; Tacitus, *Histories* 2:79 and *Annals* 15:28; Suetonius, *Vespasian* 6:3). While Philo preferred the pursuit of wisdom and the work of instructing students, his relations imply that he remained well versed in public affairs on an international scale.

Philo's Embassy

Threats to the Jewish community, in fact, thrust Philo upon the public scene in 38-40 CE, when he led a delegation to the Roman imperial court to defend Jewish liberties. In two apologetic narratives, *Against Flaccus* and *The Embassy to Gaius*, Philo recounts these turbulent years and the mortal threat they posed to the Jewish *politeuma* (also *politeia*). This political "constitution" had granted Jews autonomy to live peacefully by their ancestral laws under the Ptolemaic Empire. Yet this *politeuma* was subject to variant interpretations and required vigilant defense. With the advent of Roman rule in Egypt (30 BCE), Alexandrian Greeks suffered a humiliating demotion, leading to contentious rivalries among Greeks, native Egyptians, and Jews (Barclay 1996).

Against Flaccus recounts how the Roman prefect Auvilius Flaccus failed to deter a destructive anti-Jewish pogrom. His tacit support of anti-Jewish conspiracies "filled the civilized world with racial conflicts" (44). One flashpoint was the visit of the Jewish king Herod Agrippa to Alexandria (38 CE), an event of national pride for Jews but offensive to Alexandrian Greeks. In the violent aftermath, images of the emperor were forced into Jewish synagogues, properties were plundered, Jews were forced into one precinct within the city. The elders of Alexandria, a body traditionally representing Jewish autonomy, were horribly scourged in the public theater. Flaccus did nothing to assuage the violence. Yet his most threatening measure was a declaration that Jews were "foreigners and aliens," an exploit that Philo interprets as "the utter destruction of our constitution" (53-54). Philo dwells lovingly upon Flaccus's downfall, an admonitory tale that "the nation of the Jews is not left destitute by the providential assistance of God" (191).[1]

Embassy to Gaius reflects these events, yet now with a critical eye toward the Roman emperor Gaius (Caligula). If Flaccus was blamed for calculated passivity, Gaius's abuses were those of maniacal aggression. He irrationally regarded the Jews as a threat since their laws forbade them to recognize him as a deity. Further inflaming his hostility were anti-Jewish Alexandrian Greeks within his court. When an altar to the divine emperor was erected in the Palestinian coastal city of Jamnia, local Jewish inhabitants defiantly tore it down (202). In an audacious reprisal, Gaius ordered his effigy installed within the Jerusalem temple itself, an act that threatened "the utter destruction of the general constitution of the Jewish nation" (194).[2] Persuaded by King Herod Agrippa, Gaius relented in Jerusalem, only to make Alexandria the new object of his self-glorification (346).

Philo's appeals to Gaius did not turn the tide. Neither a recitation of the injustices committed against the Jews nor a detailed explanation of their ancestral laws swayed the emperor (367). The embassy appears to have ended in stalemate, if not failure. The underlying political issues would be addressed only after Gaius's assassination (Josephus, *Antiquities* 19:280–85). The new emperor Claudius restored Jewish religious freedoms, even as avenues toward civil and cultural advancement remained disputed. Beyond Philo's time, such tensions within Hellenistic urban environments would escalate in a destructive Diaspora revolt against Rome (116–117 CE) that devastated the way of life Philo had labored so desperately to defend.

Philo's Writings

Ultimately, Philo's greatest devotion was not to civil affairs but to the pursuit of wisdom (*Special Laws* 3:1–6). He appears to have written within a larger Alexandrian Jewish tradition, characterized by a continual dialogue between Judaism and Hellenistic philosophy. His intellectual quest survives within a collection that scholars classify into three groups: (1) historical/apologetic works (including *Flaccus* and *Embassy*), (2) exegetical works, and (3) philosophical works.

Most survive in their original Greek, although some are preserved in Armenian and Latin translations. The circumference of these writings reveals the complex roles that scripture and philosophy, Judaism and Hellenism, play within his thought (see Box 6.1).

Box 6.1 Major Writings of Philo of Alexandria

Narrative/Apologetic Works

Against Flaccus
Embassy to Gaius
Hypothetica

Exegetical Works

Questions and Answers
On Genesis
On Exodus

Allegorical Commentary
Allegorical Laws (Gen 2–3)
On the Cherubim (Gen 3:24–4:1)
On the Sacrifices of Cain and Abel (Gen 4:2–4)
The Worse Attacks the Better (Gen 4:8–16)
On the Posterity of Cain (Gen 4:16–25)
On the Giants (Gen 6:1–4)
On the Immutability of God (Gen 6:4–12)
On Husbandry/On Noah's Work as a Planter (Gen 9:20)
On Drunkenness (Gen 9:21)
On Sobriety (Gen 9:24–27)
On the Confusion of Languages (Gen 11:1–9)
On the Migration of Abraham (Gen 12:1–6)
Who Is the Heir of Divine Things? (Gen 15:2–18)
On Mating with the Preliminary Studies (Gen 16:1–6)
On Flight and Finding (Gen 16:6–14)
On the Changing of Names (Gen 17:1–22)
On Dreams (Gen 28:11–12)

> *Exposition on the Law*
> *On the Creation of the World*
> *On Abraham*
> *On Joseph*
> *On the Life of Moses*
> *On the Decalogue*
> *On Special Laws*
> *On Rewards and Punishments*
>
> **Philosophical Works**
>
> *Every Good Man Is Free*
> *On Animals*
> *On Providence*
> *On the Contemplative Life*
> (see further Kamesar 2009)

Exegetical Works

Philo composed some of the most significant hermeneutical literature in Western history. His exegesis focuses predominantly upon the Pentateuch, with occasional support from other writings. This seems to imply that Philo situated the Pentateuch on an unparalleled plane of religious authority. He interprets the Pentateuch from the Greek Septuagint. For Philo, the Septuagintal translators "prophesied" (*Moses* 2:37) by divine inspiration and spoke in harmony with the spirit of Moses himself (2:40). Philo's knowledge of an eclectic range of Greek philosophical traditions shines through much of his exegesis; so does the scriptural essence of his thought. Both "philosophy" and "scripture" take on new meanings in this creative enterprise. Three categories highlight his surviving exegetical works, each with its own distinct approach: Questions and Answers, Allegorical Commentary, and Exposition on the Law.

Questions and Answers

Philo's *Questions and Answers on Genesis and Exodus* proceeds by a **question-and-answer** method. Problems are raised about the meaning of the scriptural text, then answered by the commentator. Earlier Greek interpreters of Homeric literature had utilized this technique; Philo, immersed in Alexandrian scholarship, employed it in continuous interpretations of the Torah. For example, as Philo addresses the circumcision commandment of Genesis 17:10, he questions, "What is the meaning of, 'And every male among you shall be circumcised?'" (*Questions* 3:46).[3] His answer is "twofold." Philo does not minimize the literal command to circumcise. Yet he is also concerned with a complementary level of meaning that is abstract, intellectual, spiritual. To circumcise the intellect is to purify it from destructive thoughts of rebellion and ambition, rendering the mind so pure that it may now worship God in priestly holiness. "What is the meaning" of circumcision, then?—a liberating purification of the whole person, body and soul (cf. *Jubilees* 1:22–23). Philo's questions and answers are typically concise, suggesting that this genre served the purposes of elementary instruction.

Allegorical Commentary

Greater complexity abounds within the *Allegorical Commentary* on Genesis, which appears to have addressed advanced audiences. Philo's **allegorical exegesis** continuously interprets textual details as symbols for spiritual, cosmic, or ethical ideals. Narratives regarding Israel's ancestors become paradigms of cosmic order and the soul's journey toward wisdom. Allegorical interpretation allowed Greek scholars to distill philosophically redemptive ideals from otherwise embarrassing episodes in mythological literature. Homer himself thus became a moral-philosophical author, "the great hierophant of heaven and the gods," who wrote allegorically to deter self-destructive vices and open a path to heaven for human souls (Heraclitus, *Homeric Problems* 70, 76).

Likewise, Philo assumes that Moses taught moral-philosophical doctrines about the soul and the cosmos throughout the narratives of Genesis, which may be unfolded through the arts of allegorical interpretation (*Heir* 213–14). Alongside this sublime vision, allegorical interpretation also resolves more practical problems and ambiguities in scriptural texts (*Posterity* 1–11). In comparison with his contemporaries, Philo speaks of his allegorical method as exhibiting a balance between literal and spiritual meanings, just as body and soul dwell together. He thus rejects hyperallegorical interpretation that nullifies concrete legal observance of the divine commands (*Migration* 89–93; cf. *Abraham* 88).

The longest surviving unit within the *Allegorical Commentary* is titled *Who Is the Heir of Divine Things?*, a continuous exegesis of God's covenant with Abraham in Genesis 15:2–18. The scriptural passage embodies the emergence of the rational soul, which will ascend above the passions to inherit divine wisdom. Philo employs an arsenal of rhetorical techniques to interpret the narrative on this conceptual plane. Extended paraphrases recast the plain letter of the text (e.g., *Heir* 24–29). The abstract meanings of etymologies are explored (23, 40, 54, 58). He quotes Greek poets (5, 189) and employs question-and-answer exegesis (e.g., 313–14). **Diatribe** rhetoric raises (usually misguided) questions from an imaginary interlocutor, leading to a superior, corrective answer (e.g., 81, 90–91). At every turn, he examines Genesis 15 through the lens of myriad secondary citations from other passages of the Torah. Through these techniques, the scriptural narrative becomes an allegorical representation of the soul's journey and the structure of the cosmos.

The mysterious account of Abraham's covenant sacrifice (Gen 15:9–17) has long troubled ancient and modern interpreters.[4] For Philo, the dividing of the sacrifices into equal and opposite parts evokes the activity of the divine *Logos* as it divides all things into contrasting opposites and makes the cosmos intelligible. The *Logos* occupies a central role within Philo's philosophy, as it mediates the transcendent God's wisdom and activity throughout the cosmos. Standing between divine and human nature, the *Logos* serves as an intercessor to God on behalf of afflicted humanity and as an ambassador of God's governance to humans. The *Logos* thus offers assurance that "the merciful God will never disregard his own work" (205–6).

As he interprets the prophecy of Genesis 15:12–16, Philo turns to one of his favorite devices: he reads the exodus from Egyptian slavery as a paradigm of the soul's journey. The soul begins "enslaved to the outward senses" in Egypt. Through philosophical instruction, however, the soul "shall return," as it migrates toward the promised land of divine wisdom (293–99). This prophecy comes to Abraham as he enters into an ecstatic, visionary state (Gen 15:1, 12). At "sunset" (Gen 15:12, 17), the "light" of human reason subsides, and he is possessed by the divine spirit (*Heir* 258–63): "for the setting of reason and its darkening gave way to ecstasy and divinely inspired mania" (265; cf. 69–70; *Creation* 70–71; *Moses* 1:175). Reason and prophetic revelation thus interchange, as the wise soul becomes "the vocal instrument of God, smitten and played by his invisible hand" (*Heir* 259).[5] The allegory reveals the mystical features of Philo's thought (*Migration* 34–45; *Special Laws* 3:1–6), as he describes the interplay between the reason that allows humans to understand the created universe and inspiration in which divine realities are revealed within the soul.

As his allegorical interpretation concludes, Philo clarifies that the promise of land to Abraham (Gen 15:21) refers not to physical territory but to "the land whose fruit is . . . the wisdom of God" (*Heir* 314–15)—that truly "great river" (*Euphratou*) that overflows with everlasting "gladness" (*euphrosunēs*). In the end, the drama of redemption found in the great covenant story of Genesis 15 proceeds beyond land and territory to that which is "imperishable" (*Heir* 316).

Given this intellective, spiritualizing interpretation of the promise of land to Abraham, one may question whether Philo values the hope of a future, national restoration of Israel. Philo's thought tends to explore the soul's more immediate, existential apprehension of divine wisdom rather than a future eschatological realization. Possible glimpses into the hope of national restoration are, nevertheless, accessible elsewhere among his writings (*Rewards* 93–97, 162–72; *Moses* 1:289–91, 2:43–44). His primary concern with the soul's everlasting liberation may, secondarily, translate into the hope of temporal, political redemption (Termini 2009).

Exposition on the Law

Diverging from continuous exegesis, Philo's *Exposition on the Law* pursues a more systematic, theoretical approach. Individual units of the *Exposition* survive in books with particular titles. In *Creation of the World*, Moses introduces the laws with "a most wondrous beginning—the creation of the cosmos," so that "the cosmos sings in unison with the law, and the law with the cosmos" (*Creation* 3). Philo stands in accord with Ben Sira that the wisdom that governs the cosmos is also found in "the book of the covenant of the Most High God, the law" (Sir 24:23). However, Philo offers the fullest elaboration of this "creation-law" relationship in ancient Judaism.

In concluding the *Exposition*, Philo reviews his strategic program (*Rewards* 1–3). The oracles of the prophet Moses took three forms: (1) an account of creation, (2) a history of the ancestors, and (3) legislation. Together they advance the conviction that divine wisdom harmoniously exists in creation, Israel's history, and its laws. One who keeps the laws of the Torah, therefore, lives as a citizen of the entire cosmos and dwells in harmony with its natural order (*Creation* 3). Surprisingly few direct citations from scripture appear. For the most part, Philo proceeds theoretically and propositionally, with allegorical interpretation utilized as needed. His skills as a narrative author of the ancestors' lives are profoundly illustrated in treatises on *Abraham, Joseph,* and especially his monumental *Life of Moses*. Given these formal characteristics, some scholars view the *Exposition* as addressing mixed audiences of Jews, Greeks, and proselytes.

The treatise *On the Creation of the World* begins and ends with basic claims. The physical world is a creation and depends upon the providence of some primary cause, namely the one eternal God (*Creation* 7–12, 170–72). In his treatment of the two complementary creation accounts of Genesis, Philo distinguishes between an earlier, incorporeal, intelligible creation (Gen 1) and a later, physical, visible creation (Gen 2–3). The "visible" creation has been made according to the "intelligible world" that preexisted it eternally within the mind of the divine *Logos* (*Creation* 15–25). The visible world is thus a secondary copy of this incorporeal reality. Human creation is also fashioned according to this model. The "mind" (*nous*), the rational dimension of the human soul, has been created according to the divine "image," the *Logos* (20–25; *Heir* 230–31). The soul is thus fashioned in accord with the principles of divine law that fill creation, and the original human lived as a citizen of the world, following its inherent laws as though they were a harmonious constitution (*Creation* 142–44).

Human life, however, shared not only in the divine, immortal reason but also in earthly substance and physical sensation (135). The first human was a composite of divine reason and earthly substance (cf. *Heir* 57). Problems thus arose through the senses and pleasure. Philo reads these allegorically in the Genesis text through Eve (the senses) and the serpent (pleasures), as pleasures seduce the senses and dominate the mind (*Creation* 166). Reason became "a subject instead of a ruler, a slave instead of a master, an alien instead of a citizen, and a mortal instead of an immortal" (165).[6] The philosophy found in the Torah, however, teaches how the mind may be restored to its eternal model, mercifully delivered from destructive pleasures, and advanced upon the path toward immortality.

Philosophical Writings

Philo also composed works dedicated to noteworthy philosophical questions. Although compatible with his exegesis, they proceed without reliance upon scriptural tradition. In one example, Philo defended a traditional Stoic claim, writing *Every Good Man Is Free* and *Every Bad Man Is a Slave*. Only the former work survives. In this treatise, only the virtuous soul is truly free amid the changing fortunes of life. Philo argues on comparative, universal grounds, spanning the Greek "seven sages," the Persian Magi, the Indian gymnosophists, and the Essenes of Syria-Palestine (*Good Man* 75–87). Quotations from philosophers and poets proliferate, as do examples from athletic games, historical events, and cultural norms of slavery and freedom.

Philo and the New Testament

Philo is not directly mentioned in the New Testament. Nevertheless, his writings likely reflect rhetoric, interpretive methods, and theologies that circulated more broadly within synagogue instruction in the Jewish Diaspora. For Gregory Sterling (2003, 252), this makes Philo's works "the single most important body of material" from ancient Judaism for understanding the expansion of Christian thought beyond its Palestinian origins. More than theology, Philo's embassy reveals the turbulent climate of Jewish and Greek relations that the early church sought to navigate as it developed in urban social environments. Paul's letters and the Gospel of John attest intersections with Philo that may reflect the church's thorough interaction with the traditions of Diaspora Judaism.

Paul's Letters

Philo offers immense value for contextualizing some of the more obscure moments in Paul's letters. One of the most frequently discussed instances concerns Corinthian rejection of resurrection (1 Cor 15:35–50) (Horsley 1978; Sterling 2003). Paul is at pains to convince the Corinthians that the fullest spiritual existence is not presently attainable by "wisdom" (1 Cor 1:17–25) but only through the cross and future eschatological redemption. He thus argues that the "first Adam" was the human physically created "from the earth" in Genesis 2:7 and subject to mortality; the "last Adam became a life-giving spirit," namely Christ himself, "the man from heaven" (15:45–47). His sequential argument insists that "the physical" is first, then "the spiritual" at the time of final redemption (15:47, 49).

The specific Corinthian "wisdom" Paul seeks to counteract may find its closest surviving correspondence in the writings of Philo, for whom the physical creation secondarily reflects a preexistent ideal world that is qualitatively superior (*Creation* 20–25; *Heir* 230–31). The "first," "heavenly" human created in Genesis 1:27 bears "the image of God" and does not participate in the material corruption of "the earthly" human formed in Genesis 2:7 (*Allegorical Laws* 1:31–32; *Creation* 134). Some Corinthians may have followed a similar logic in which sapiential, spiritual liberation beyond the corruptible body obviated any need for resurrection and apocalyptic redemption. The apostle known as Apollos, "a Jew... from Alexandria" (Acts 18:24), became popular at

Corinth (1:12, 3:4–6, 4:6, 16:12) and may have popularized the kind of spiritualizing, "Philonic" interpretation of redemption that Paul seeks to correct.

While 1 Corinthians presents Paul arguing against the grain of Philonic reasoning, Romans exhibits greater accord. Paul reinterprets circumcision on a spiritual plane, emphasizing that "circumcision is not merely external and physical ... circumcision is circumcision of the heart by the spirit" (Rom 2:28–29).[7] Abraham's circumcision becomes a physical "sign" and "seal" of the righteousness he already possessed through faith (4:11–12). The tendency to interpret circumcision on both a physical and intellectual/spiritual plane can be found repeatedly in Philo (*Questions* 3:46; *Special Laws* 1:1–11; *Migration* 89–93). By contrast, Paul's radical position in Galatians 5:1–12 lacks the more balanced, Philonic treatment found in Romans.

Paul also explains how righteous Gentiles may keep the law by nature: "Indeed, when the Gentiles, who do not have the law, do by nature the things required by the law, these are a law for themselves" (Rom 2:14). For such persons, the demands of the law are "written upon their hearts," as their own conscience testifies to divine righteousness (2:15). Although Philo does not advance this specific argument, his *Exposition* portrays Israel's ancestors as "unwritten laws" (*Decalogue* 1), "living and rational laws" (*Abraham* 5), even prior to the Sinai revelation. The ancestors "embraced a line of conduct consistent with nature, from attending to their own natural impulses, and from being prompted by an innate virtue" (*Abraham* 6).[8] Paul's argument in Romans 2:14–15 applies to righteous Gentiles, who have no written law, the very kind of "unwritten," "natural" virtues that Philo saw in Israel's ancestors prior to the written Torah. Once again, arguments that can be identified in Philo serve Paul especially well in Romans, as he interprets his gospel "to the Jew first and also to the Greek" (1:16–17).

Although Paul was hardly an allegorical interpreter of Philo's caliber, he desperately employs his own version of allegorical interpretation in Galatians 4:21–31 during one of the most urgent conflicts of his career. Abraham's two sons (Ishmael and Isaac) and their two mothers (Hagar and Sarah) allegorically depict (*allēgoroumena*) two different religious conditions, "two covenants" (4:24): one of law, slavery, and flesh (Ishmael and Hagar); the other of faith, freedom, and the promise of the spirit (Isaac and Sarah). Philo, too, interprets Hagar and Sarah allegorically. Hagar embodies the encyclical studies that prepare the soul for the pursuit of wisdom. However valuable, these "slavish and concubine arts" (*Preliminary Studies* 36) must ultimately lead beyond themselves to wisdom, allegorically represented by Sarah.[9] Paul utilizes allegorical interpretation to distinguish his gospel of freedom from the teachings of his early church opponents, who, in his view, advocate circumcision, law, and slavery.

John's Gospel

Philo's extensive development of the divine *Logos* poses a crucial intellectual predecessor to the Gospel of John. Even as the gospel relies heavily upon wisdom theology, its Prologue (1:1–18) ultimately prefers the term *Logos* ("Word"), not *Sophia* ("Wisdom"), as a designation for the preexistent Christ. Philo, too, was an heir of earlier wisdom and developed its concerns through an extensive dialogue with philosophy, including the redemptive role of the *Logos* as God's "interpreter and prophet" (*Immutability* 138). Philo closely interrelates the roles of *Sophia* and *Logos* (*Flight* 97). In this sense, Philo may serve as "an important bridge figure between the earlier wisdom texts and the Fourth Gospel" (Ringe 1999, 44).

Several of the Prologue's assumptions about the *Logos* can be identified in Philo:

> . . . the highest Word of God, which is the fountain of wisdom, in order that by drinking of that stream, he may find everlasting life instead of death. (*Flight* 97)

> . . . his first-born Word, the eldest of his angels, as the great archangel of many names; for he is called, the authority, and the name of God, and the Word, and man according to God's image. (*Confusion* 146)

> Now the image of God is the Word, by which all the world was made. (*Special Laws* 1:81; cf. *Sacrifices* 8)

[N]o mortal thing could have been formed on the similitude of the supreme Father of the universe, but only after the pattern of the second deity, who is the Word of the supreme Being. (*Questions* 2:62)[10]

For John, the *Logos* executes God's creation (1:3, 10), can be called "god" or "divine" (1:1), offers everlasting life, and enlightens all people with the capacity of understanding (1:4, 9). The Prologue also appears to share the claim that the supreme God is accessible to mortals only through the intermediary power of the *Logos* (1:18).

The Prologue, of course, adapts the *Logos* theology more radically than does Philo, who could hardly have asserted that the "*Logos* became flesh" exclusively within the humanity of one person (see *Heir* 234). For Daniel Boyarin (2001, 261), this claim marks "the moment that the Christian narrative begins to diverge" from what is otherwise fully continuous with Jewish reflection upon the *Logos*. Thus, even as the Prologue builds upon the philosophical foundations of earlier Hellenistic-Jewish thinkers like Philo, it also innovates as it applies the fullest potency of the *Logos* theology to the figure of Jesus himself.

Josephus

If Philo illustrates philosophical inquiry, Josephus exhibits the arts with which Jews represented their own history in the genres of Hellenistic historiography. He was not the first to walk this path. He was preceded by Artapanus, Cleodemus Malchus, Demetrius the Chronographer, Eupolemus, and Pseudo-Eupolemus. Yet only fragments of their works remain, while the voluminous writings of Josephus yield some of the most significant—and, in many cases, the only—testimonies for events that transpired in the Hellenistic and Roman eras.

Josephus's Autobiography

Thanks to his late autobiographical *Life* (ca. 93/94 CE), we know more about the biography of Josephus than of Philo—at least what Josephus chose to reveal. Josephus's story begins as Philo's ends. Born in the first year of Gaius Caesar (37–38 CE), he claims descent from a Hasmonean priestly heritage on his mother's side (*Life* 1–2). Even in childhood, he became an adept legal scholar. At sixteen, he sought specialized knowledge among Pharisees, Sadducees, and Essenes, even spending three years with a wilderness ascetic (10–12). Returning from this philosophical quest, he aligned himself with the Pharisees. In his twenty-sixth year (63–64 CE), he sailed to Rome to petition for the release of priestly associates. His delegation succeeded, and he gained many favors from Poppaea, the wife of Nero (16). Josephus's self-portrait as philosopher, diplomat, and ascetic addresses the rhetorical problems he confronted in the *Life*.

This laudatory self-presentation introduces the decisive years of Josephus's existence and the complex roles he played within the Great Jewish Revolt. Josephus returned from his Roman delegation to find that revolutionary fervor had gained momentum, yet he claims to have discouraged revolt (17–19). When violence between Greeks and Jews escalated, however, there was no turning back. The Jews' revolt was not voluntary; "they were forced by necessity to enter into it" (27; cf. 351).[11] Under these desperate circumstances, "the principal men of Jerusalem" sent Josephus to Galilee with two associates to persuade the local populace to lay down their arms (28–29). Throughout this Galilean peace mission (66–67 CE), Josephus operates as a benevolent diplomat, resolving conflicts through cleverness rather than violence. He exercises clemency, faithfulness to Jewish law, moderation toward all.

The rationale for this moderate, forbearing self-presentation emerges later in the *Life*, where Josephus refutes the allegations of Justus of Tiberias, a fellow survivor of the revolt. Justus appears to have accused Josephus of forcing Galilean cities into revolt, while enriching himself at their expense (336–67; cf. 259–61, 284, 295–98, 302–3, 314–15). Josephus's ascetic, priestly background, his denunciation of revolt and avoidance of bloodshed are intentionally stylized to refute these allegations. The question, however, remains: Had Josephus acted "more like a tyrant than a governor" (261)?[12]

The picture is complicated by an earlier account in the *Jewish War* (2:562–3:408), where Josephus presents himself as an ideal general who raised an army and fortified the cities of the Galilee. At Jotapata

(Yodefat), he met Rome face to face (*War* 3:141), ferociously defending the city for forty-seven days through "many glorious and bold actions" (3:150–54).[13] At its fall in the summer of 67, Josephus hides with compatriots in a pit, but is discovered. He then reveals prophetic visions that herald Rome's inevitable might and the rise of the general Vespasian to emperor. Josephus surrenders to the Romans, not "as a deserter of the Jews, but as a minister" from God to prophesy that all must submit to Rome (3:354).[14] Even so, his comrades demand a death pact rather than surrender. After a philosophical oration against suicide fails to persuade, Josephus escapes by enticing them to kill one another by lot. When only two men remain, Josephus surrenders to Vespasian (3:355–91).

Diplomat, priest, ascetic, philosopher, Pharisee, prophet, general, tyrant—Josephus's self-aggrandizing accounts leave behind a tangled description of his Galilean mission. Did Josephus exaggerate peaceful intentions in *Life* to refute the accusations of Justus? Or did he idealize military heroism in *War* to praise Vespasian and discourage revolt? If Josephus's goal had ever been peace, events surely took a different turn. Even as he defends his integrity, his accounts betray his confiscation of property, his brutality, his liaisons with revolutionary leaders (*Life* 72, 128, 424; *War* 2:610–13), and attempts to mitigate his complicity in embarrassing episodes (*Life* 64–67, 262–65, 373–80) (Cohen 1979). The very Jerusalem authorities who originally commissioned him also attempted to remove him (*Life* 189–203). Perhaps they had good reason. His accounts reveal his ambitious, manipulative, pretentious character, even as he became engulfed by events that quickly spiraled beyond control.

After his surrender to Vespasian, Josephus's roles clarify. As a war prisoner, he encouraged surrender at the siege of Jerusalem, offering himself as living testimony to Rome's inevitable triumph. When Vespasian became emperor in 69, he freed Josephus, made him a Roman citizen, and provided him with lands in Judaea, a palatial apartment at Rome, and an annual pension (*Life* 422–29). As a valued member of the imperial court, Josephus received Vespasian's own family name, Flavius. The decades after the Revolt became a crucial period for Josephus's vast literary production. His activity fades from view ca. 100 CE.

The many roles that Josephus played within one of the most important events in Western history leave behind a complex legacy. Scholars continue to weigh the self-serving maneuvers of his political career alongside his more noble religious aspirations as priest, historian, and Jeremiah-like prophet who failed to deter the downfall of Jerusalem (Bilde 1988; Klawans 2012). If he leaves behind essential information regarding ancient Judaism, such promise also remains intertwined with his rhetorical self-presentation, dramatic arts, and interpretive tendencies (Mason 2003). While historians have traditionally studied Josephus as evidence for earlier history in Palestine, he equally represents a vital resource for understanding the Jewish community at Rome in the decades after the Revolt.

Jewish War (Judaean War)

Josephus's earliest literary work, the *Jewish War*, recounts the history of Judaea from the Maccabees to the aftermath of the Great Revolt (see Box 6.2). *War* appears to have been written in stages, with Books 1–6 reaching their completion ca. 79–81 CE. Josephus originally composed an Aramaic account to discourage Jews in Mesopotamia from revolution (1:3–6; cf. 2:388–89). This work served as the basis for a greatly expanded translation into Greek that had an additional, apologetic purpose: to refute accounts that praised the Romans at the expense of the Jews. Portions of the work were presented to Vespasian prior to his death (in 79). Since Book 7, however, mentions Domitian's reign (81–96 CE), it appears to have been composed later. Its tendencies often align with Josephus's later works (*Antiquities*, *Life*, *Apion*).

The major thematic tendencies of *War* are communicated by Josephus's own incisive narrative commentary (4:84–86, 104, 131–34, 148–50, 314–25; 5:19–20, 255–57, 351–55, 442–45; 6:260–70, 288–315), as well as in monumental orations by pivotal figures within the drama (2:345–404; 3:362–82, 472–84; 4:238–69, 271–82; 5:360–419; 6:34–53, 96–110, 327–50; 7:320–36, 341–88). Through these devices, *War* offers a multifaceted explanation of the causes that led to the Revolt. The exploitation of Judaea by the Roman procurators Albinus and Florus (62–66 CE) inflame hostilities (2:271–83). Violent conflicts

> **Box 6.2 Contents of the *Jewish War***
>
> Book 1 Preface; Maccabean Revolt to the death of Herod the Great (167–4 BCE)
> Book 2 Heirs of Herod, Procurators, Outbreak of Revolt (4 BCE–66 CE)
> Book 3 Conquest of Galilee (66–67 CE)
> Book 4 End of Galilean Campaign; Nero's Death; Vespasian's Rise (67–69 CE)
> Book 5 Siege of Jerusalem
> Book 6 Fall of Jerusalem/Burning of the Temple (70 CE)
> Book 7 Aftermath; Masada; Epilogue (70–79 CE)

erupt between Jews and Greeks in major Hellenistic cities (2:266–70, 284–96). These burgeoning troubles give revolutionary factions a raison d'être and drive even the aristocracy to war.

Yet above all, Josephus consistently blames Jewish revolutionary leaders and their poisonous ideologies for the doom of Jerusalem. In light of their atrocities, the Roman victory was an act of divine justice that purified Jerusalem from their reign of terror. The modern reader will recognize that his unrelenting criticism tells one side of a deeper story. The revolutionaries themselves operated from religious ideologies that had precedent among the diverse currents of Judaism in the first century. Josephus's narrative reveals the variety of revolutionary movements and their own internal conflicts with one another:

1. Judas the Galilean. Long before the war (6 CE), Judas rejected direct Roman rule and taxation, arguing that Jews owed devotion to God alone and not to the empire (*War* 2:118; cf. Exod 20:1–3; Deut 6:4–5). Judas's ideology suddenly inspired a "Fourth Philosophy" alongside the traditional sects of the Pharisees, Sadducees, and Essenes. Yet this anomalous innovation had never previously existed within Judaism (cf. also *Antiquities* 18:1–10, 20:102).
2. The Sicarii. Among the "first" revolutionaries (*War* 7:262), the "Sicarii," a group of knife-wielding (*sicae*, short swords) urban

assassins, targeted members of the priestly aristocracy and supporters of Rome. By canceling debts, they presented themselves as socioeconomic liberators (2:427). After early defeats in Jerusalem, they made Masada their Judaean desert stronghold (4:398-409). Under the leadership of Eleazar ben Jair, whom Josephus calls a descendant of Judas the Galilean (7:252-54), the Masada Sicarii proved eternally faithful to their ideology, choosing death by their own hands rather than surrender to Rome (73/74 CE).

3. John of Gischala. The evils of Judas and the Sicarii, however, pale before the unalloyed wickedness of John of Gischala (7:263), Josephus's former rival in Galilee (2:585-94). Of humble origin, John prospered in the olive oil trade, amassed an army, and fortified his native city of Gischala. When besieged by the Romans, he fled to Jerusalem, where he galvanized a force of displaced revolutionaries, calling themselves "zealots" (4:84-134, 389-97; cf. Num 25:10-13). With zealot support, John fought other factions and gained control of the temple (5:98-105). He was captured at the fall of Jerusalem and imprisoned at Rome. Josephus describes his ambitions as intent on establishing a monarchy (4:389-97).

4. Eleazar son of Simon. Many "zealots" distrusted John's ambitions and formed a separate faction under Eleazar (5:5-10), a capable leader of priestly status (2:564-65, 4:225). Eleazar's zealots held sway within the inner court of the temple. When they welcomed all to celebrate Passover, John exploited their sincerity to seize full control of the temple (5:98-105).

5. Simon bar Giora. Simon's patronym implies that his family had converted (Aramaic: *gîyôr'*, "proselyte") to Judaism. He initially roamed freely outside Jerusalem, gathering an army (4:508-44) and proclaiming "liberty to those in slavery" (cf. Isa 61:1). His ideology of "liberty" implies the sociopolitical, possibly even royal-messianic character of his movement. By 69 CE, John's opponents had invited Simon into the city (*War* 4:574-84, 5:527-33), where the two fought for control. After Jerusalem's fall, Simon suddenly appeared, clothed in a purple robe, "in the place where the temple had formerly been" (7:29), as though he

were the king of this fallen city.[15] Simon was executed during the triumph that celebrated Rome's victory (7:116–62), an indication that Rome regarded him as the principal leader of the Revolt.

Josephus consistently blames revolutionary leaders for the destruction of Jerusalem. They made it impossible for the priestly aristocracy to unify conflicting factions and achieve an advantageous settlement with Rome. Their actions defiled the holy city by their impurities, bloodshed, and abominable treatment of the temple (2:449–56, 538–39; 4:147–92, 199–207, 314–25, 380–86, 558–63; 5:7–20, 380, 402–15, 562–66; 6:1–8, 93–110, 118–28, 259–60). It was thus a divinely ordained act of judgment that brought about the fall of Jerusalem. This perspective can even lead Josephus to the radical claim that "God had doomed this city to destruction as a polluted city, and was resolved to purge his sanctuary by fire" (4:323; cf. *Antiquities* 20:166; 2 Kings 21:1–15; Ezek 1–10).[16] The Romans thus appear not as hateful conquerors but as agents of God's will (*War* 6:95–128, 228, 236–66; 7:158–62).

Amid the tragic story Josephus tells, several apologetic devices defend the broader integrity of Judaism against the anomalous ambitions of the revolutionaries. A detailed description of the glory of Jerusalem and its temple reveals the grandeur of Judaean civilization prior to its destruction (5:136–247). The failed efforts of "legitimate" leaders, including Josephus himself, counterbalance the sedition of the revolutionaries (2:336–407, 569–71; 4:151–95, 236–325). Prophecy, too, plays a decisive role. Even as Rome's divinely ordained triumph had been prophetically revealed to Josephus (3:350–54, 399–408; 5:375–419), false prophecy proliferated, and the revolutionaries fanatically misinterpreted oracles that accelerated their demise (4:387–88, 6:285–315). In yet another stroke, the philosophical sects of Judaism—the Pharisees, Sadducees, and Essenes—represent the perennial vitality within Jewish tradition, over and against the sudden atrocities of the revolutionaries (2:117–66).

As Josephus's writings survived within later Christianity, his legitimation of the divine wrath unleashed in the destruction of the temple outweighed his apology for the greater Jewish tradition. By the fourth century, Josephus offered some Christian authors an incriminating indictment of Judaism in light of the death of Jesus. The historian known as Pseudo-Hegesippus, for example, extensively paraphrases Josephus, with the interpretation that the fall of Jerusalem was divine punishment for the death of Jesus himself (*Ruin of the City of Jerusalem* 2:12, 5:32) (Feldman and Hata 1987). Such tendentious, anti-Jewish misinterpretations of Josephus supported Christian claims that God had rejected the Jews and temple sacrifice in favor of the Gentile church.

Jewish Antiquities (Judaean Antiquities)

To achieve the fullest picture of Josephus, the tendencies of *War* must be balanced with those of his later writings. *Jewish Antiquities* often records alternative accounts of the same episodes found in *War*. The *Antiquities* may thus attest a number of developments in his treatment of history. In comparison with *War*, the *Antiquities* is a vast composition, ranging from creation to the Revolt. An immediate implication of this structure is that Josephus wrote to interpret not the anomalies of the Revolt but the greatness of Judaism throughout time. Books 1–10 chronicle Jewish history from creation until the Babylonian conquest; the second half tells the story of the postexilic eras. In this laborious undertaking, Josephus utilizes scriptural sources and a vast range of other materials. *Antiquities* reached its completion near 93/94 CE, when Josephus was fifty-six years of age (*Antiquities* 20:267), with his autobiographical *Life* added as an appendix.

Josephus claims to write for all who love learning, including Greeks interested in Judaism. When composing *War*, he already had it in mind to set those unusual events within the context of "who the Jews originally were," their constitution, laws, and customs (*Antiquities* 1:5–6).[17] He compares himself with the Septuagintal translators, who labored to render their laws into Greek for the greater advancement of human learning (1:10–12). His narrative will vindicate God's righteous governance of history and promote useful virtues: those who keep the divine laws prosper, while breaking them leads to calamity. The *Antiquities* will thus reveal both history and the "philosophy" of "the wisdom of Moses, our legislator" (1:14–23).

Scholars have compared this style of apologetic, "didactic" history with the *Roman Antiquities* of Dionysius of Halicarnassus (first century BCE) (Attridge 1976). Dionysius covers the mythic origins of the Romans, their "antiquities," leading up to the First Punic War (265 BCE). He writes to "remove erroneous impressions" about the Romans from the minds of Greeks critical of their culture (*Roman Antiquities* 1:4-8). Josephus likewise composes an **antiquity** that will vindicate Judaism through a moralizing presentation of its customs, laws, and history, an urgent need in the political aftermath of the Revolt.

In the first half of *Jewish Antiquities* (Books 1-10), Josephus depends heavily upon scriptural sources, recasting them in methods familiar to "rewritten scriptural" compositions. These techniques may be observed in his presentation of Abraham. Like *Jubilees* and *LAB*, Josephus offers a prehistory, in which Abraham observes the heavenly bodies and discovers that only one God rules the cosmos, "the first" to have made this assertion. When Abraham turns aside into Egypt (Gen 12:10-20), he does so not only to avoid famine but also to dialogue with Egyptian priests, teaching them Chaldean astronomy. It was thus Abraham who mediated the most advanced Near Eastern cosmology to Egypt, whence the Greeks themselves would later discover it (cf. *Apion* 1:166-68). The Egyptians establish friendly relations with Abraham, foreshadowing a major agenda of the *Antiquities*: the legitimation of Jewish rights throughout the ancient world.

In his version of the *Aqedah*, Josephus psychologizes Abraham's great "love" for Isaac. The deity's inner motivations are also explained: God tests Abraham's devotion to worship, especially whether he will offer sacrifice for the many blessings he has received. Abraham responds with perfect sacrificial devotion. He is willing to sacrifice his son, "since all creatures that live enjoy their life by [God's] providence" (*Antiquities* 1:225).[18] In a moving oration, Abraham explains directly to Isaac (1:228) that he will now send him back to God as a holy sacrifice. Isaac will enjoy immortality in the divine presence, even as his sacrifice will grant Abraham everlasting divine favor (1:231). Isaac (twenty-five in Josephus's story) is willing to be sacrificed in gratitude for the gift of life. As in *Jubilees* (18:14), the "mountain" (Gen 22:2, 14) is identified as the future temple mount in Jerusalem (*Antiquities*

1:226). Josephus alleviates the terror of the episode, explaining that the benevolence of the deity could never have allowed Isaac's death.

As he treats Israel's law, Josephus explains how God revealed to Moses a divinely ordained "government" and its "laws." Any future "constitution of government" that deviates from these laws will bring swift destruction upon the nation, even as keeping them will lead to life and blessing. Moses reiterates these basically Deuteronomistic principles in his final oration (*Antiquities* 4:302-14; cf. Deut 28-30). Yet whereas Deuteronomy speaks of Israel's "covenant" with God, Josephus utilizes the term "constitution of government" (*diataxis politeias*), language more conversant with Greek political theory than with the Pentateuch (Plato, *Republic* 587a-e; Aristotle, *Politics* 1274b-88b; *Athenian Constitution*; Aeschines, *Timarchus* 1:4). This language may represent an apologetic cultural translation by Josephus, as he represents Jewish law in the language of Greek political theory. Philo's defense of the endangered Jewish "constitution" reveals the immediate political seriousness of Josephus's strategy.

The Jewish "constitution" of "government" was inherently moral, "friendly to all" (*Antiquities* 16:174-78), and compatible with imperial rule (1:5, 10; 3:83-88, 213, 287, 322; 4:45, 177-98, 230, 294-98, 309-14; 5:97-98, 132-35, 179-81; 6:35-37; 10:275-79; 11:139-44; 15:280-83; 18:9; cf. *Apion* 2:164-66, 287). On the basis of this humane constitution, Jewish rights should flourish throughout the world (*Antiquities* 12:119-28, 279-81; 14:143-55, 185-267, 306-23; 16:160-78; 19:278-85). While Israel's ideal government was originally instituted as a priestly aristocracy, its polity could allow for constitutional monarchy, provided that kings faithfully observed its laws (4:223-24; 6:83-85; 8:125-29, 187-89, 277-81; 9:281-82; 10:59-60; 11:111-13). Yet as Moses forewarned, legal transgressions would inevitably lead to later historical disasters. Through this theoretical and legal structure, Josephus offers a moralizing interpretation of the rise and fall of Israel's monarchy and of the very course of history itself.

This interpretive paradigm remains active as Josephus turns to events of the Hellenistic and Roman eras. The *Antiquities* tends to discourage further pursuit of monarchy, especially in its treatment of Herod the Great (14:165-67, 172-76; 15:5-7, 50-70, 80-87, 164-82, 202-66; 16:150-59, 392-404; 17:146-81). Josephus's account of Herod relies heavily upon the work of Nicolaus of Damascus, who had composed a favorable history of his reign (16:183-87). Yet Josephus's editorial comments equally highlight Herod's tyrannical character. This combination of perspectives is valuable, since it allows glimpses into Nicolaus's pro-Herodian ideology (e.g., 15:380-423; 16:12-65, 335-52; 17:99-130), as well as Josephus's more critical stance.

While Herod had been courageous, fortunate, and useful to Rome, he had also been psychologically tormented by the passions of love and envy (16:150-59, 17:191-92). Ultimately, these led him to violate the cardinal rule of the *Antiquities*: he deviated from the divinely ordained constitution (15:266-82, 373-79; 16:1-5), bringing destruction upon himself, his family, and his people. Josephus's psychologizing treatment of Herod is again conversant with ancient political theory, in which the passions of a tyrannical ruler endanger the entire nation (Herodotus, *Histories* 3:80; Plato, *Republic* 565d-580c; Aristotle, *Politics* 1310b-15b; cf. *Aristeas* 221-24; Philo, *Moses* 1:148-54). In light of such dangers, Josephus stands within his own priestly Hasmonean heritage, arguing that priestly aristocracy offers the best political structure for living out Israel's law (*Antiquities* 4:223, 16:187).

The Revolt itself takes on new perspective in the *Antiquities*. In line with the larger political themes of the work, the calamities that came upon the nation arose due to its deviation from the divinely revealed constitution. While Josephus continues to malign revolutionary leaders (*Antiquities* 18:1-10), blame is no longer so easily assigned to their atrocities alone. War had come upon the Jews by "necessity," due to a confluence of events that forced them "unwillingly" to fight the Romans (1:6, 20:258), a view also found in his *Life* (27, 351; cf. *War* 7:358, 387). This interpretation of the Revolt may express a more sympathetic historical perspective in Josephus's later years. More removed from the events, he appears to have contemplated more deeply the unavoidable confluence of bewildering circumstances that thrust Judaea tragically into revolution. In his struggle to interpret the historical catastrophe within a theological framework, Josephus shares a concern with theodicy, so richly illustrated within the dialogues of his apocalyptic contemporaries, *4 Ezra*, *2 Baruch*, and *Apocalypse of Abraham*.

Against Apion

In spite of his *Antiquities*, Josephus complains that antagonists have questioned the antiquity of the Jews and criticized their absence from Greek history. *Against Apion* defends Judaism amid such accusations, documenting its presence throughout historical memory. The modern title *Against Apion* arises from the second half of the work (Book 2), where Josephus refutes Apion, a principal opponent of Philo's earlier embassy. Apion was a Hellenized Egyptian grammarian who had accused the Jews of Alexandria before Gaius. Although he was already dead (*Apion* 2:143), Josephus's apology shows that the anti-Jewish accusations of Hellenized Egyptians (1:223-24) remained potent throughout the end of the first century.

The larger structure of the apology documents the presence of the Jews in ancient historical sources (1:28-218), and then refutes the false claims of such authors as Manetho (1:227-87), Chaeremon (1:288-303), Lysimachus (1:304-20), and Apion (2:1-144). The negation of their outlandish claims offers valuable insights into Greek anti-Judaism. Josephus advances his own rhetorical, at times even fictional strategies for defending the antiquity and integrity of Judaism. The apology concludes with an encomiastic presentation of Moses and the law, one that emphasizes the timeless unity of Judaism (2:145-296). Josephus explains laws on diet, the temple, sacrifice, marriage, sexuality, family, and burial of the dead. Israel's law made virtue a matter of daily practice and should be regarded as a treasure to the entire human race. It commands moderation, courage, sanctity, and peace with all people.

Josephus and the New Testament

In spite of the challenges of interpreting this fluid personality, Josephus's writings remain essential for contextualizing the church's origins within its formative historical environment. Josephus mentions numerous political and religious figures named in New Testament literature, often providing fuller, alternative accounts of their activities. He further mentions John the Baptist, James the brother of the Lord, and probably Jesus himself. These figures are marginal to his history, yet he treats them as they intersect his primary concerns. This is especially the case in *Antiquities* 18–20, a loosely edited collection of accounts dealing with varied Jewish experiences after the reign of Herod's heir, Archelaus (6 CE).

John the Baptist

While explaining how Herod Antipas's army was destroyed by the Arabians, Josephus offers a remarkable testimony to John the Baptist. Antipas had planned to divorce an Arabian princess to marry Herodias, the wife of his half-brother Philip. The clever princess, however, secretly escaped to her father, King Aretas IV, who marched against Antipas (*Antiquities* 18:109–15). "Some of the Jews" believed that the consequent destruction of his army was an act of God "as a just punishment of what Herod had done against John, who was called the Baptist" (18:116). Antipas had earlier become paranoid about John's powerful following and determined "to prevent any mischief he might cause by putting him to death" (18:118–19).[19]

In the Synoptic Gospels, the immediate cause of John's execution differs. John criticizes Antipas's controversial remarriage, provoking the wrath of Herodias and her daughter Salome. Antipas himself bore no ill will toward John and even "liked to listen to him" (Mark 6:17–29). He was persuaded somewhat unwillingly to execute John through the wiles of Herodias and Salome. In Josephus's account, however, it was Antipas's paranoia, not Herodias's wrath, that doomed John. The two accounts, which offer different (if not entirely contradictory) explanations, nevertheless reveal how John's sudden execution inspired a variety of popular religious interpretations.

For Josephus, John's preaching emphasizes a combination of ritual and moral purity: the "cleansing of their bodies" in baptism must be accompanied by "souls that had already been purified by righteousness" (*Antiquities* 18:117). This summation of John's preaching, which emphasizes both ritual washing and moral purity, aligns well with the Synoptic Gospels, where baptism demands moral impetus to "bring forth fruits in keeping with repentance" (Matt 3:8; cf. Luke 3:10–14).

Josephus never mentions any association between John and Jesus. Rather than a forerunner to Jesus, John stands in his own right as a "good man" and one of the most formidable popular religious leaders of his time.

James, the Brother of Jesus

Josephus recounts the death of James, "the brother of Jesus who was called 'Christ,'" at the hands of the high priest Ananus (*Antiquities* 20:197-203). In the wealth of information that he supplies concerning the priesthood, Josephus highlights the powerful exploits of the Annas family. After serving as the first high priest under direct Roman rule (6-15 CE), Annas the elder had "five sons" serve in the office, an anomaly within Jewish history. His son Ananus orchestrated the death of James "and some others" during a transition between Roman governors. Ananus exploited the interim to convene "a council of judges" before whom he accused these "breakers of the law"; he delivered them to execution by stoning. The targeting of James indicates his prominent standing within the early church community at Jerusalem (cf. Gal 2:9; Acts 15:13-21). Josephus criticizes Ananus for exceeding the limits of his authority. The power to assemble councils and execute capital punishments belonged to Roman governors.

Annas's son-in-law was no less than Joseph Caiaphas, the high priest associated with Jesus's trial and accusation before Pilate (Matt 26). Annas himself appears in the Gospel of John as an interrogator of Jesus (John 18:13-14, 19-23) and as a powerful influence after his high priesthood (cf. Luke 3:2; Acts 4:6). It seems no coincidence that both Jesus and James stood accused by members of the specific priestly family of Annas, which apparently took a hardline stance against religious innovation.

Testimonium Flavianum

The most famous passage of Josephus's writings, offering a description of Jesus himself (*Antiquities* 18:63-64), is known as the *Testimonium*

Flavianum (i.e., "Flavius" Josephus's "testimony" to Jesus). There is no question that in its present form the *Testimonium* reflects Christian presuppositions. Where the *Testimonium* flatly declares Jesus "was the Christ" (*Antiquities* 18:63), this cannot have arisen from Josephus. Christian assumptions recur where Jesus "appeared on the third day alive, as the divine prophets had spoken" (*Antiquities* 18:64; cf. 1 Cor 15:3-6). Such clearly Christian elements have often led to the conclusion that the entire passage represents an inauthentic insertion into Josephus's works.

Yet other features seem unlikely to have been composed by Christians. Jesus was a "wise man" and "teacher" (*Antiquities* 18:63), descriptors insufficient to Christians but characteristic of Josephus's style (e.g., *War* 3:376; *Antiquities* 3:49; 8:53; 10:203, 237, 241; 11:57-58; 13:114). He is a "doer of wondrous deeds," a likely reference to Jesus's reputation for the miraculous. The description invites comparison with other wonder-workers in Josephus, including the prophet Elisha (*Antiquities* 9:182; cf. 2:267, 295, 345; 3:1, 14; 5:28). Josephus's characterization of Jesus as a wise man and wonder-worker resonates well with traditions preserved in the Synoptic Gospels, where Jesus develops a reputation precisely for "wisdom" and "mighty works" (Mark 6:2).

Regarding Jesus's death, the "leading men among us" formed a legal accusation, on the basis of which "Pilate condemned him to a cross" (*Antiquities* 18:64). This balance of priestly accusation and Roman condemnation genuinely reflects the political situation in the first century, yet is reported in a cool, neutral tone uncharacteristic of Christian sources. Josephus's final claim—"the tribe of the 'Christians,' so named after him, did not cease"—expresses wonder that this "tribe" had survived at all, sentiments unusual for Christians. The explanation of the name "Christians" further indicates that Josephus was familiar with the messianic claims of his followers. Indeed, he describes James as "the brother of Jesus who was called 'Christ'" (*Antiquities* 20:200).

When the probable Christian, as well as plausibly Josephan, characteristics of the passage are weighed, they support the theory that Christian editors altered an originally Josephan description of Jesus. Such editorial activity reflects the "Christianizing" of Josephus as a historical authority for the church. It has its corollary in the church's reception of Philo, who became an honored source for early Christian exegesis, philosophy, and apologetics (Eusebius, *Church History* 2:16–18).

Popular Religion

Josephus documents a variety of popular messianic and prophetic figures during the era of Christian origins. Some of these very figures are mentioned in the New Testament. Such accounts reveal that Early Judaism was not simply defined by priestly circles, erudite philosophical sects, or elite scribes. Living prophets, messiahs, and wonder-workers played episodic yet powerful roles within Jewish society in the first century (Horsley and Hanson 1999). Josephus therefore remains an invaluable source for contextualizing the popular movement that arose around Jesus himself and came to regard him as "prophet" and "messiah" (Mark 8:27–30; Luke 24:19–27).

In *Antiquities* 17, Josephus continually describes a series of three royal claimants who arose after the death of Herod the Great (4 BCE):

1. Judas, son of Ezekias, raided the royal armory at Sepphoris and armed his compatriots, "zealous of royal honor" (*Antiquities* 17:271–72). Ezekias had been a "chief brigand" imprisoned by Herod. Judas sought the kingship "not by virtue but by force," that is, not by royal lineage but through armed revolt.
2. Simon, a slave of Herod, raided royal palaces at Jericho and initiated a popular uprising (17:273–74). A physically gifted, charismatic figure (cf. 1 Sam 9:2, 16:12), Simon "dared to put on the crown" and was "proclaimed king" by his followers. The Romans swiftly intervened, and Simon was beheaded.
3. Athronges, the shepherd, rose from obscure origins on the basis of bodily strength and courage (*Antiquities* 17:278–85). He "dared set his mind upon the kingship" and "put on the crown." Organizing authority among his four brothers, he attacked Roman and Herodian targets until suppressed by Archelaus. The catalogue indicates that the end of Herod's reign triggered social upheavals in which popular royal-messianic movements flourished.

Prophetic activity also abounds within Josephus's histories. As we have seen, prophecy became essential to Josephus's own identity and interpretation of history. It is little wonder that he takes interest in popular prophets of his time:

1. An unnamed Samaritan prophet (ca. 36 CE) led a multitude up Mount Gerizim, claiming to reveal "the holy vessels in the spot where Moses had placed them" (*Antiquities* 18:85–87). The prophet thus aspires to restore the Samaritan holy mountain, rather than Jerusalem, as the divinely ordained site of worship. The prophet's activity may reflect Samaritan hope in the *Taheb*, a Moses-like restorer of true worship on Mount Gerizim (Deut 18:15–18). Pilate quickly dispels the movement.
2. Claiming the title "prophet," Theudas (ca. 45 CE) guided many "commoners" to the Jordan River, promising to divide its waters and to walk across it (*Antiquities* 20:97–98). Roman troops "cut off his head and carried it to Jerusalem." The book of Acts remembers him as leading a failed popular uprising (Acts 5:36).
3. An Egyptian "prophet" (ca. 56 CE) led multitudes to the Mount of Olives, promising that "at his command the walls of Jerusalem would fall down" (*Antiquities* 20:169–72; cf. *War* 2:261–63). The Roman governor disperses the crowd, and the prophet escapes. His memory is reflected in Acts, where Paul is mistaken for the missing prophet (Acts 21:38).[20]

The messianic claimants featured by Josephus tend to be charismatic figures who raid imperial and Herodian fortresses and arm the populace. The prophets tend to be action prophets with authority to command powerful wonders configured upon the primal saving events of Israel's past, like the exodus and conquest of the land. Such messianic and prophetic movements appeal to the populace but are typically disdained by Josephus and perceived as destabilizing to Roman governance. Josephus's testimonies offer valuable evidence that messianism and prophecy were not simply ideals of a sacred past; they were courageously lived out by those who acted to overthrow the political settlement of their time and to inaugurate a new order beyond Roman rule.

Notes

Chapter 1

1. Trans. *Old Testament Pseudepigrapha* (ed. Charlesworth 1983–85) = *OTP*.
2. Codex Alexandrinus, Codex Venetus, Codex Claromontanus (Gallagher and Meade 2017).

Chapter 2

1. Translations of Ben Sira and Wisdom follow NRSV.
2. Babylonian Talmud, *Sanhedrin* 100b.
3. Chrysostom, *Sermons on Matthew* 9, 47, 80; Augustine, *Sermons on New Testament Lessons* 10, 11, 32, 47.
4. Epicurus, *Letter to Menoeceus* 124–27; *Key Doctrines* 19–21.
5. Philo, *Moses*, 1:96–146.
6. Translations of NT follow NRSV.
7. Trans. NRSV, with revision.
8. *On the Gospel of John* 111, trans. Roberts and Donaldson.
9. Trans. NRSV, with revision.
10. Trans. NRSV, with revision.
11. Translations of Paul's letters follow NRSV.

Chapter 3

1. Trans. Charles.
2. Trans. Nickelsburg (2012).
3. *Gilgamesh Epic*, X–XI; *Odyssey* 11:8–22, 639–41; 12:1–27.
4. Trans. *OTP*.
5. Trans. *OTP*.

6. Trans. Charles; Henze 2011.
7. Trans. *OTP*.
8. Trans. *OTP*.
9. Trans. Gurtner.
10. Trans. Gurtner.
11. Trans. *OTP*.
12. Esp. ch. 7, 29:3–13, 22:5, 20:5, 20:7; possibly also 9:7, 23:4–10, 10:6–12, 17:8b–19.
13. Trans. Kulik.
14. See *LAB* 23:6, Philo, *Heir* (258–65).
15. Trans. Kulik.
16. Trans. Kulik.
17. Trans. Kulik.
18. Translations of NT follow NRSV.
19. Trans. Charles.
20. Trans. Charles.
21. Trans. *OTP*.
22. Amos 5:18–20; Isa 2:12, 13:6–9; Zeph 1:7–16; Jer 46:10; Ezek 13:5, 30:3, 39:8–13; Obad v15; Zech 14:1–7; Mal 3:1–4:5; Joel 1:15; 2:1–3:21; cf. Zech 12:1–13:6.
23. Trans. Gurtner.

Chapter 4

1. Trans. Vermes.
2. Trans. García Martínez and Tigchelaar.
3. Trans. *OTP*.
4. Trans. *OTP*.
5. Trans. Charles.
6. Trans. Charles.
7. Cf. *Midrash Rabbah*, Genesis 55:7.
8. Mishnah, *Avot* 5; *Pirkei de Rabbi Eleazar* 31; *Midrash Tanḥuma Vayera* 22; *Midrash Numbers Rabbah* 17.
9. Trans. Charles, with revision.
10. Trans. *OTP*.
11. Trans. *OTP*.

12. Trans. *OTP*.
13. *Targum Neophiti* Gen 11:31, 15:7; *Genesis Rabbah* 38:13.
14. Cf. *Pirkei de Rabbi Eliezer* 26.
15. Trans. *OTP*.
16. Trans. NRSV.
17. Trans. James.
18. Cf. Babylonian Talmud, *Sanhedrin* 89b.
19. Trans. *OTP*.
20. Trans. *OTP*.
21. Trans. James, with revision.
22. Trans. *OTP*.
23. Trans. *OTP*.
24. Trans. *OTP*.
25. Translations of Paul's letters follow NRSV.
26. Trans. *OTP*.
27. Trans. Neusner.
28. Trans. CDE.
29. Trans. *OTP*.
30. Trans. *OTP*.
31. Trans. García Martínez and Tigchelaar.
32. Cf. *Numbers Rabbah* 17:2; *Mekhilta De-Rabbi Ishmael*, 7:78–82.
33. Trans. Jacobson.
34. For example, *Genesis Rabbah* 56:1–2; *Pirkei de Rabbi Eleazar* 31; *Pesikta de Rab-Kahana* 31/32.

Chapter 5

1. Trans. Vermes.
2. Trans. Yadin.
3. Trans. Vermes.
4. Trans. García Martínez.
5. E.g., *4QPsalm^f, 11QPsalm^b, 11QPsalmAp^a*.
6. Trans. D. Harrington.
7. Trans. García Martínez.
8. Trans. García Martínez, with revision.
9. Trans. García Martínez
10. Trans. NRSV.

Chapter 6

1. Trans. Yonge. Cf. *Moses* 1:34–36.
2. Trans. Yonge.
3. Trans. Yonge, with revision.
4. Cf. *ApAbr* 9–14; *LAB* 23:6; *4 Ezra* 3:13–14; *2 Baruch* 4:4.
5. Trans. Colson and Whitaker.
6. Trans. Colson and Whitaker.
7. Translations of NT follow NRSV.
8. Trans. Yonge.
9. Trans. Yonge.
10. Trans. Yonge.
11. Trans. Whiston.
12. Trans. Whiston.
13. Trans. Whiston.
14. Trans. Whiston.
15. Trans. Whiston.
16. Trans. Whiston.
17. Trans. Whiston.
18. Trans. Whiston.
19. Trans. Whiston, with revision.
20. Trans. Whiston.

Glossary

Aggadah (Hebrew: "narration," "tale"): A term for the nonlegal traditions of Rabbinic Judaism that concern narratives, folklore, morals, and spiritual-mystical teachings.

allegorical exegesis: A method of interpreting literary classics that reads textual details as symbols for spiritual, cosmic, or ethical ideals.

anthologies: Compositions that select disparate scriptural texts and cite them together as they illumine a common theme.

antiquity: A type of narrative history that explains the origins and customs of a nation from the mythic past to the recent present, often with an apologetic/didactic purpose.

apocalypse: A genre of literature in which a divine revelation is disclosed to a chosen human being, often in symbolic discourse. **Temporal apocalypses** concern the course of past, present, and future history. **Cosmic-spatial apocalypses** unveil the mysteries of creation, often including the deity's throne and the places of the dead. **Dialogue apocalypses** present a deliberative conversation between the visionary recipient and heavenly beings.

apocalypticism (apocalyptic thought): The concepts found within formal literary apocalypses that may also occur in other writings.

Apocrypha (or **Deuterocanonical** Books): Writings that circulated with Septuagintal and Latin versions of the Old Testament, yet not within the canon of the Hebrew Bible.

apology: A literary document composed to defend the beliefs and practices of an individual or group.

Bar-Kochba Revolt (132–135 CE): A failed revolt by Jews in Palestine against Rome, led by Simon bar-Kochba.

beatitudes: Poetic declarations of blessedness upon a particular type of person, often beginning with the word "Blessed" or "Happy."

biblical manuscripts: Early copies of books that would later appear in the Bible.

canon: An exclusive collection of scriptural books.

Christology: Theological reflection upon Jesus as the Christ, especially his relationship to God and to humanity.

Deuteronomistic paradigm: A theological interpretation of history informed by the blessings and curses of Deuteronomy (e.g., chs. 28–30).

Diaspora: The "scattering abroad" of the Jewish people beyond Judaea, especially in Egypt, Greece, Italy, and Babylonia.

Diaspora Revolt (115–117 CE): A failed Jewish revolt in Egypt, Cyrene, Cyprus, and Mesopotamia.

diatribe: Rhetorical argumentation, in which a question from an imaginary interlocutor leads to a superior, corrective answer.

dualism: A form of religious thought that structures reality into two opposite principles or powers.

encyclical paideia: A form of ancient Hellenistic education in grammar, music, geometry, and logic.

epistemology: The philosophical question of what humans can know and how they know it.

Essene hypothesis: The hypothesis proposes that an ancient community of Essenes preserved and copied many Dead Sea Scrolls.

Euhemerism: The ancient theory, associated with the Greek mythographer Euhemerus, that the gods had originally been human heroes and kings.

explicit interpretation: A commentator quotes a passage from a scripture text, then interprets it, making a clear distinction between scripture and commentary.

flood typology: Frequent apocalyptic motif in which the primeval flood foreshadows the end of the age.

Great Jewish Revolt (66–70 CE): A failed rebellion by Jews in Palestine against Rome, resulting in the destruction of the Jerusalem temple.

Halakhah (Hebrew: "path," "way"): A term for the collective body of Jewish law, including the oral laws transmitted by early rabbinic sages and codified in the Mishnah.

harmonization: Scriptural passages dealing with compatible subject matter are fused into a single, unified version.

Hasmonean Dynasty (ca. 140–63 BCE): The Jewish priestly kingdom established by the heirs of the Maccabean revolutionaries.

Hellenization: The spread of Greek culture, especially after the conquests of Alexander the Great.

implicit interpretation: A scriptural passage is represented with interpretive alterations interwoven into the text.

Lady Wisdom: The literary personification of wisdom as a transcendent heavenly being.

Logos: The divine "reason" or "word" that structures the cosmos and makes it intelligible to human inquiry.

Maccabean Revolt (167–164 BCE): A successful Jewish revolt against the Seleucid Empire and pro-Hellenistic Jews, led by the Maccabean family.

miqveh (pl. *miqva'ot*): A stepped bathing pool constructed to accommodate purification rituals.

polis (Greek: "city"): A fortified Hellenistic-style city-state, often featuring central cult sites, theaters, and gymnasia.

politeuma (also *politeia*): This political "constitution" granted Jews autonomy to live peacefully by their ancestral laws under the Ptolemaic Empire.

predeterminism: The belief that God has already determined the course of creation, history, and human existence.

Pseudepigrapha: Writings that did not feature within the Jewish or most Christian canons of scripture. The title reflects the pseudonymous authorship of many of these writings.

pseudonymity: Literary strategy in which a text is intentionally written as though it had been composed by someone else, usually an idealized figure of the past (e.g., Enoch).

Q-source: A theoretical source of Jesus's sayings, believed to have been independently edited in the gospels of Matthew and Luke.

question-and-answer: A method of scriptural interpretation in which questions are raised about a scriptural passage, then answered by the interpreter.

Rabbinic Judaism: The movement that would lay the foundations of modern Judaism, guided by belief in a written and an oral Torah codified in the Mishnah (ca. 200 CE).

scribes: Literary and legal specialists who cared for, copied, and interpreted religious literature.

sectarian literature: Dead Sea Scrolls believed to have been composed or edited within the sectarian religious movement featured in the *Rule of the Community*.

Septuagint: A Greek translation of scriptural books. The title "Septuaginta" (abbrev., LXX) reflects the legend in which *seventy*-two Jewish scholars produced this inspired translation.

Tannaim: Jewish sages, ca. 10 BCE–200 CE, whose views contributed strongly to the Mishnah.

testament: A literary device that portrays the final admonitions of illustrious figures of the past, often teaching morality and forecasting future events.

Testimonium Flavianum: A much disputed "testimony" in the *Antiquities* of "Flavius" Josephus that offers a brief description of Jesus.

textual plurality: Since there was no official version of scripture in antiquity, a scriptural book might be preserved and studied in multiple versions.

theodicy: A conceptual attempt to understand how "divine" (*theo-*) "justice" (*-dikē*) operates amid the imperfections of the world.

universalism: Religious thought concerned with all creation and human life; often contrasted with "nationalism," which focuses on a specific people.

wisdom hymn: A poetic genre within wisdom literature that explores topics such as creation or Lady Wisdom.

wisdom instruction: An instructional genre within wisdom literature in which a sage teaches an envisioned audience.

Works Cited

Attridge, Harold W. 1976. *The Interpretation of Biblical History in the Antiquitates Judaicae of Flavius Josephus*. SBLDS. Missoula, MT: Scholars Press.

Attridge, Harold W. 1989. *The Epistle to the Hebrews: A Commentary on the Epistle to the Hebrews*. Hermeneia. Minneapolis, MN: Fortress Press.

Barclay, John M. G. 1996. *Jews in the Mediterranean Diaspora from Alexander to Trajan (323 BCE–117 CE)*. Edinburgh: T&T Clark.

Bauckham, Richard, James R. Davila, and Alexander Panayotov. 2013–. *Old Testament Pseudepigrapha: More Noncanonical Scriptures*. Grand Rapids, MI: Eerdmans.

Becker, Adam H., and Annette Yoshiko Reed. 2003. *The Ways That Never Parted: Jews and Christians in Late Antiquity and the Early Middle Ages*. TSAJ 95. Tübingen: Mohr Siebeck.

Beker, J. Christiaan. 1980. *Paul the Apostle: The Triumph of God in Life and Thought*. Philadelphia, PA: Fortress Press.

Bilde, Per. 1988. *Flavius Josephus between Jerusalem and Rome*. JSPSup 2. Sheffield: JSOT Press.

Blackwell, Ben C., John K. Goodrich, and Jason Maston, eds. 2016. *Paul and the Apocalyptic Imagination*. Minneapolis, MN: Fortress Press.

Blackwell, Ben C., John K. Goodrich, Jason Maston, and Loren T. Stuckenbruck, eds. 2019. *Reading Revelation in Context*. Grand Rapids, MI: Zondervan Academic.

Blount, Brian K. 2009. *Revelation: A Commentary*. Louisville, KY: Westminster/John Knox Press.

Boccaccini, Gabriele, and John J. Collins, eds. 2007. *The Early Enoch Literature*. Leiden: Brill.

Boyarin, Daniel. 1999. *Dying for God: Martyrdom and the Making of Christianity and Judaism*. Stanford, CA: Stanford University Press.

Boyarin, Daniel. 2001. "The Gospel of the *Memra*: Jewish Binitarianism and the Prologue to John." *Harvard Theological Review* 94: 243–84.

Bultmann, Rudolf. 1997. "The History of Religions Background of the Prologue to the Gospel of John" (1923). In *The Interpretation of John*, edited by John Ashton, 27–46. Edinburgh: T&T Clark.

Charles, R. H., ed. 1913. *The Apocrypha and Pseudepigrapha of the Old Testament in English*. Oxford: Clarendon Press.

Charlesworth, James H., ed. 1983–85. *The Old Testament Pseudepigrapha*. 2 vols. New York: Doubleday.

Cohen, Shaye J. D. 1979. *Josephus in Galilee and Rome: His Vita and Development as a Historian*. Leiden: Brill.

Collins, John J. 1997. *Jewish Wisdom in the Hellenistic Age*. Old Testament Library. Louisville, KY: Westminster John Knox Press.

Collins, John J. 1998. *The Apocalyptic Imagination: An Introduction to Jewish Apocalyptic Literature*. Grand Rapids, MI: Eerdmans.

Collins, John J. 2009. *Beyond the Qumran Community: The Sectarian Community of the Dead Sea Scrolls*. Grand Rapids, MI: Eerdmans.

Collins, John J. 2022. "The Pseudepigrapha and Second Temple Judaism." In *Fountains of Wisdom: In Conversation with James H. Charlesworth*, edited by Gerbern Oegema, Henry Rietz, and Loren Stuckenbruck, 311–22. London: T&T Clark.

Crawford, Sidney White. 2008. *Rewriting Scripture in Second Temple Times*. Grand Rapids, MI: Eerdmans.

Crossan, John Dominic. 1992. *The Historical Jesus: The Life of a Mediterranean Jewish Peasant*. San Francisco, CA: HarperSanFrancisco.

Davila, James R. 2005. *The Provenance of the Pseudepigrapha: Jewish, Christian, or Other?* JSJSup 105. Leiden: Brill.

de Boer, Martinus C. 2020. *Paul, Theologian of God's Apocalypse: Essays on Paul and Apocalyptic*. Eugene, OR: Cascade Books.

DeSilva, David. 2004. *Introducing the Apocrypha: Message, Context, and Significance*. Grand Rapids, MI: Baker Academic.

de Vaux, Roland. 1973. *Archaeology and the Dead Sea Scrolls*. Oxford: Oxford University Press/British Academy.

Dunn, James D. G. 1988. *Romans 1–8*. Waco, TX: Word Books.

Enns, Peter E. 1996. "The 'Moveable Well' in 1 Cor 10:4: An Extrabiblical Tradition in an Apostolic Text." *Bulletin for Biblical Research* 6: 23–38.

Fabricius, J. A. 1713, 1723. *Codex pseudepigraphus Veteris Testamenti*. Hamburgi et Lipsiae: sumptu Christiani Liebezeit.

Feldman, Louis H., and Gohei Hata, eds. 1987. *Josephus, Judaism, and Christianity*. Leiden: Brill.

Fisk, Bruce Norman. 2001. *Do You Not Remember? Scripture, Story and Exegesis in the Rewritten Bible of Pseudo-Philo*. JSPSup 37. Sheffield: Sheffield Academic Press.

Gallagher, Edmon L., and John D. Meade. 2017. *The Biblical Canon Lists from Early Christianity: Texts and Analysis*. Oxford: Oxford University Press.

García Martínez, Florentino, and Eibert J. C. Tigchelaar, eds. 1997–98. *The Dead Sea Scrolls Study Edition*. 2 vols. Leiden: Brill.

Goodman, Martin. 2002. "Jews and Judaism in the Second Temple Period." In *Oxford Handbook of Jewish Studies*, edited by Martin Goodman, Jeremy Cohen, and David Sorkin, 36–52. Oxford: Oxford University Press.

Gurtner, Daniel M. 2009. *Second Baruch: A Critical Edition of the Syriac Text*. New York: T&T Clark.
Harrington, Daniel J. 1996. *Wisdom Texts from Qumran*. London: Routledge.
Harrington, Hannah. 2004. *The Purity Texts*. New York: T&T Clark.
Henze, Matthias. 2011. *Jewish Apocalypticism in Late First Century Israel*. TSAJ 142. Tübingen: Mohr Siebeck.
Himmelfarb, Martha. 2018. "Second Temple Literature outside the Canon." In *Early Judaism: New Insights and Scholarship*, edited by Frederick Greenspahn, 29–51. New York: New York University Press.
Hogan, Karina Martin. 2008. *Theologies in Conflict in 4 Ezra: Wisdom Debate and Apocalyptic Solution*. JSJSup 130. Leiden: Brill.
Horsley, Richard A. 1978. "'How Can Some of You Say That There Is No Resurrection of the Dead?' Spiritual Elitism in Corinth." *Novum Testamentum* 20: 203–31.
Horsley, Richard A., with Scott S. Hanson. 1999. *Bandits, Prophets, and Messiahs: Popular Movements at the Time of Jesus*. Harrisburg, PA: Trinity Press International.
Jacobson, Howard. 1996. *A Commentary on Pseudo-Philo's Liber Antiquitatum Biblicarum, with Latin Text and English Translation*. 2 vols. AGJU 31. Leiden: Brill.
James, M. R. 1917. *The Biblical Antiquities of Philo*. London: S.P.C.K.
Kamesar, Adam. 2009. *The Cambridge Companion to Philo*. Cambridge: Cambridge University Press.
Käsemann, Ernst. 1969. *New Testament Questions of Today*. Translated by William John Montague. London: SCM.
Kautzsch, Emil. 1900. *Die Apokryphen und Pseudepigraphen des Alten Testaments*. Tübingen: Mohr.
Keck, Leander E. 1988. *Paul and His Letters*. Philadelphia, PA: Fortress Press.
Klawans, Jonathan. 2012. *Josephus and the Theologies of Ancient Judaism*. New York: Oxford University Press.
Kohler, Kaufmann. 1918. *Jewish Theology Systematically and Historically Considered*. New York: Macmillan.
Kraft, Robert A. 1994. "The Pseudepigrapha and Christianity." In *Tracing the Threads: Studies in the Vitality of Jewish Pseudepigrapha*, edited by John Reeves, 55–86. SBLEJL 6. Atlanta, GA: Scholars Press.
Kugel, James L. 2012. *A Walk through Jubilees: Studies in the Book of Jubilees and the World of its Creation*. JSJSup 156. Leiden: Brill.
Kulik, Alexander. 2004. *Retroverting Slavonic Pseudepigrapha: Towards the Original of the Apocalypse of Abraham*. Atlanta, GA: SBL Press.
Lim, Timothy H. 2013. *The Formation of the Jewish Canon*. AYBRL. New Haven, CT: Yale University Press.
Magness, Jodi. 2021. *The Archaeology of Qumran and the Dead Sea Scrolls*. 2nd edition. Chicago: Eerdmans.

Mason, Steve. 2003. *Josephus and the New Testament*. 2nd edition. Peabody, MA: Hendrickson.

McDonald, Lee Martin. 2012. *Formation of the Bible: The Story of the Church's Canon*. Peabody, MA: Hendrickson.

Mueller, James R. 1982. "The Apocalypse of Abraham and the Destruction of the Second Jewish Temple." In *Society of Biblical Literature Seminar Papers*, 341–49. Chico, CA: Scholars Press.

Murphy, Frederick J. 1993. *Pseudo-Philo: Rewriting the Bible*. New York: Oxford University Press.

Murphy, Frederick J. 2012. *Apocalypticism in the Bible and Its World: A Comprehensive Introduction*. Grand Rapids, MI: Baker Academic.

Najman, Hindy. 2014. *Losing the Temple and Recovering the Future: An Analysis of 4 Ezra*. New York: Cambridge University Press.

Neusner, Jacob. 2002. *The Tosefta: Translated from the Hebrew with a New Introduction*. Peabody, MA: Hendrickson.

Nickelsburg, George W. E. 2001. *1 Enoch 1: A Commentary on the Book of 1 Enoch, Chapters 1–36; 81–108*. Hermeneia. Minneapolis, MN: Fortress Press.

Nickelsburg, George W. E., and James C. VanderKam. 2012. *1 Enoch 2: A Commentary on the Book of 1 Enoch, Chapters 37–82*. Hermeneia. Minneapolis, MN: Fortress Press.

Philo Volume IV. 1932. Translated by F. H. Colson and G. H. Whitaker. Loeb Classical Library 261. Cambridge: Harvard University Press.

Portier-Young, Anathea. 2011. *Apocalypse against Empire: Theologies of Resistance in Early Judaism*. Grand Rapids, MI: Eerdmans.

Reed, Annette Yoshiko. 2009. "The Modern Invention of 'Old Testament Pseudepigrapha.'" *Journal of Theological Studies* 60: 403–36.

Ringe, Sharon H. 1999. *Wisdom's Friends: Community and Christology in the Fourth Gospel*. Louisville, KY: Westminster/John Knox Press.

Roberts, A., and J. Donaldson, eds. 1986–89. *Ante-Nicene Fathers*. 10 vols. Grand Rapids, MI: Eerdmans.

Sanders, Jack T. 1983. *Ben Sira and Demotic Wisdom*. SBLMS 28. Chico, CA: Scholars Press.

Sayler, Gwendolyn B. 1984. *Have the Promises Failed? A Literary Analysis of 2 Baruch*. SBLDS 72. Chico, CA: Scholars Press.

Schiffman, Lawrence H. 1995. *Reclaiming the Dead Sea Scrolls*. ABRL. New Haven, CT: Yale University Press.

Segal, Michael. 2007. *The Book of Jubilees: Rewritten Bible, Redaction, Ideology and Theology*. JSJSup 117. Leiden: Brill.

Sterling, Gregory E. 2003. "'Philo Has Not Been Used Half Enough': The Significance of Philo of Alexandria for the Study of the New Testament." *Perspectives in Religious Studies* 30: 251–69.

Stone, Michael. 1990. *Fourth Ezra: A Commentary on the Book of Fourth Ezra*. Hermeneia. Minneapolis, MN: Fortress Press.

Stone, Michael. 2011. *Ancient Judaism: New Visions and Views*. Grand Rapids, MI: Eerdmans.
Stuckenbruck, Loren T. 2007. *1 Enoch 91–108*. Berlin: de Gruyter.
Suter, David. 1979. "Fallen Angel, Fallen Priest: The Problem of Family Purity in 1 Enoch 6–16." *Hebrew Union College Annual* 50: 115–35.
Tabor, James, and Michael Wise. 1995. "4Q521 'On Resurrection' and the Synoptic Gospel Tradition: A Preliminary Study." In *Qumran Questions*, edited by James Charlesworth, 161–63. Sheffield: Academic Press.
Termini, Cristina. 2009. "Philo's Thought within the Context of Middle Platonism." In *Cambridge Companion to Philo*, edited by Adam Kamesar, 95–123. Cambridge: Cambridge University Press.
Tiller, Patrick A. 1993. *A Commentary on the Animal Apocalypse of 1 Enoch*. SBLEJL 4. Atlanta, GA: Scholars Press.
Tov, Emmanuel. 2001. *Textual Criticism of the Hebrew Bible*. 2nd revised edition. Minneapolis, MN: Augsburg Fortress.
Ulrich, Eugene, and Peter W. Flint. 2011. *Discoveries in the Judaean Desert XXXII: Qumran Cave 1: II. The Isaiah Scrolls: Part 2: Introductions, Commentary, and Textual Variants*. Oxford: Oxford University Press.
VanderKam, James C. 1984. *Enoch and the Growth of an Apocalyptic Tradition*. CBQMS 16. Washington, D.C.: Catholic Biblical Association.
VanderKam, James C. 2001. *Book of Jubilees*. London: A&C Black.
VanderKam, James C. 2018. *Jubilees: A Commentary in Two Volumes*. Hermeneia. Minneapolis, MN: Fortress Press.
Vaux, Roland de. 1973. *Archaeology and the Dead Sea Scrolls*. Oxford: Oxford University Press/British Academy.
Vermes, Geza. 1973. *Scripture and Tradition in Judaism: Haggadic Studies*. StPB 4. 2nd revised edition. Leiden: Brill.
Vermes, Geza. 1997. *The Complete Dead Sea Scrolls in English*. New York: Penguin Books.
Whiston, William. 1980. *The Works of Josephus: Complete and Unabridged*. New updated edition. Peabody, MA: Hendrickson.
Winston, David S. 2003. "Theodicy in the Wisdom of Solomon." In *Theodicy in the World of the Bible*, edited by Antii Laato and Johannes de Moor, 525–45. Leiden: Brill.
Witherington, Ben, III. 2000. *Jesus the Sage: The Pilgrimage of Wisdom*. Revised edition. Minneapolis, MN: Fortress Press.
Yadin, Yigael. 1983. *The Temple Scroll*. 3 vols. Jerusalem: Israel Exploration Society.
Yonge, C. D. 1993. *The Works of Philo: Complete and Unabridged*. New updated edition. Peabody, MA: Hendrickson.
Zahn, Molly M. 2012. "Genre and Rewritten Scripture: A Reassessment." *Journal of Biblical Literature* 131: 271–88.

Index of Sources

For the benefit of digital users, indexed terms that span two pages (e.g., 52-53) may, on occasion, appear on only one of those pages.

Boxes are indicated by *b* following the page number

1. Hebrew Bible (Old Testament)
Genesis, 9, 16–17, 39, 59–60, 61, 69, 80, 81–82, 95, 99–100, 102–12, 109*b*, 111*b*, 113, 114–17, 119, 123–27, 136–38, 162–64, 167, 174, 178
Exodus, 9, 31–32, 34–35, 39, 81, 102, 113, 118–19, 120–23, 136–37, 174
Leviticus, 99–100, 103, 118, 144
Numbers, 113, 116, 120–23, 175
Deuteronomy, 7–8, 9, 59–60, 81, 99–100, 113–14, 115, 136–37, 139–40, 141–44, 153–54, 179, 186
Joshua, 99–100, 105, 113, 114, 116–17, 152
Judges, 113, 114, 117–18
1–2 Samuel, 113–14, 146, 185
1–2 Kings, 37–38, 113–14, 176
Isaiah, 7, 9, 32, 36, 56, 58, 64, 66, 80, 95, 98, 116–17, 119–20, 129, 135–38, 145, 149–50, 154–55, 175–76
Jeremiah, 135
Ezekiel, 149–50, 176
Amos, 141
Habakkuk, 130, 137–38
Psalms, 5–6, 7–8, 9, 26, 64, 119–20, 136–37, 141–42, 145–46, 149–50, 154–55
Proverbs, 7–8, 13, 23, 24, 25–26, 28, 31, 36, 37–38, 47, 148
Job, 7–8, 13, 23–24, 30, 33, 36, 74–75
Qoheleth (Ecclesiastes), 13, 23, 24, 26, 33, 36
Esther, 7

Daniel, 5–6, 7–8, 54–59, 61–62, 64, 65, 67–68, 69, 70, 77, 85, 86, 87, 93, 94, 102, 115–16, 137–38, 150
Ezra-Nehemiah, 125
1–2 Chronicles, 113–14

2. Apocrypha (Deuterocanonical Books)
1 Esdras, 10, 11–12
1 Maccabees, 10, 11*b*, 11–12, 14, 102, 125, 141–42
2 Maccabees, 10, 11–12
3 Maccabees, 11–12
2 Esdras. See *4 Ezra*
4 Maccabees, 15, 47*b*
Baruch, 10, 11*b*, 11–12, 41–42, 49–50
Bel and the Dragon, 10, 12
Judith, 10, 11*b*, 12, 15, 41–42
Letter of Jeremiah, 10
Prayer of Azariah and Song of the Three Young Men, 10, 12
Prayer of Manasseh, 10
Psalm 151, 10, 145
Psalm 154, 145
Psalm 155, 145
Wisdom of Jesus Ben Sira (Sirach, Siracides, Ecclesiasticus), 8, 9, 10, 13, 14, 23–34, 36, 41, 43, 44, 47–49, 54, 59, 62, 75, 97, 125, 145, 165
Susannah, 10, 12
Tobit, 10, 11*b*, 12, 15, 41–42, 136–37
Wisdom of Solomon, 10, 11*b*, 13, 23–27, 34–42, 37*b*, 44, 45, 46, 47–49, 51–53, 51*b*, 52*b*, 53*b*, 59, 69, 97

3. Old Testament Pseudepigrapha
1 Enoch, 9, 15, 16, 54, 59–70, 60*b*, 81–82,
    91, 102, 136–37
  Book of Watchers, 56–57, 59–60, 61–63,
    68, 85, 91
  Parables (Similitudes) 49–50, 63–65,
    64*b*, 83, 85, 87, 91
  Astronomical Book, 65–66
  Dream Visions, 66–68, 70, 82, 83
  Epistle of Enoch, 59–60, 68–69,
    70, 93, 94
  Apocalypse of Weeks, 69–70
2 Enoch, 16, 80
2 Baruch, 15, 16, 54, 70–73, 71*b*, 74*b*, 75,
    77, 78–80, 81, 82, 85, 86, 90, 92, 93,
    94, 95–96, 180
4 Ezra (2 Esdras), 8, 9, 10, 13, 15, 16, 54,
    70–77, 71*b*, 74*b*, 78, 80, 81, 82, 83,
    85, 86, 90, 91, 92, 94, 95–96, 119–
    20, 180
Ahiqar, 13–14, 15, 42
Apocalypse of Abraham (ApAbr), 16, 54,
    70–72, 80–83, 87, 90, 116–17, 180
Apocalypse of Daniel, 13–14, 16
Artapanus, 170
*Biblical Antiquities (Liber Antiquitatum
    Biblicarum, LAB)*, 17, 97–101, 113–
    23, 126, 178
Cleodemus Malchus, 170
Demetrius the Chronographer, 170
Eupolemus (and Pseudo-Eupolemus), 170
Joseph and Aseneth, 15, 17
Jubilees (Jub.), 9, 15, 17, 59, 65–66, 70, 94,
    97–69, 104*b*, 106*b*, 109*b*, 111*b*, 113,
    117, 120, 124–25, 127, 136–37, 142–
    43, 144, 162, 178–79
Letter of Aristeas (Aristeas), 17, 42, 180
Odes of Solomon, 15, 18
Psalms of Solomon, 15, 18
Sentences of Pseudo-Phocylides, 18, 42
Sibylline Oracles, 15, 16, 127
Testament of Job, 16–17
Testaments of the Twelve Patriarchs,
    15, 16–17

4. Dead Sea Scrolls
Angelic Liturgy, 147
Aramaic Apocalypse, 149, 150
Astronomical Enoch, 60–61
Beatitudes, 148
Bless, O My Soul, 147
Catena A, 138
Commentary on Genesis A, 149
Commentary on Habakkuk, 130, 137–38
Commentary on Nahum, 138
Consolations, 137
Damascus Document, 102, 127, 129–
    30, 131, 136–37, 138–39, 141,
    149, 151–54
Enoch^{c,d,e} (4QEn^{c,d,e}), 60–61
Florilegium, 138
Genesis Apocryphon, 100
Great Isaiah Scroll (1QIsa^a), 135–36
Great Psalms Scroll (11QPs^a), 28, 145
Halakah A–C, 144–45
Instruction for a Student
    (4QInstruction), 148
Jeremiah^{a-e} (4QJer^{a-e}), 135
Lady Folly, 148
Melchizedek, 138
Messianic Apocalypse, 149–50, 154–55, 155*b*
New Jerusalem, 149–50
Ordinances, 144–45
Pseudo-Ezekiel, 100
Pseudo-Jubilees^a, 125
Reworked Pentateuch, 137
Rule of Blessings (1QSb), 138–39, 140–
    41, 149
Rule of the Community (1QS), 98, 129,
    131–34, 135, 138–41, 139*b*, 144–45,
    148–49, 151–54, 155–56
Rule of the Congregation (1QSa), 138–39,
    140–41, 149
Sapiential Work, 148
Some Works of the Torah, 130,
    142, 143–44
Targum of Job, 137
Targum of Leviticus, 137
Testimonia, 137
Thanksgiving Hymns, 146–47
Tohorot, 144–45
Temple Scroll (11QT^a) 99–101, 137,
    141–43, 151–52
    (4QT^b) 99
War Scroll, 138–39, 141–42
Words of the Luminaries, 147

INDEX OF SOURCES 203

5. New Testament
Matthew, 42–46, 43b, 151–52, 153–55, 182–83
Mark, 11b, 42–43, 84–87, 88–89, 182, 184, 185
Luke, 8, 11b, 42–46, 43b, 154–55, 155b, 182–83, 185
John, 11b, 46–50, 155–56, 169–70, 183
Acts, 88–89, 127, 152–53, 183, 186
Romans, 50–53, 51b, 52b, 53b, 89–90, 91, 92, 121, 125, 126–27, 167–68
1–2 Corinthians, 42, 89, 90, 91–92, 120–23, 167–68, 183–84
Galatians, 89, 91, 125, 127, 168–69, 183
Philippians, 89, 91, 92
1 Thessalonians, 50, 88–89, 90, 91–92
1–2 Timothy, 127
Hebrews, 11b, 123–27
James, 11b
1–2 Peter, 11b, 88–89
1–3 John, 11b
Jude, 9, 11b, 15, 59–60, 61
Revelation (Apocalypse of John), 54, 56, 83, 92–96

6. Philo of Alexandria, 19–20, 157–71, 160b
Against Flaccus (Flaccus), 158–59
Allegorical Laws, 123, 167–68
Embassy to Gaius (Embassy), 158–59
Every Good Man Is Free (Good Man), 166
On Abraham (Abraham), 163, 165, 168
On Dreams (Dreams), 127
On Drunkenness (Drunkenness), 123
On Flight and Finding (Flight), 169
On Joseph (Joseph), 165
On Mating with the Preliminary Studies (Preliminary Studies), 157–58, 168–69
On Providence (Providence), 157–58
On Special Laws (Special Laws), 159–60, 169
On the Confusion of Languages (Confusion), 169
On the Creation of the World (Creation), 164, 165–66, 167–68
On the Decalogue (Decalogue), 168
On the Immutability of God (Immutability), 169
On the Life of Moses (Moses), 127, 161, 164, 165, 180
On the Migration of Abraham (Migration), 123, 163, 164, 168
On the Posterity of Cain (Posterity), 163
On Rewards and Punishments (Rewards), 164, 165
On the Sacrifices of Cain and Abel (Sacrifices), 169
On the Special Laws (Special Laws), 164, 168
Questions and Answers on Genesis and Exodus (Questions), 162, 168, 170
The Worse Attacks the Better (Worse Attacks Better), 123
Who is the Heir of Divine Things? (Heir), 163–64, 165–66, 167–68

7. Josephus, 19–20, 170–86
Against Apion (Apion), 8, 173, 178, 179, 181
Jewish Antiquities (Ant.), 4, 37–38, 99–100, 126, 127, 131–32, 151–52, 157–58, 159, 173, 174, 176, 177–80, 181–86
Jewish War (War), 4, 71b, 131–32, 152–53, 157–58, 171–72, 173–77, 174b, 180, 184, 186
Life, 170–73, 177, 180

8. Rabbinic Literature
Mishnah, Sabbath, 109
Yadayim, 143–44
Babylonian Talmud, Sanhedrin, 95–96
Tosefta, Sukkah, 122

9. Other Ancient Sources
Aeschines
Timarchus, 179
Aristotle
Athenian Constitution, 179
Politics, 179, 180
Athanasius
Festal Letter 39, 10–11
Augustine
On the Gospel of John, 47–48
Cave of Treasures, 101

Cleanthes
  Hymn to Zeus, 47b
Diogenes Laertius
  Lives, 45
Dionysius of Halicarnassus
  Roman Antiquities, 178
Epistle of Barnabas, 61
Euhemerus
  Sacred History, 40b
Eusebius
  Church History, 184–85
Heraclitus
  Homeric Problems, 162
Herodotus
  Histories, 180
Instruction of Phibis (*Phebhor*), 28
Palaea Historia, 101

Plato
  Republic, 179, 180
Pliny the Elder
  Natural History, 131–32
Pseudo-Hegesippus
  Ruin of the City of Jerusalem, 176–77
Suetonius
  Vespasian, 157–58
Syriac History of Joseph, 101
Tacitus
  Histories, 157–58
  Annals, 157–58
Tales of the Prophets, 101
Tertullian
  Apparel of Women, 61
Theognis of Megara, 28

General Index

For the benefit of digital users, indexed terms that span two pages (e.g., 52-53) may, on occasion, appear on only one of those pages.

Abraham, 80–83, 105–12, 115–17, 123–27, 163–64, 168, 178–79
Aggadah, 4–5, 101b, 127
allegory, 162–65, 168–69. *See also* interpretation; symbolism
angels and demons, 35, 60, 61–63, 65, 67, 69, 73–76, 81–82, 102–3, 107, 109, 110–11, 127, 139–40, 145, 155–56, 169
Antiochus IV Epiphanes, 3, 56, 150
apocalypticism (and eschatology), 13, 16, 32–33, 36–37, 37b, 41, 45–46, 54–96, 112, 115, 116–17, 121, 129, 136, 141–42, 146, 147–50, 151–52, 167–68
Apocrypha (Deuterocanonical Books), 1, 10–13, 11b, 134
apologies, 17, 18–19, 157–59, 173, 176–77, 178, 181, 184–85
Aqedah, 110–12, 111b, 116–17, 123–27, 178–79

baptism, 121, 151–52, 182–83
Bar-Kochba Revolt, 2b, 3–4, 70–72, 84
beatitudes, 26–27, 148
biblical manuscripts, 128, 134–37

calendar, 65–66, 103–4, 104b, 107–8, 143, 146, 147
canon, 6–19, 11b, 134, 136–37
Catholicism, 6–7, 10, 11b
Christology, 46–50, 167
circumcision, 102, 108–10, 109b, 125, 162, 168–69
Codex Alexandrinus, 15

Codex Ambrosianus, 15, 78
Codex Sinaiticus, 15
conversion, 17, 175–76
creation, 30–31, 39–41, 46–53, 51b, 56–57, 58–59, 62–63, 81–82, 145, 165–66, 169, 177

Dead Sea Scrolls, 7, 9, 15, 19, 28, 42, 60–61, 65–66, 98, 100–1, 102, 128–56
death and afterlife, 4b, 33–34, 36, 38, 41, 49, 69, 74, 75, 79, 89, 90, 125–27, 166, 178–79, 181. *See also* resurrection
Deuteronomistic theology, 113–15, 139–40, 144, 179
diaspora, 2, 2b, 3–4, 10, 52–53, 157–59, 166–67
diatribe, 163
dualism, 24b, 35, 57–58, 82, 91, 107, 110–11, 129, 139–40, 148–49, 155–56

Eastern Orthodoxy, 6–7, 10–11
education, 25–26, 28, 31, 37–38, 148, 157–58, 162, 164, 168–69
Egypt, 2b, 17, 27, 34, 39–41, 157–66, 178
epistemology, 24–25, 30, 37–38, 74–75, 76, 89, 155–56
esoteric books, 9, 72–73, 77
Essenes, 3, 4b, 131–32, 151–53, 166, 170–71, 174, 176–77
Ethiopian Orthodox Church, 15, 61, 102

flood, 59–60, 61, 66, 69, 114–15, 127
"Fourth Philosophy", 174
freewill, 4b, 33–34, 75, 82–83

GENERAL INDEX

Gentiles, 39–41, 62–63, 68, 80, 91, 109, 118, 156, 168
Great Jewish Revolt, 2b, 3–4, 70–72, 71b, 80, 85–87, 128, 157–58, 170–77

Halakhah, 4–5, 101b, 138. *See also* law
Hasmonean Dynasty, 3, 11–12, 64, 130, 143, 170–71
heavenly tablets (celestial documents), 59–60, 68–69, 94, 102–3, 107–8, 109–10
Hellenization, 2b, 3, 25, 27, 28, 32, 45, 62, 70, 105, 157–86
Herod the Great, 2b, 3, 179–80, 185
Historical Jesus, 42–46, 151, 182–85

idolatry, 39–41, 40b, 50–53, 51b, 81–82, 88, 105–7, 113–14, 116, 118–19, 120–21
inspiration, 32–33, 164
interpretation, 97–127, 137–38, 157–69
Islam, 101

John of Gischala, 175
John the Baptist, 43, 151–52, 181–83

Khirbet Qumrān, 132–34, 133b
Kingdom of God, 45–46, 84–85
kingship, 3, 17, 37–39, 68, 85, 143, 179–80, 184–85
kinship, 25–26, 28–29, 31–32, 181

Latin Vulgate, 10, 13
law (also Torah), 1, 4–5, 7–8, 9, 19, 25, 31–32, 41–42, 59–60, 66–67, 73, 75–76, 77, 98, 99–100, 102–12, 118, 128–30, 138–45, 159–61, 165–66, 168–69, 177, 179–80, 181
leadership, 58, 68, 70–115, 117–18, 129–30, 149, 158, 171, 174–76, 179–80
logos, 47–50, 47b, 163–64, 165–66, 169–70

Maccabean Revolt, 2b, 3, 11–12, 25, 27, 28–29, 30, 55, 67–68, 70, 102, 173
magic, 62, 118, 127

marriage, 17, 31–32, 99–100, 113–14, 118, 131–32, 143–45, 151–52, 181, 182
martyrdom, 11–12, 58, 86, 115–16
Masada, 174–75
Masoretic Text (MT), 135–36
messianism, 64–65, 64b, 68, 77, 79, 83, 85, 94–96, 140–41, 149–50, 154–55, 155b, 175–76, 184–85
midrash, 101b, 127
millennium, 94–96
miracles, 184, 185, 186
Mishnah, 2, 2b, 4–5, 101
morality, 12, 18, 32–33, 35–36, 37–38, 52, 53b, 58, 88–89, 108, 109–10, 162, 168, 181, 182–83
Moses, 13, 66–67, 81, 98, 102–3, 105, 108, 109, 118–20, 121–22, 127, 142–43, 161–63, 165, 177, 179, 181

narrative, 11–12, 17, 18–19, 81, 102–20, 162, 165

Oriental Orthodoxy, 6–7, 10–11

Parousia, 88–89
Pharisees, 3, 4b, 8, 19, 70–72, 138, 143–44, 150, 170–71, 174, 176–77
philosophy, 4b, 11–12, 19–20, 32–33, 34, 35–36, 38, 45, 46–47, 47b, 159–66, 184–85
polis, 3
politeia (also Jewish liberties), 17, 158–59, 177, 178, 179–80
prayers, hymns, odes, 11–12, 18, 26–27, 32–33, 78, 140–41, 145–47
predeterminism, 4b, 57, 62, 94, 132
priesthood, 19, 28–29, 31–32, 47–48, 62, 107–8, 111, 131, 138, 140, 143–44, 149, 150, 170–72, 176, 179, 180, 183
prophecy and prophets, 1, 7–8, 9, 32–33, 44, 45–46, 55, 56, 58, 66–67, 93, 98, 114, 129–30, 137–38, 146, 151–52, 161, 164, 171–72, 176–77, 185, 186
Protestantism, 6–7, 10–11, 11b
Pseudepigrapha, 13–19, 134
pseudonymity, 13, 34–35, 55, 113

Q-Hypothesis, 42–46, 43*b*, 154

Rabbinic Judaism, 2, 4–5, 8, 19–20, 27, 34, 70–72, 98, 113, 128
resurrection, 11–12, 58–59, 63, 65, 78, 88–89, 91–92, 94–96, 123–24, 125–26, 149–50, 154–55, 155*b*, 167–68
revelation, 54–57, 59–60, 75–76, 77, 79, 81, 91, 93, 103, 113, 129–30, 147–49, 164
rewritten scriptures, 17, 100–20, 137, 142–43, 178
Roman Empire, 2, 2*b*, 3–4, 56, 70–72, 71*b*, 77, 79, 88, 92, 138, 141–42, 157–59, 170–77

Sabbath, 3, 27, 106*b*, 141, 144–45, 147
Sadducees, 3, 4*b*, 170–71, 174, 176–77
Samaritan Pentateuch (SP), 135
Samaritans, 156, 186
scribes, 25, 28, 44, 59–60
sectarianism, 3, 4*b*, 25, 59–60, 129
Septuagint (LXX), 1, 2*b*, 10, 17, 135–36, 161, 177
sexuality, 50–53, 52*b*, 88–89, 99–100, 109–10, 121, 141, 148, 181
Sicarii, 174–75
slavery, 29, 166, 168–69, 175–76, 185
symbolism, 55–56, 66–68, 82, 116–17, 119–20
synagogue, 1, 158–59, 166–67

Talmud, 4–5, 101
Tannaim, 4–5
targum, 101*b*, 137
temple (Jerusalem), 1–5, 11–12, 28–29, 31–32, 39, 48–49, 58–59, 66–67, 69–70, 76–77, 78–79, 82, 85, 97, 102, 111, 113, 118, 130, 141, 142–43, 145, 149–50, 157–58, 178–79
testaments, 16–17, 68–69, 85
theodicy, 24–25, 24*b*, 28–29, 33, 34–35, 41, 70–72, 74, 82, 180
translation, 10, 14, 17, 27, 30, 73, 78, 80, 102, 113, 173, 177

warfare, 36–37, 68, 71*b*, 77, 80, 85–86, 141–42
wealth and poverty, 28–29, 32, 45, 69, 132, 141, 144–45, 152–53, 174–75
wisdom, 13, 18, 23–53, 54, 63–64, 65, 89, 123, 146, 147–49, 159–60, 163–64, 167–69, 184
women, 12, 17, 29, 76–77, 80, 112, 117–18, 129, 131–32, 141, 148, 162, 169, 182

Zealots, 175